IN ROUGH COUNTRY

ALSO BY JOYCE CAROL OATES

The Edge of Impossibility: Tragic Forms in Literature (1972)

New Heaven, New Earth:
The Visionary Experience in Literature (1974)

Contraries (1981)

The Profane Art: Essays and Reviews (1983)

On Boxing (1987)

(Woman) Writer: Occasions and Opportunities (1988)

George Bellows: American Artist (1995)

Where I've Been, and Where I'm Going:
Essays, Reviews, and Prose (1999)

The Faith of a Writer: Life, Craft, Art (2003)

Uncensored: Views and (Re)views (2005)

IN ROUGH COUNTRY

ESSAYS AND REVIEWS

JOYCE CAROL OATES

An Imprint of HarperCollinsPublishers

HarperCollins books may be purchased for educational, business, or
sales promotional use. For information, please write: Special Markets
Department, HarperCollins Publishers, 10 East 53rd Street, New York,
NY 10022.

FIRST EDITION

Designed by Mary Austin Speaker
Frontispiece photograph by Kramer O'Neill

Library of Congress Cataloging-in-Publication Data has been applied for.

ISBN: 978-0-06-196398-8

10   11   12   13   14   /RRD / 10   9   8   7   6   5   4   3   2   1

For Barry Qualls

ACKNOWLEDGMENTS

Many thanks are due to the editors of the publications in which, in slightly different forms and with varying titles, the essays in this volume originally appeared.

The New York Review of Books: "The Woman in White: Emily Dickinson and Friends"; " 'Cast a Cold Eye': Jean Stafford"; "The Art of Vengeance: Roald Dahl"; " 'Large and Startling Figures': The Fiction of Flannery O'Connor"; "In Rough Country I: Cormac McCarthy"; "In Rough Country II: Annie Proulx"; "*Enchanted!* Salman Rushdie"; "A Photographer's Lives: Annie Leibovitz"; " 'The Great Heap of Days': James Salter's Fiction"; "Margaret Atwood's Tales"; "In the Emperor's Dream House: Claire Messud"; "The Story of X: Susanna Moore's *In the Cut*"; "Boxing: History, Art, Culture: Kasia Boddy's *Boxing: A Cultural History.*"

The New Yorker: "After the Apocalypse: Jim Crace's *The Pesthouse.*"

The Times Literary Supplement: " 'As You Are Grooved, So You Are Grieved': The Art and the Craft of Bernard Malamud's Fiction."

Playboy: "Revisiting Nabokov's *Lolita*"

Vogue: "Nostalgia 1970: Detroit"

The Humanist: "Why Is Humanism Not the Preeminent Belief of Human-Kind?" Acceptance speech on the occasion of being named 2007 Humanist of the Year.

Atlantic Monthly: "The Myth of the American Idea"

Smithsonian Magazine: "Revisiting Lockport, New York"

" 'Cast a Cold Eye': Jean Stafford" is the introduction to *The Collected Stories of Jean Stafford* (Farrar, Straus & Giroux)

"Shirley Jackson's Witchcraft" is the afterword to Jackson's *We Have Always Lived in the Castle* (Penguin U.K.)

"In the Absence of Mentors/Monsters" originally appeared in *Narrative* and in *Mentors, Muses & Monsters: 30 Writers on the People Who Changed Their Lives*, edited by Elizabeth Benedict, and in *Narrative*.

CONTENTS

PREFACE

In Rough Country

The "rough country" of my title has a double meaning: it refers to both the treacherous geographical/psychological terrains of the writers who are my subjects—Flannery O'Connor, Shirley Jackson, Cormac McCarthy, Annie Proulx, Margaret Atwood among others—and also the emotional terrain of my life following the unexpected death of my husband Raymond Smith in February 2008 after forty-eight years of marriage.

As literature is a traditional solace to the bereft, so writing about literature can be a solace to the bereft as it was to me during the days, weeks, and months when the effort of writing fiction often seemed beyond me, as if belonging to another lifetime when I'd been younger, more resilient and reckless. Overnight everything seemed to change for me, and inside me—the death of a "loved one" is a universal experience yet, to the bereaved, it is singular as a mountain thundering downhill in an avalanche that swallows you up utterly, batters your brain and fills your mouth with rubble. I could compose short stories—slowly and painstakingly—with perhaps one-tenth of the efficiency I'd formerly taken for granted—bizarre and surreal stories about loss, grief, "surviving"—but I have not been able to imagine anything so ambitious as a novel, even a short novel. Like a person whose vision has become blurred following a blow to the head, I can't seem to *see* beyond the relatively brief span of the short story.

Reading and taking notes, especially late at night when I can't sleep, has been the comfort for me that saying the rosary or reading *The Book of Common Prayer* might be for another. Immersing myself in the imaginations of other writers, constructing a line of argument which is the structure of a literary essay—in contrast to the less calibrated and predictable swerves and leaps of fiction—has been a lifeline. Reading, which had always been, in my former life, my reward for a full day of writing, became, in my new, uncharted life as a widow, an end in itself of almost mystical significance. "These fragments I have shored against my ruins"—this line from T. S. Eliot's "The Waste Land" echoed obsessively in my thoughts. I came to feel that I was making my way word by word, sentence by sentence, across something like a narrow swaying footbridge above an abyss—this footbridge wasn't my construction but comprised of others' work, for which I was infinitely grateful. Working into the early hours of the morning— as I'd never done when I was married and our lives adhered to a conventional and commonplace domestic routine—reading in bed still partly dressed amid a nest of pillows, my mother's knitted quilt, papers, books, and bound galleys, and when I was very lucky one or another of our two cats—who were slow to forgive me for the abrupt and mysterious disappearance of the individual who by custom fed them their breakfast each morning as well as "talked" to them through the day as required—became the new center of my life, an oasis of quiet in contrast to the nightmare cacophony of daytime: the phone ringing, ceaseless e-mails, "death-duties" to be executed *ad infinitum*. Days were filled with other people and none of them my missing husband: people in whose eyes I saw sympathy, pity, uneasiness, concern. By night, I was an avid reader and writer; by day, a widow.

What a widow *is*, is defined by an absence.

What a widow *is not*, is a whole/unmaimed individual.

Working late into the night was a melancholy sort of pleasure but when I did sleep, in the way of the insomniac's sudden stuporous coma-like sleep like a précis of death, it was very difficult to wake up—to wake fully—in the morning—whatever "morning" was. Where getting out of bed had once been effortless, unthinking, now the very concept *getting out of bed* acquired an almost supernatural significance: fraught with danger, terror, dread. What is more awful than *waking, getting up*?—when you want so very badly to sleep; when your brain aches for the extinction of all thought, especially the awareness of time. Sleep becomes if not happiness, a reminder of happiness; a respite from the duties of daylight that involve memory, thinking, making decisions and *actions*. There were mornings in the late winter and early spring of last year when it seemed to me that the very air of my bedroom had turned viscous and heavy; that gravity exerted some sort of new, palpable pressure, as if I were lying on the bottom of the ocean. My brain was a kind of cotton batting which deep-ocean-thoughts of menace could make their way only slowly and what a risk, to disturb this paralysis! Nothing is so exhausting and daunting to the insomniac as *getting out of bed* and so my remedy was to forestall this by propping myself up against pillows and returning to whatever I'd been doing when I'd finally turned out the light and tried to sleep a few hours before. In this way though I had committed myself to *opening my eyes* yet I need not yet complete the ordeal of *getting out of bed*. I recalled that Edith Wharton famously wrote her novels in long-hand in a similar posture in her enormous canopied bed, tossing sheets of paper onto the floor for a maid to gather up. I had no maid, nor did I toss my notes onto the floor, but I quite understood Wharton's instinct in this case to forestall contending with whatever— in Wharton's case house-guests, "social life"—awaits beyond one's bed.

During these months, and well into this new year of 2009, Robert Silvers of the *New York Review of Books* has been my cherished friend. Like his late co-editor Barbara Epstein, my beloved editor for more than twenty years at *NYR*, Bob is the most exacting of editors as he is a warmly encouraging and thoughtful reader. There is something thrilling—if also daunting—about undertaking to review a book one hasn't yet read and assessed; if your inclination is, like my own, to wish not to publicly criticize any work of art, in acknowledgment of the difficulty of creating anything whether meritorious or otherwise, it's an endeavor in which the reviewer risks exposure, as in a fun house mirror. The most painful of the essays included here is "Boxing: History, Art, Culture" for this was undertaken in February 2008 before my husband was stricken with pneumonia and hospitalized at the Princeton Medical Center; during Ray's week in the hospital I worked on the essay in frantic bursts in the interstices of driving to the hospital, teaching my classes at Princeton University, and dealing with household duties; at night, after visiting hours at the hospital, I researched and worked on the essay until 2 A.M. or so—I was proud of myself in the small ridiculous ways in which we are proud of ourselves at such desperate times; my husband, who did not usually read my fiction, was looking forward to reading this essay, or so he said. No one could know the effort that went into this single "review" that would appear in a May 2008 issue of NYR—out of all proportion to its length and significance as a text; no one could guess that there is a break in the essay between the second section and the section that begins with the words "From the bare-knuckle era of John L. Sullivan"—the pages before were written by a woman with a husband, the pages following were written by a woman who had lost her husband. It was Nietzsche who said *Between one and none there gapes . . . an infinity.*

After my husband's sudden death, of what was called a hospital infection, only a few hours after we'd been discussing his discharge within a few days, I could return to this essay only sporadically, with a residual sort of excitement, as there might be observed, in the waning light of the iris of the eye of a decapitated beast, some residual alertness to stimuli, but it was not revised and completed for some time. Yet in the immediate aftermath of my husband's death, in a kind of vigil that night, when several friends of ours came to stay with me,

stunned as I was, and tenderly solicitous, it happened that—
for something to say of an abstract and impersonal nature, I
suppose—I spoke about the essay I was writing, the ambitious
scholarly book I was reviewing, and of the very long history of
boxing—how what seems to us recent may in fact have its roots
in antiquity, in almost pre-history. How minuscule, how finite,
how fleeting the *individual*. Whatever else I managed to say
that night, I don't remember, and I have little memory of what
my friends said, but this "profound" thought remains. There is
pathos here, but perhaps a kind of beauty as well. Ideas, literature, art remain after much else falters and falls away. It is not
a permanent victory by any means, but it is a victory of a kind
and it is a victory we all share.

Joyce Carol Oates
June 1, 2009

I.

CLASSICS

A POE MEMOIR

Here was a mystery!—in our near-bookless farmhouse in upstate New York twenty miles north of Buffalo and approximately that distance south of Lake Ontario, in the region known stoically by its inhabitants as the Snow Belt, there was a book—battered as if water-stained, aged-looking, austere in its dark binding—intriguingly titled *The Gold Bug*.

The Gold Bug!—my childish imagination was stirred by this intriguing image. Of bugs—insects of all species, especially flies and mosquitoes—we had many, in the country; on a farm, especially. But a *gold bug*, what could this be? The author's name—EDGAR ALLAN POE—was striking, "poetic"—but unknown to me, a child of ten with a precocious interest in books and storytelling and all that was not-real but imagined, as a kind of waking dream.

The other great books of my childhood were Lewis Carroll's *Alice's Adventures in Wonderland* and *Through the Looking-Glass*. Superficially very different, yet Lewis Carroll and Edgar Allan Poe would have understood each other perfectly, I think. Both wrote surreal/nightmare/"gothic"/

fairy-tale-like stories to be read, if not fully comprehended, by children as well as adults.

As it turned out, it wasn't the overwrought, maddeningly slow-moving long story "The Gold Bug" that turned out to be one of my favorite Poe stories but other, shorter tales like "The Black Cat," "The Fall of the House of Usher," "The Pit and the Pendulum," "The Tell-Tale Heart," that most captivated me and were deeply imprinted on my memory, always with admiration, wonderment, and trepidation. (Especially since, as a child, I wasn't altogether certain that these strange short stories with their elevated language, so very different from the plain, vernacular English spoken by the inhabitants of Millersport, New York, and their bizarre nightmare plots weren't "real"— in the way that events described in newspapers were "real" though wholly beyond my ability to comprehend as beyond the perimeters of Millersport, New York.)

Of the great, classic stories of Poe, it was "The Tell-Tale Heart" that exudes the most immediate and sheerly visceral power. Here we find the fated/doomed/ecstatic/quintessential voice of Poe:

> True!—nervous—very, very dreadfully nervous I had been and am; but why *will* you say that I am mad? The disease had sharpened my senses—not destroyed—not dulled them.

In this very short masterpiece, Poe evokes the "voice" of interior madness, as it is a voice that is speaking to us with disturbing intimacy if not complicity. A crime has been committed—a terrible, unspeakable crime—parricide?—the senseless murder of an elderly, unnamed man with what the narrator believes to be an Evil Eye. In order to protect himself from this Evil Eye, the narrator has to exorcise it, for otherwise he will succumb to abject terror:

> Many a night, just at midnight, when all the world slept, [terror] has welled up from my own bosom, deepening, with its dreadful echo, the terrors that distracted me . . .

As in most stories by Poe, terror precedes any object: terror simply *is*, as primordial as life itself. Yet in a most bizarre ritualistic fashion the elderly man must be murdered—improbably smothered, or crushed, beneath a bed.

"I then smiled gaily, to find the deed so far done."

So a younger generation hopes to exorcise and replace their elders. But no story of Poe is lacking in recrimination and punishment. And so the gloating murderer is betrayed by what he believes to be the amplified beating of the (murdered) old man's heart—which is in fact the murderer's own heart— the "tell-tale heart"—growing louder and more accelerated when police officers come to investigate: "*a low, dull, quick sound—much such a sound as a watch makes when enveloped in cotton.*" (How typical it is of Poe, a navigator of Gothic landscapes that have no physical existence, to so carefully describe the sound of this runaway ghost-heart!) Soon then, the murderer is driven mad and confesses to the crime:

> "I admit the deed!—tear up the planks!—here, here!—it is the beating of his hideous heart!"

When I first read this eerie, fluent story, I was very young and hardly not a conscious, still less an analytical reader. What a story is about would have seemed to me precisely what it seems to be about, and nothing more. In later years, reading Poe, often teaching Poe—as I teach exemplary stories of Poe to my writing students at Princeton University—I came to see the subtlety of effects in this brief story, the mastery of the madman's lurid reasoning, the quick setting of the scene, the rapid development of "plot," the abrupt denouement as final and irrevocable as the slamming of a door. Now, first-person narrations by the eloquently deranged are hardly novelties, but in the mid-nineteenth century, when literary English was stately, formal and unfailingly elevated, as if statues were speaking in echo-laden marble halls, Poe's voice of scarcely suppressed hysteria would have been astonishing—if not repellent—to most readers.

It was only a coincidence, but "Edgar Allan Poe" was also a character in his own right, in a card game called *Authors*, popular in the 1950s in that bookish/literate era when television was only just beginning its conquest of American households. Poe's somewhat effeminate deathly-pale "poetic" face framed by very black curly hair was reproduced on playing cards in the company of such staid luminaries as Ralph Waldo Emerson, Nathaniel Hawthorne, Herman Melville, James Fenimore Cooper and Washington Irving. While Hawthorne was the most conventionally handsome of the *Authors*, and Emerson the most sternly Transcendental, it was Poe who exuded the air, both melancholy and menacing, of the glamorously doomed writer/poet—it was Poe for whom a literary-minded girl might feel some tug of (innocent? precocious?) infatuation.

One day I would learn that, in fact, Poe is perhaps the most mysterious of our classic American writers, along with his younger contemporary Emily Dickinson with whom he shared a number of writerly obsessions—mortality, loss, death above all. Like his similarly gifted/accursed twentieth-century counterpart H. P. Lovecraft, another doomed purveyor of "weird tales," Poe led a life beset from the start by misfortune and nightmare, as in one of the darker of Grimms' fairy tales: his actor-father abandoned his mother when Poe was an infant, and his mother died when he was three; he was rejected at the age of nineteen by the well-to-do Richmond merchant who'd adopted him; prone to gambling and alcohol he was "withdrawn" from the University of Virginia and expelled from West Point; his cousin-bride Virginia whom he'd married when she was fourteen—and he was twenty-eight—collapsed of a "burst blood vessel" while singing, at the age of twenty, never regained her health and died a few years later. His great achievements—*Tales of the Grotesque and Arabesque* and *The Raven and Other Poems* (1845)—sold poorly. Though Poe's work is far from realistic in any external way its Gothic excess is surely a psychological mirror of his beleaguered personal life.

I was sick—sick unto death with that long agony; and when they at last unbound me, and I was permitted to sit, I felt that my senses were leaving me. The sentence—the dread sentence of death—was the last of distinct accentuation which reached my ears. ["The Pit and the Pendulum"]

In fact it is not merely "I" but an accursed collective "we" of whom Poe speaks:

We stand upon the brink of a precipice. We peer into the abyss—we grow sick and dizzy. Our first impulse is to shrink from the danger. Unaccountably we remain . . . [For] we now the most vividly desire it. And because our reason violently deters us from the brink, *therefore*, do we the most impetuously approach it. ["The Imp of the Perverse"]

(How I identified with such peculiar epiphanies, though I'd never seen an abyss, let alone peered into it; let alone felt myself drawn to its brink! Yet I felt the same sympathy reading this Poe story that I would feel years later reading Dostoyevsky's *Notes from the Underground* and the terrifying prophetic tales of Franz Kafka imagined in the years before the Holocaust—a sense of kinship, a predilection for uttering the truth that "will not be comforted.")

Though Poe's prose and poetry are saturated with a kind of high-voltage Gothic sexuality, in fact Poe's men—and women—(a single female-type)—are asexual as mannequins. They never touch one another—or, if they do, their touch isn't caressing or provocative but, as in "The Fall of the House of Usher," fatal as a cobra's bite. As a literary sensibility, Poe was unapologetically sexist: famous—or infamous—for having stated explicitly what others assume implicitly, from the most revered Romantic poets to our tabloid cable TV news:

> "Of all melancholy topics, what, according to the *universal* understanding of mankind, is the *most* melancholy?" Death—was the obvious reply. "And when," I said, "is this most melancholy of topics most poetical?" . . . The answer . . . is obvious—"When it most closely allies itself to *Beauty:* the death, then, of a beautiful woman is, unquestionably, the most poetical topic in the world . . ." ["The Philosophy of Composition"]

A woman writer/reader is bemused to discover how very many beautiful dead or near-dead females abound in Poe's prose and poetry—in fact, there is not a "living" female character in all of Poe, of any significance. The attraction is to the (safely) deceased female from Roderick Usher's ghastly pale sister Madeleine—one of the "living dead"—and the vampire-like Ligeia to the more innocent child-heroine of "Annabel Lee"— inspiration for Nabokov's obsessive pedophile Humbert Humbert of *Lolita*. The Gothic imagination has no interest in, not the slightest awareness of, ordinary women and men and their erotic relations, still less their relations as mature individuals in society. As a woman writer, I make no more or no less of this than it requires: we read our classic writers because they are visionary geniuses, not because they are "politically correct" or adhere in any way to shifting political/cultural sentiments.

Poe suffuses my fiction, in particular my "Gothic" fiction,

in the way that Lewis Carroll suffuses my fiction, as a kind of distant model, not an immediate predecessor. Once in a playful/surreal mood, I wrote a story titled "The White Cat," included in my Gothic fiction collection *Haunted: Tales of the Grotesque* (1994)—the very obverse of Poe's famous story "The Black Cat"—for in my story, the female triumphs over the male; in Poe's story, the male triumphs over the female, at least temporarily. And how appropriate it seemed to me, when writing my long quasi-historical novel *My Heart Laid Bare* (1998), a post-Modernist Gothic saga about a purely American family of confidence-men and -women, to preface it with this enigmatic quote from Poe, in 1848:

> If any ambitious man have a fancy to revolutionize, at one effort, the universal world of human thought, human opinion, and human sentiment, the opportunity is his own— the road to immortal renown lies straight, open, and un-encumbered before him. . . . All that he has to do is write and publish a very little book. Its title should be simple—a few plain words—"My Heart Laid Bare.". . . But this little book must be *true to its title*. . . . No man dare write it. . . . No man *could* write it, even if he dared. The paper would shrivel and blaze at every touch of the fiery pen.

Has any writer succeeded in writing such a book? I think so, yes—many writers have since Poe's time, especially in the twentieth century when the taboo against "naturalism" in literature, as in society, began to dissolve. To name just one: James Joyce's *Ulysses*, a masterly amalgam of the symbolic, the allegoric, the "realistic" and the "naturalistic." Poe would have been astonished—and perhaps appalled.

Another curious absence in Poe is "history"—any hint in his prose fiction of a recognizable time, place, "real people." No reader would ever guess that the author was an ambitious writer/editor steeped in the cultural and political turbulence of his time, determined to be a successful magazine editor of such popular magazines as *Burton's Gentleman's Magazine* and *Graham's Magazine* as well as a best-selling writer with a worldwide audience of readers; that, as one associated with the Old South, he scorned mere "regional" writing, and never dealt with a single "southern" issue (like slavery) in his work. One could never guess from the frenetic obsessions of Poe's poetry and prose that here was a thoroughly "professional"—if not a "hack"—writer who'd written hundreds of reviews of mediocre and long-forgotten books for such journals as the *Southern Literary Messenger* and essays with such pedantic titles as "The Poetic Principle" and "The Philosophy of Composition" ("Beauty is the sole legitimate province of the poem"—"Melancholy is . . . the most legitimate of all the poetical tones"). Except in surreal distorted forms Poe's actual, autobiographical life is missing from his work, along with what might be called "historical context"—though Poe lived in New York City, Philadelphia, and Richmond, Virginia, during the Mexican War (1846–1848), the rise of the virulent "patriotic" movement called the Know-Nothings (whose anti-Catholic/anti-immigrant platform in 1844 featured proposals to ban all naturalized citizens from public office and to extend the waiting time for citizenship to twenty-one years), and the imperialist incursions of Manifest Destiny, not to mention the enslavement of hundreds of thousands of abducted Africans in the southern states, there isn't a glimmer of any of these issues in his work.

In this, Poe resembles his younger contemporary Emily Dickinson, whose poetry is similarly timeless and "ahistoric," though Poe was far from being otherworldly or reclusive like Dickinson. Of the thousands—millions?—of speculative critical remarks inspired by Edgar Allan Poe perhaps the most insightful is that of a fellow "outlaw" writer of the twentieth century, D. H. Lawrence:

> Moralists have always wondered helplessly why Poe's "morbid" tales need have been written. They need to be written because old things need to die and disintegrate, because the old white psyche has to be gradually broken down before anything else can come to pass . . . Poe had a pretty bitter doom. ["Edgar Allan Poe," *Studies in Classic American Literature*]

Is this true? Is art a kind of catharsis, with the power to transform culture? We no longer believe this, if we ever did, for art has come to seem to us a phenomenon of the solitary individual, and not the collective, for whom politics has become all-engulfing as a state religion. But it is surely true, Edgar Allan Poe had a "pretty bitter doom"—from which, in his bravely imagined art, he seems never to have wavered.

THE WOMAN IN WHITE:
EMILY DICKINSON AND FRIENDS

A Summer of Hummingbirds: Love, Art, and Scandal in
the Intersecting Worlds of Emily Dickinson, Mark Twain,
Harriet Beecher Stowe, and Martin Johnson Heade
by Christopher Benfey

White Heat: The Friendship of Emily Dickinson &
Thomas Wentworth Higginson
by Brenda Wineapple

> The Riddle we can guess
> We speedily despise.
> —EMILY DICKINSON (#1220)

A mysterious "confluence of hummingbirds" is the start-
ing point for Christopher Benfey's engagingly impressionistic work of literary and cultural criticism, focusing on the
summer of 1882 when Americans as gifted and temperamentally disparate as Emily Dickinson, Thomas Wentworth Higginson, Harriet Beecher Stowe and Henry Ward Beecher, and
Mabel Todd and Martin Johnon Heade seem to have become
"fanatical" about hummingbirds:

They wrote poems and stories about hummingbirds; they painted pictures of hummingbirds; they tamed wild hummingbirds and collected stuffed hummingbirds; they set music to the humming of hummingbirds; they waited impatiently through the winter months for the hummingbirds' return.

In addition to what Benfey calls his "motley assemblage" of *dramatis personae* he has also included Mark Twain, Henry James, John Greenleaf Whittier, the capitalist investor Henry Morrison Flagler and the suffragette activist Victoria Woodhull, and the twentieth century artist Joseph Cornell; there is even room in this leisurely constructed narrative for an exploration and exegesis of the Gilded Age phenomenon of the lavish "hotel-world" of South Florida. As if to suggest an aestheticism seemingly at odds with our more customary sense of American pragmatism and Puritanism, Benfey begins his book with a curious epigraph from John Ruskin—

I have wasted my life with mineralogy, which has led to nothing. Had I devoted myself to birds, their life and plumage, I might have produced something myself worth doing. If I could only have seen a hummingbird fly, it would have been an epoch in my life.

—and he includes in his final chapter a passage of adulatory prose from Henry James describing the gigantic Hotel Ponce de Leon in St. Augustine, in 1905, by all reports a bizarre Disneyland of conspicuous consumption:

It is difficult to render the intensity with which one feels the great sphere of the hotel close round one, covering one in as with high shining crystal walls, stretching out beneath one's feet an immeasurable polished level, revealing itself as, for the time, for the place, the very order of nature and the very form, the only one, of the habitable world.

All of which is to argue, the reader surmises, that the post–Civil War/pre–World War I America of which Benfey writes bears a significant relationship to *fin de siècle* English culture, and that the individuals whom Benfrey discusses—Emily Dickinson, for one, of whom it's said by her sister-in-law neighbor Susan Dickinson that the reclusive Amherst poetess had not "any idea of morality"—are aesthetic epicureans of a sort, finding profound meaning in "routes of evanescence" unexpectedly akin to the Pateresque ideal of burning with a hard gem-like flame.

Christopher Benfey, poet, critic, and professor of literature at Mount Holyoke, whose previous critical works include *Emily Dickinson and the Problem of Others* (1984), *Emily Dickinson: Lives of a Poet* (1986), *The Double Life of Stephen Crane* (1994), *The Great Wave: Gilded Age Misfits, Japanese Eccentrics, and the Opening of Old Japan* (2004), and most recently *American Audacity: Literary Essays North and South* (2007), has constructed an intricately woven bird's nest of a book arguing that the "seismic upheaval" of the Civil War and its protracted aftermath precipitated a psychic crisis in the national consciousness as Americans tried to retain traditional beliefs, values, and conventions in the face of ever-shifting new social, political, and racial realities. Both during and after the war, Benfey speculates, Americans "gradually left behind a static view of existence, a trust in fixed arrangements and hierarchies":

> In science and in art, in religion and in love, they came to see a new dynamism and movement in their lives, a brave new world of instability and evanescence . . . (A) dynamism . . . (that) found perfect expression in the hummingbird.

And the hummingbird as a creature of mysterious otherworldly beauty is most brilliantly evoked by the watercolors of Martin Johnson Heade—see Heade's masterpiece "Cattleya Orchid and Three Brazilian Hummingbirds," 1871, which Benfey discusses in detail—and the poetry of Emily Dickinson—see the riddlesome poem indexed as #1463, which Benfey calls the poet's "signature poem" since Dickinson frequently sent it to correspondents and sometimes signed it "Humming-Bird"—"as though she herself were its evanescent subject."

> A Route of Evanescence
> With a revolving Wheel—
> A Resonance of Emerald—
> A Rush of Cochineal—
> And every Blossom on the Bush
> Adjusts its tumbled Head—
> The mail from Tunis, probably,
> An easy Morning's Ride—
>   (c. 1879)

A *Summer of Hummingbirds* is richly populated by eccentric personalities in addition to Dickinson and Higginson: the itinerant and obsessive Martin Heade, one of the greatest of nineteenth-century nature painters, who yearned to evoke a kind of New World Eden in his highly stylized, symbolic paintings; the beautiful and uninhibited Mrs. Mabel Loomis Todd, whom Heade loved at a distance, and who conducted a scandalous love affair virtually in public, in staid Amherst, Massachusetts, with the older brother of Emily Dickinson; the flamboyant hedonist preacher Henry Ward Beecher of whom Benfey says admiringly that he was "drawn to things that flickered and flashed . . . He liked to tell people that he was intoxicated by art"; and Beecher's Christian-messianic sister Harriet Beecher Stowe, famous as the author of *Uncle Tom's Cabin* but the author as well of a curious book-length polemic titled *Lady Byron Vindicated* (1869). More a skeptical observer than a participant of the genteel cultural scene, Mark Twain emerges intermittently in Benfey's narrative as a kind of measuring-rod for the author: the most famous writer of his time and yet harshly judged by such envious New Englanders as Higginson, who claimed to have found Twain "something of a buffoon," and an anonymous critic for a local Amherst newspaper who, after Twain lectured in Amherst to a large audience, reported: "As a lecturer we are of the opinion that he is a first-class failure."

Though *A Summer of Hummingbirds* thrums with the interlocking tales of these idiosyncratic individuals, with inspired vignettes and gossipy asides, and the author's prevailing Olympian perspective, in a manner to suggest Louis Menand's

The Metaphysical Club: A Story of Ideas in America (2002), at the core of the story Benfey finds so intriguing is an impassioned portrait of Emily Dickinson—what might be called Dickinson's most inward and erotic self, of which Benfey has written in such earlier essays as "The Mystery of Emily Dickinson" (in *American Audacity*), and here attaches to the "route of evanescence" that finds its ideal expression in the hummingbird. It isn't just that Dickinson is the most original and provocative of the individuals in Benfey's book but she remains the most enigmatic, a perennial goad to critical speculation: despite the enormous attention she has received, Dickinson "remains almost as mysterious as Shakespeare . . . She is part of our language without being part of our history" (*Emily Dickinson: Lives of a Poet*). As Brenda Wineapple concedes with disarming candor at the midway point in her wonderfully evocative double portrait of Dickinson and Dickinson's friend/editor/"Master" Colonel Thomas Wentworth Higginson, *White Heat*:

> Emily Dickinson stops my narrative. For as the woman in white, *savante* and reclusive, shorn of context, place, and reference, she seems to exist outside of time, untouched by it. And that's unnerving. No wonder we make up stories about her, about her lovers, if any, or how many or why she turned her back on ordinary life and when she knew the enormity of her own gift (of course she knew) and how she combined words in ways we never imagined and wish we could.

As Benfey's subtitle suggests, for all its shimmering web of interlocking ideas, the "scandal" of Eros is the driving force here, culminating in two seemingly ecstatic adulterous relationships—the affair of the most famous Protestant preacher of his era, Reverend Henry Ward Beecher, and one of his female admirers, Mrs. Elizabeth Tilton—"The biggest sex scandal in the history of American religion," as Benfey breathlessly notes—which resulted in a highly publicized adultery trial in 1874; and the remarkably protracted affair of Emily Dickinson's brother Austin and the much younger Mrs. Mabel Loomis Todd, the wife of an Amherst College astronomy professor. While Emily Dickinson's connection with the dashing Reverend Beecher was slight, Dickinson was well aware of her brother's longtime affair with Mrs. Todd and seems to have been, with her sister Vinnie, in some way a confidante of the illicit lovers who used the Homestead, the Dickinson family house, for their trysts. And there were Emily Dickinson's shadow-lovers, among them the "Master" to whom Dickinson alludes tantalizingly in numerous poems, and the Massachusetts Supreme Court justice Otis Lord, Dickinson's elder by eighteen years and a "crusty conservative" who emerges in Dickinson's life after the death of Dickinson's father, as a source of solace and affection, even as possible fiancé.[1] Unhappily for Dickinson, the one man who seems to have unequivocally loved her and may have wished to marry her died of a stroke in 1884, before anything like a formal engagement was announced. Broken in spirit by this loss, as by numerous others including the terrible typhoid death of a beloved little nephew, Dickinson herself grew ill and died in 1886, at the age of fifty-five.

Benfey locates in the poetry of Dickinson's younger years an obsession with Lord Byron—Byron's famous poem "The Prisoner of Chillon" becomes "the Rosetta stone of (Dickinson's) tortured destiny"—and a frankly sexual undertone to Dickinson's elliptically imagistic poetry of the 1860s:

> I tend my flowers for thee—
> Bright Absentee!
> My Fuschzia's Coral Seams
> Rip—while the Sower—dreams—
>
> Geraniums—tint—and spot—
> Low Daisies—dot—
> My Cactus—splits her Beard
> To show her throat—
> (339, c. 1862)

The passive female being is overcome—seemingly ravished—by the mysterious Byronic "Master" who has never been definitely named by countless biographers and commentators but whose presence in Dickinson's most ardent poetry is unmistakable:

> My life had stood—a Loaded Gun—
> In Corners—till a Day
> The Owner passed—identified—
> And carried me away—

And now We roam in Sovereign Woods—
And now We hunt the Doe—
And every time I speak for Him
The Mountains straight reply—

. . .

Though I than He—may longer live
He longer must—than I—
For I have but the power to kill,
Without—the power to die—
   (754, c. 1863)

Benfey suggests that Dickinson's "Master" poems are addressed to three prominent men in the poet's life, with whom she corresponded in terse, playful, enigmatic letters very like her verse—the "handsome and worldly editor of the *Springfield Daily Republican*" Samuel Bowles; the "brooding . . . Byronic" Protestant preacher Reverend Charles Wadsworth of whom it was thrillingly said that his "dark eyes, hair and complexion (had) a decidedly Jewish cast"; and Colonel Higginson, the prominent Boston literary man to whom Dickinson sent her verse in the pose of a schoolgirl eagerly seeking advice from a distinguished elder, though Dickinson was thirty at the time and had already written— and published, in Samuel Bowles's newspaper—a poem as assured as the one beginning "Safe in their Alabaster Chambers . . ." (21, c. 1862) (The romantic relationship with elderly Judge Lord came later in Dickinson's life.) Here is Dickinson's now-famous letter of appeal, dated April 15, 1862:

Mr Higginson,

Are you too deeply occupied to say if my Verse is alive?

The mind is so near itself—it cannot see, distinctly—and I have none to ask—

Should you think it breathed—and had you the leisure to tell me, I should feel quick gratitude—

If I make the mistake—that you dared tell me—would give me sincerer honor—toward you—

I enclose my name—asking you, if you please—Sir—to tell me what is true?

That you will not betray me—it is needless to ask—since Honor is its own pawn—

We can surmise that Higginson replied with encouragement and a predictable sort of advice, to which Dickinson responded with enigmatic dignity:

You think my gait "spasmodic"—I am in danger—Sir—
You think me "uncontrolled"—I have no Tribunal.

As Benfey notes, Dickinson didn't change a thing in her poems, and assures Higginson that she has no wish to be published: "I smile when you suggest that I delay 'to publish'—that being foreign to my thought, as Firmament to Fin."

Both Benfey and Wineapple are very good at presenting the ways in which Dickinson and Higginson "invented themselves and each other" in their epistolary friendship; in both their books, though at greater length in Wineapple's, Colonel Higginson unexpectedly emerges not as the contemptibly

pompous figure who dared to "correct" the most original poet
of the nineteenth century as if he were indeed her schoolmaster,
which is our usual sense of Higginson, but as a person of considerable courage, imagination, generosity, and achievement.
Unlike his distinguished New England literary mentor Ralph
Waldo Emerson, Higginson managed to combine the intellectual life with the life of a vigorous activist: as a young man he
was a Protestant minister who lost his church as a consequence
of fervent Abolitionist beliefs; a radical in New England re-
formist circles, he was a staunch supporter of John Brown; in
the Civil War he was a colonel who led a contingent of nine
hundred ex-slaves in the occupation of the city of Jacksonville,
Florida. (Higginson later wrote movingly of this experience in
Army Life in a Black Regiment, 1869: "a minor masterpiece"
in Brenda Wineapple's estimation.)

With astonishing zeal and steadfastness Higginson was
an early advocate of women's suffrage as he was a vociferous
advocate of civil rights for Negroes during Reconstruction; he
was a quasi-mystical nature-writer, in the mode of his model
Henry David Thoreau; his *Young Folks' History of the United
States* (1875) became a best-seller. Higginson's first love had
been poetry, in which he may have been slightly discouraged by
a rejection letter from Emerson at *The Dial* that in its devastating brevity deserves enshrinement like the pithier aphorisms of
Oscar Wilde:

[Your verses] have truth and earnestness and a happier hour
may add that external perfection which can neither be com-
manded nor described.

Yet Emily Dickinson seems to have virtually idolized Higginson, having committed to memory much of his published writing in *The Atlantic* and elsewhere and constantly deferring, or seeming to defer, to his "superior" judgment. As Benfey notes, "she told him, twice, that he had saved her life." Their famous first meeting in August 1870, at the Dickinson family home in Amherst, Massachusetts, is preserved solely in Higginson's prose, in a letter to his wife Mary:

> A step like a pattering child's in entry & in glided a little plain woman with two smooth bands of reddish hair & a face . . . with no good features—in a very plain & exquisitely clean white pique & a blue worsted shawl. She came to me with two day lilies which she put in a sort of childlike way into my hand & said "These are my introduction" in a soft frightened breathless voice—& added under her breath, Forgive me if I am frightened; I never see strangers & hardly know what I say—but she talked soon & thenceforward continuously—& deferentially—sometimes stopping to ask me to talk instead—but readily recommencing. [*A Summer of Hummingbirds*]

And, later, somewhat defensively:

> I never was with anyone who drained my nerve power so much . . . Without touching her, she drew from me. I am glad not to live near her. She often thought me *tired*.

Though convinced of Dickinson's originality and of the possibility of her genius, yet Higginson persists in seeing in her something frankly repugnant; he suspects "an excess of tension . . . something abnormal" in her.

Within the loosely constructed space of *A Summer of Hummingbirds*, the epistolary friendship/romance of the self-styled "scholar" Emily Dickinson and her "master" Higginson is but one thread in an entanglement of erotic yearnings, while in the aptly titled *White Heat* the primary focus is a tenderly voyeuristic evocation of the literary couple's relationship, as in these Jamesian elocutions of Wineapple's:

> Totemic assumptions about Emily Dickinson and Thomas Wentworth Higginson do not for a moment let us suppose that she, proffering flowers and poems, and he, the courtly feminist, very much married, were testing the waters of romance. But about their correspondence is its faint hint or, if not of that, then of a flirtation buoyed by compassion, consideration, and affection. . . . (Each) of (Dickinson's) notes bursts with innuendo, attachment, warmth, flattery. . . . She admired his gravitas. "Your thought is so serious and captivating, that it leaves one stronger and weaker too, the Fine of Delight." She admired his probity. "That it is true, Master . . . is the Power of all you write."

How crushed Dickinson must have been by Higginson's remarriage, and by his obvious reluctance to visit her, yet, admirably, as so admirably Dickinson weathered any number of personal blows, in some fusion of female stoicism and pragmatism she seems to have re-channeled her attention upon the elderly widower Judge Otis Lord, a resident of Salem, Massachusetts, to whom she wrote letters of unfettered longing:

> My lovely Salem smiles at me. I seek his Face so often—but I have done with guises.
>
> I confess that I love him—I rejoice that I love him—I thank the maker of Heaven and Earth—that gave him me to love—the exultation floods me. I cannot find my channel—the Creek turns Sea—at the thought of thee—

At the same time, Dickinson continued to write to her "Master" Higginson in elevated, occasionally elegiac terms, as in this final poem sent to Higginson shortly before her death in 1886:

> Of glory not a Beam is left
> But her Eternal House—
> The Asterisk is for the Dead,
> The Living, for the Stars—
>   (1647)

The concluding chapters of Wineapple's *White Heat* are a detailed scrutiny of Dickinson's posthumous career—"posthumous" being the only career possible for one of such startlingly original gifts, as if, in the midst of the revered Hudson Valley landscape painting of the nineteenth century there might have appeared the unsettling canvases of Cézanne. How does one *see* what is so radically new, still more how does one draw *meaning* from it? Leaving 1775 poems of varying degrees of legibility and completion, often in teasingly variant forms, Emily Dickinson presented a considerable puzzle for scholars of her work through the decades, and particularly for her first, at times overwhelmed editors Higginson and the indefatigable Mabel Todd, who could not resist correcting Dickinson's punctuation and other seeming flaws in her verse. It may even be—this would constitute another radical strangeness in Dickinson, amid the staid formality of her era—that "her poems were always in progress, meant to be revised, reevaluated, and reconceived, especially when dispatched to different readers." As Richard Howard suggests, finishing poems may not have interested Dickinson: "her true Flaubert was Penelope, to invert a famous allusion, forever unraveling what she had figured on the loom the day before." It seems like a simple query, why a poem must be *singular* and not rather *plural*, as musical compositions in the mode of John Cage are not fixed and finite but ever-improvised. Perhaps it's only a convention, that the *gravitas* of print seems to insist upon permanence, and it's the "route of evanescence" so magically embodied by Dickinson's poems that is the truest nature of poetry.

Though critical responses were inevitably mixed, with British critics the most roused to contempt, the first edition of Dickinson's *Poems* sold out rapidly through eleven printings in 1891 and the second, "swathed in white, like its author," was another best seller later in the same year. Tireless Mabel Todd, thrilled by her new mission of bringing a New England poetess of genius to the attention of the public, set on the road as a sort of precursor of Julie Harris in *The Belle of Amherst*, giving lectures and readings throughout New England.

Benfey concludes *A Summer of Hummingbirds* with a lyric epilogue titled "Toward the Blue Peninsula" in which, as in a cinematic flash-forward, he breaks the nineteenth-century frame of his gossamer narrative to bring us to Joseph Cornell who, in the mid-1950s, so brilliantly incorporated images from Dickinson's poetry—birds and flowers and jewels and planets—in his box-sculptures "with a ghostly majesty and strangeness." Appropriately, Benfey's ending isn't a critical summing-up or a statement of fact but an evocative poetry: "The window is open. The perch is empty. The bird has flown."

CAST A COLD EYE: JEAN STAFFORD

"This is the day when no man living may 'scape away."
Whenever she tried out a new typewriter, Jean Stafford typed this oracular remark from *Everyman*, the medieval morality play in which, as an undergraduate at the University of Colorado in the early 1930s, she'd played the role of Good Deeds. Recalling the experience decades later, in the preface to the 1971 reprint of her novel *The Mountain Lion*, Stafford notes with characteristic irony: "I spoke [Good Deeds'] lines because I had (and have) the voice of an undertaker."

Of the distinguished short story writers of her era—one that includes Eudora Welty, Peter Taylor, John Cheever, Katherine Anne Porter, and Flannery O'Connor—Jean Stafford (1915–1979) is perhaps the most versatile. Her writerly voice is very aptly described as an "undertaker" voice, never oracular or self-conscious but quite often jarringly jocular in its Doomsday revelations. A virtuoso of that demanding sub-genre the "well-crafted short story," Stafford is yet the author of several novels of which one, *The Mountain Lion*, remains a brilliant achievement, an exploration of adolescence to set beside

Carson McCullers's masterwork *The Member of the Wedding*. Unlike Welty, Taylor, Cheever, and O'Connor, whose fiction is essentially regional in its settings, Stafford has written fiction set as convincingly in Europe ("Innocents Abroad") as in New England ("The Bostonians, and Other Manifestations of the American Scene"); in New York City and environs ("Manhattan Island") as in the semi-fictitious town of Adams, Colorado ("Cowboys and Indians, and Magic Mountains"), that is an amalgam of Covina, California, where Stafford was born, and Boulder, Colorado, where she grew up and attended the University of Colorado. Impatient with all pieties, not least the piety of familial/cultural heritage, Stafford remarks in her preface to these *Collected Stories* that she could not wait to escape her "tamed-down" native grounds: "As soon as I could, I hot-footed it across the Rocky Mountains and across the Atlantic Ocean." Though, into middle age and beyond, Stafford lived in the New York/Long Island area, the evidence of her fiction suggests an essential restlessness, or restiveness: "Most of the people in these stories are away from home, too, and while they are probably homesick, they won't go back."

Stafford's versatility is perhaps most in evidence in the range of tone in her fiction: from the gently melancholic to the savagely comic, from a delicately nuanced mimicry of the waywardness of interior speech to sudden outbursts of shocked clarity ("But the fact is that there has been nothing in my life," as the narrator of "I Love Someone" confides) and concise images that take us beyond mere speech ("The weather overhead was fair and bland, but the water was a mass of little wrathful whitecaps," at the conclusion of "Beatrice Trueblood's Story").

There are numerous animals in Stafford's fiction, always indi-
vidually noted no matter the smallness of their roles: the fat,
comatose tabby cats of "A Country Love Story" who mimic
their mistress's gradual descent into emotional torpor over the
course of a long New England winter; the pet capuchin mon-
keys of "In the Zoo" observed as unnervingly humanized, "so
small and sad and sweet, and so religious-looking with their
tonsured heads that it was impossible not to think their gibber-
ish was really an ordered language with a grammar that some
day some philologist would understand"; and the foundling
German shepherd Laddy, also of "In the Zoo," who plays a
principal, tragic role in the story:

> He grew like a weed; he lost his spherical softness, and his
> coat, which had been sooty fluff, came in stiff and rusty
> black; his nose grew aristocratically long, and his clever,
> pointed ears stood at attention. He was all bronzy, lustrous
> black except for an Elizabethan ruff of white and a tip of
> white at the end of his perky tail ... He escorted Daisy and
> me to school in the morning, laughing interiorly out of the
> enormous pleasure of his life.

In "An Influx of Poets," Cora Savage observes her pet cat Pretty
Baby, whose blissful pride in motherhood is an ironic, in time
bitterly ironic expression of the vulnerability of Cora's emotional state:

> [The kittens] were still blind and [Pretty Baby] was still
> proud, cosseting them with her milk and her bright, abra-

sive tongue and the constant purr into which, now and then, she interjected a little yelp of self-esteem. When she nestled down, relaxed among her produce, I knelt and strongly ran the knuckle of my thumb down the black stripes that began just above her nose and terminated in the wider, blacker bands around her neck, and then I left her to her rapturous business of grooming her kittens, nursing in their blindness and their sleep.

A gambling casino in Knokke-le-Zoute, Belgium, a grubby downscale version of Monte Carlo, nonetheless exerts an almost preternatural spell on a young woman named Abby in "The Children's Game" who succumbs to the hypnotic frenzy of roulette:

> She was still ahead when the wheel was spun for the last time; and when everything was finished she was giddy as she struggled out of her cocoon-like trance. The croupiers' fatigue humanized them; they rubbed their eyes and stretched their legs and their agile hands went damp. Abby was a little dashed and melancholy, let down and drained; she was, even though she had won, inconsolable because now the table, stripped of its seduction, was only a table. And the croupiers were only exhausted workingmen going to bed.

So appalled is Abby by the "monstrous" Belgian town, her appalled fascination inspires Stafford to a tour de force of description as charged with kinetic energy as Dickens's most animated city scenes:

[Knokke-le-Zoute] possessed houses that looked like buses threatening to run them down and houses that looked like faces with bulbous noses and brutish eyes . . . The principal building material seemed to be cobblestones, but they discovered a number of houses that appeared to be made of cast iron. In gardens there were topiary trees in the shape of Morris chairs and some that seemed to represent washing machines. The hotels along the sea were bedizened with every whimsy on earth, with derby-shaped domes and kidney-shaped balconies, with crenellations that looked like vertebrae and machicolations that looked like teeth, with turrets, bow-windows, dormers and gables, with fenestrations hemstitched in brick or bordered with granite point lace. Some of the chimneys were like church steeples and some were like Happy Hooligan's hat. The cabanas, in the hot, dark haze, appeared to be public telephone booths. Even the flowers dissembled and the hydrangeas, looked like utensils that belonged in the kitchen . . . The plazas were treeless plains of concrete where big babies sunned. . . . There was an enormous smell of fish.

And Stafford's characters are a wonderfully motley lot, outsized and garrulous as cartoon bullies, meekly repressed and virginal as the hapless observers in Henry James; adolescent girls and women who struggle to define themselves against their adversaries, and deeply conflicted, self-lacerating women who seem to have succumbed to sexist stereotypes despite their high intelligence. Here, as intelligent as any of Stafford's characters, yet utterly miserable, is Ramona Dunn of "The Echo and the Nemesis," an American graduate student who has come to post-war Heidelberg to study philology:

> Ramona Dunn was fat to the point of parody. Her obesity fitted her badly, like extra clothing put on in the wintertime, for her embedded bones were very small and she was very short, and she had a foolish gait, which, however, was swift, as if she were a mechanical doll whose engine raced. Her face was rather pretty, but its features were so small that it was all but lost in its billowing surroundings, and it was covered by a thin, fair skin that was subject to disfiguring afflictions, now hives, now eczema, now impetigo, and the whole was framed by fine, pale hair that was abused once a week by a *Friseur* who baked it with an iron into dozens of horrid little snails.

Of Stafford's three novels, her first, *Boston Adventure* (1944), published when she was twenty-eight, became a surprise best seller and launched her public career ("The most brilliant of the new fiction writers," *Life* proclaimed, in tandem with a photograph of the strikingly attractive young woman). Subsequent novels *The Mountain Lion* (1947) and *The Catherine Wheel* (1952) were critically well received but not so commercially successful as *Boston Adventure*; Stafford's energies came to be channeled into her short fiction which was prominently published in *The New Yorker* and collected in *Children Are Bored on Sundays* (1954) and *Bad Characters* (1965). Though Stafford wrote books for children and the remarkable *A Mother in History* (1966), a portrait of the mother of Presidential assassin Lee Harvey Oswald, the culmination of her career was *Collected Stories* (1969), nominated for a National Book Award and recipient of the Pulitzer Prize in 1970.

Throughout her career, Stafford drew upon her personal life in her most engaging and fully realized work, but there is virtually nothing in her writing that is self-indulgent, self-pitying or self-aggrandizing. Her most powerfully sustained single work, *The Mountain Lion*, a tragic coming-of-age story set in Stafford's childhood California and Colorado, has elements to suggest autobiography ("what, other than books, could there be for that scrawny, round-shouldered, tall thing [Molly], misanthropic at the age of twelve?") but is narrated with an Olympian detachment that eases in, and out, of its principal characters' minds to stunning effect. Similarly, Stafford's most frequently anthologized stories, "The Interior Castle," "A Country Love Story," and "In the Zoo," bring us into painful intimacy with their female characters only to draw back at climactic moments, like a coolly deployed camera. Indeed, *Cast a Cold Eye*, the title of a collection of pointedly autobiographical stories by Stafford's controversial, slightly older contemporary Mary McCarthy, would have been an ideal title for Stafford's collected stories.

Stafford seems to have defiantly reversed the westward migration of her family, leaving Colorado for Europe soon after graduation from college, with the grandiose and surely quixotic plan of studying philosophy in Heidelberg. She was known to boast to friends that she'd left home at the age of seven; friends commented on her "desperate" wish to have been an orphan.

Like the doomed Molly of *The Mountain Lion*, Stafford was bookish and inclined to writing at a young age. Her early literary heroes were as disparate as Charles Dickens and Proust, Mark Twain, Henry James, and Thomas Wolfe, icons of masculine literary success. Like Willa Cather before her, though without Cather's wish to invent her writing self as male, and like Sylvia Plath to come, Stafford nursed a lifelong contempt for feminine pieties and "nice" behavior; her fierce dislike of her mother's clichéd optimism is very like Plath's for her self-sacrificing mother Aurelia. Where Plath gritted her teeth and wrote determinedly upbeat letters home to Aurelia from England, after Plath's death to be gathered in *Letters Home* in an attempt to correct "cruel and false caricatures" of the mother-daughter relationship in Plath's poetry, Stafford transcribed her mother's letters to her with jeering annotations, to be sent to her friends for their amusement.

"Nothing can more totally subdue the passions than familial piety" it's observed with a shudder in the Colorado-set story "The Liberation." Here, a desperate young woman barely manages to escape from her smothering older relatives, who want to appropriate, like genteel vampires, her imminent marriage. On the train headed east, Polly Bay thinks, "How lonely I have been. And then, 'I am not lonely now.' " Stafford seems to have both despised and feared her father, by her account an obsessive, brutal, bigoted man from whom escape was imperative; in the preface to the *Collected Stories* she speaks glibly of him as the author of a western novel called *When Cattle Kingdom Fell*, which she never troubled to read. (Nor did Stafford read *A Stepdaughter of the Prairie*, a memoir of a

Kansas girlhood by a cousin.) Yet, ironically, as John Stafford toiled for thirty years on a crank analysis of government deficit spending, so Stafford herself would toil for more than twenty years on a novel unfinished at the time of her death, titled "The Parliament of Women." Ironically also, though perhaps unsurprisingly, Stafford was drawn to the volatile, domineering, manic-depressive poet Robert Lowell who wreaked havoc in her life even before she married him, remarking in a letter to a friend that, though Stafford sometimes hated Lowell, "he does what I have always needed to have done to me and that is that he dominates me." (This domination included even such physical abuse as attempted strangulation.)

One of Stafford's most famous stories is "The Interior Castle," an eerie, hallucinatory account of the ordeal of a young woman named Pansy Vannerman who has suffered a terrible injury to her face and head following a traffic accident in a taxi; like Stafford, who was disfigured in an accident caused by Robert Lowell's drunken driving, Pansy must undergo facial surgery that involves extreme pain:

[The surgeon] had now to penetrate regions that were not anesthetized and this he told her frankly . . . The knives ground and carved and curried and scoured the wounds they made; the scissors clipped hard gristle and the scalpels chipped off bone. It was as if a tangle of tiny nerves were being cut dextrously, one by one; the pain writhed spirally. . . . The pain was a pyramid made of a diamond; it was an intense light; it was the hottest fire, the coldest chill, the highest peak.

In this ecstasy of pain, Stafford's normally restrained prose soars to astonishing heights as if the subject were not pain but an unspeakable violation of the self: "[Pansy's] brain trembled for its life, hearing the knives hunting like wolves . . ." It's significant that in Stafford's story, the driver of the crashed car has died, while in life, Robert Lowell survived relatively uninjured, and prevailed upon Stafford to marry him against her better judgment. Their eight-year marriage, far more tempestuous than that of May and Daniel in "A Country Love Story," would end in a painful divorce in 1948 from which Stafford seems never to have fully recovered: she would marry and divorce again, twice; during the final twenty years of her life she would make herself and everyone who knew her miserable with her alcoholism, ill health, and highly vocal misanthropy.

Narrated in the cool, detached tone of a fairy tale, "A Country Love Story" evokes the experience of living with a brilliant man who has become mentally ill. Daniel isn't a celebrated confessional poet but rather a professor given to "private musings" and obsessive work on a research project "of which he never spoke except to say that it would bore [his wife, May.]" To insulate herself from Daniel's unpredictable mood swings, and from the loneliness of their lives in a beautiful but isolated old farmhouse in Maine, May fantasizes a lover who appears in an antique sleigh in the front yard of the house. The lover exudes a ghostly seductiveness: "there was a delicate pallor on his high, intelligent forehead and there was an invalid's languor in his whole attitude. He wore a white blazer and gray flannels and there was a yellow rosebud in his lapel. Young as he was, he did not, even so, seem to belong to her generation, rather, he seemed to be the reincarnation of someone's uncle as he had been fifty years before." Through the long winter in their close quarters, as Daniel becomes increasingly deranged, suspecting May of infidelity, so May becomes increasingly enthralled by her phantom lover: "She took in the fact that she not only believed in this lover but loved him and depended wholly on his companionship." When Daniel demands of her, "Why do you stay here?" May has no answer, as if a spiritual paralysis has overcome her. At the story's end, Daniel has survived the winter and seems to be recovering his sanity while May, exhausted and broken by her ordeal, is "confounded utterly." In a daze she goes outside to sit in the antique sleigh from which her phantom lover has now departed, "rapidly wondering over and over again how she would live the rest of her life."

"A Country Love Story" is reminiscent of Henry James's "The Turn of the Screw" (1899) and Charlotte Perkins Gilman's "The Yellow Wallpaper" (1892), similar tales of seclusion, sexual repression, and psychological disintegration. Stafford would certainly have known James's famous ghost story but isn't likely to have known "The Yellow Wallpaper," long forgotten in Stafford's time but subsequently rediscovered by feminist scholars and now frequently reprinted. Stafford's story strikes the contemporary reader as a missive from a bygone pre-feminist era when marital loyalty, not running for one's life, was the married woman's ideal. Stafford's vision of woman's fate at the hands of men is a dark one, passivity to the point of masochism.

Set in Adams, Colorado, and narrated in the forthright

tone of a middle-aged western woman very different from the
fatally sensitive May, "In the Zoo" is another of Stafford's
tales of what might be called domestic Gothicism. Again, a tyrannical, mentally unbalanced individual dominates a household; Mrs. Placer, or, as she wishes to be called by her charges,
"Gran," becomes a foster mother to two orphaned sisters after
their parents' deaths. Mocked and bullied by Gran, treated,
like servants, the girls grow up "like worms" in an unrelent-
ing atmosphere of "woe and bereavement and humiliation."
The story erupts into physical violence rare in Stafford's fiction, when a vicious watchdog trained by Gran kills a pet mon-
key owned by an elderly friend of the sisters. It's a traumatic
memory both women bear through their lives, as the sinister
influence of Gran seems to have permanently altered their
personalities.

Stafford's last published story, the corrosively memoirist "An Influx of Poets," (1978), is a cold eye cast upon that
post-war era in our cultural history when (male) poets exuded
a Heathcliffian glamour as remote to us now as the smugly
self-congratulatory Norman Rockwell covers of the *Saturday
Evening Post*:

> There was an influx of poets this summer in the state of
> Maine and ours was only one of many houses where they
> clustered: farther down the coast and inland all the way to
> Campobello, singly, in couples, trios, tribes, they were circu-
> lating among rich patronesses in ancestral summer shacks
> of twenty rooms, critics on vacation from universities who

roughed it with Coleman lamps and outhouses but sumptu-
ously dined on lobster and blueberry gems, and a couple
of novelists who, although they wrote like dogs (according
to the poets), had made packets, which, because they were
decently (and properly) humble, they were complimented to
share with the rarer breed.

No more glamorous poet-figure than Theron Maybank, who
attracts women with his "brilliant talk and dark good looks
somehow reminiscent of the young Nathaniel Hawthorne";
a casual anti-Semite ("I would never have a Jew as a close
friend") who nonetheless betrays his desperately vulnerable
wife with a *zaftig* Jewish beauty, encourages her incipient alcoholism and hurtles her "off the brink on which [she] had
hovered for so long into a chasm." This late story of Stafford's
reads like recklessly disguised memoir, giving off sparks of raw,
pained vitality in counterpoint to the more detached rhythms
of "A Country Love Story," its obvious predecessor, concluding
with the most poignant of ritual deaths:

> We had killed Pretty Baby and killed her kittens. Theron him-
> self had put them in a gunnysack and weighted it with stones
> and had rowed halfway out to Loon Islet and dropped them
> among the perch and the pickerel.

Stafford is at her brilliant and tragic best in the unnerving mode of domestic Gothicism, but, elsewhere, she's enormously funny, capable of withering satiric portraits as pitiless

as those by Mary McCarthy, with whom she shares a zestful
disdain for hypocrisy, pretension, and feminine "niceness." The
Manhattan-based stories "Children Are Bored on Sundays,"
"Beatrice Trueblood's Story," and "The End of a Career" por-
tray social types who verge upon caricature, while the obese,
gluttonous egotist Ramona Dunn of "The Echo and the Nemesis" is a clownish type who shocks us with her sudden humanity. (Is Ramona an incest victim? Stafford seems to hint
so, with admirable subtlety.) Lottie Jump, the aptly named
shoplifter-friend of eleven-year-old Emily Vanderpool of "Bad
Characters," is a bold, brash daughter of Oklahoma migrant
workers whose humanity registers upon us belatedly; so too,
Angelica Early of "The End of a Career," who is blinded by the
world's admiring yet condescending attention, fails to develop
a personality and is devastated by even the first, mild ravages
of aging: "her heart, past mending, had stopped." (A virtual
word-for-word replication of the ending of James's *The Turn
of the Screw*.) Several of Stafford's memorable stories elude
definition, striking a chord somewhere between comedy and
horror: in "Cops and Robbers," the drunken, bullying father of
five-year-old Hannah takes her to a barber to have her beautiful long hair shorn, as a way of punishing her mother with
whom he has a quarrel; in "The Captain's Gift," the elderly,
genteel widow of an army general receives from her grandson,
an army captain stationed in Germany in the early 1940s, an
unexplained, alarming gift: "a braid of golden hair . . . cut off
cleanly at the nape of the neck, and so long it must have hung
below her waist."

The impersonal pronoun *her*, unobtrusively inserted here, is a typically chilling Stafford touch.

In her wittily ironic view of humanity, Jean Stafford is reminiscent of Jonathan Swift for whom humankind was divided about evenly into "fools" and "knaves"—naive victims, evil aggressors. Stafford's indignation is hardly less savage than Swift's, though the terms of her moral satire are likely to be realistic. Her most mordant story, "A Modest Proposal," takes its title from Swift's famous satire, providing, in a milieu of rich Caucasian tourists in the Caribbean, the most extreme image in Stafford's fiction: the "perfectly cooked boy"—a native, black baby victim of a house fire—offered to the racist Captain Sundstrom by a jovial friend:

> It was charred on the outside, but I knew it was bound to be sweet and tender inside. So I took him home . . . and told [Sundstrom] to come along for dinner. I heated the toddler up and put him on a platter and garnished him with parsley . . . and you never saw a tastier dish in your life. . . . And what do you think he did after all the trouble I'd gone to? Refused to eat any of it, the sentimentalist! And *he* called *me* a cannibal!

Is the story authentic? Is it a grotesque tall tale, meant to tease Captain Sundstrom's genteel guests? In the shocked aftermath of the narration, one of the guests throws a glass onto the stone floor of the terrace where it "exploded like a shot"—an enigmatic response that, ironically, summons the native kitchen boy to the scene. Stafford's contempt for the gathering, as for the privileged white class to which they belong, is perfectly evoked: "[The kitchen boy] ran, cringing, sidewise like a land crab, and the Captain, seeing him, hollered, "Now, damn you, what do *you* want? Have you been eavesdropping?"

THE ART OF VENGEANCE: ROALD DAHL

Collected Stories
by Roald Dahl,
with an introduction by
Jeremy Treglown

B orn in Llandaff, Wales, of well-to-do Norwegian parents, educated in England and a pilot with the Royal Air Force for part of the Second World War, Roald Dahl (1916–1990) is the author of numerous books for children[1] and a relatively small but distinct body of prose fiction for adults, *Over to You* (1946), *Someone Like You* (1953), *Kiss Kiss* (1960), *Selected Stories* (1970), *Switch Bitch* (1974), and *Eight Short Stories* (1987). The *Collected Stories*, with an excellent introduction by Dahl's biographer Jeremy Treglown, is a gathering of forty-eight stories of considerable diversity, ambition, and quality, with settings ranging from Kenya to rural England, London, and New York City and narrative styles ranging from realistic to the fabulist and surreal. Though a number of Dahl's most engaging stories, particularly in his early career, are cast in a realist mode, Dahl's reputation is that of a writer of macabre, blackly jocose tales that read, at their strongst, like artful variants of the Grimms' fairy tales; Dahl is of that select society of Saki (the pen name of H. H. Munro), Evelyn Waugh, Muriel

Spark, and Iris Murdoch, satiric moralists who wield the English language like a surgical instrument to flay, dissect, and expose human folly. As a female character says in the ironically titled "My Lady Love, My Dove": "I'm a *nasty* person. And so are you—in a secret sort of way. That's why we get along together." Given Dahl's predilection for severely punishing his fictional characters, you might expect this nasty lady to be punished, but Roald Dahl is not a writer to satisfy expectations.

Though in his fiction for adults as in his books for children Dahl exhibits the flair of a natural storyteller, for whom no bizarre leap of the imagination is unlikely, he seems to have begun writing, at the urging of C. S. Forester, as a consequence of his wartime experiences in the RAF, which included crash-landing in the African desert and participating in highly dangerous air battles during the German invasion of Greece. Such early stories as "An African Story," "Only This," "Someone Like You," and "Death of an Old Old Man" draw memorably upon these experiences and suggest that, if Dahl had not concentrated on the short-story form, and more or less abandoned realism for the showy detonations of plot made popular in Dahl's youth by Saki and O. Henry, who both published first collections of stories in the early 1900s, he might have developed into a very different sort of writer altogether. The first story in this volume, "An African Story," is a tale of primitive revenge recounted in the most laconic of voices, as chilling as any of Paul Bowles's parable-like tales of North Africa: an adventurous young RAF pilot develops engine trouble while flying solo above the Kenyan Highlands, makes a forced landing and finds himself on a desert plain where he is given aid by an elderly farmer who tells the pilot an unnerving story, or confession, "so strange that the young pilot wrote it down on paper as soon as he got back to Nairobi . . . not in the old man's words but in his own words," to be discovered by others in his squadron after his death. The anonymous narrator of "An African Story," speaking of his dead colleague, might be speaking as aptly of the young Roald Dahl himself:

> He had never written a story before, and so naturally there were mistakes. He did not know any of the tricks with words which writers use, which they have to use just as painters have to use tricks with paint, but when he had finished writing . . . he left behind him a rare and powerful tale.

In "Only This," a woman lies sleepless with anxiety after having heard a squadron of RAF bombers fly overhead en route to an air battle with the Germans; one of the pilots is her son, whose death by fire, vividly imagined, dissolves the barrier between reality and dreams and between a mother and her son, in this story of Lawrentian subtlety and intimacy that must have been, to Dahl's readers in the early 1940s, deeply moving, like its companion piece "Death of an Old Old Man," a mesmerizing account of the final, excruciatingly protracted minutes of a fighter pilot whose plane has been struck by a German Focke Wulf, forcing him to parachute out, and down, to his death in a muddy pond: "I won't struggle, he thought. There is no point in struggling, for when there is a black cloud in the sky, it is bound to rain." In "Someone Like You," a spare, minimalist story in a heavily ironic Hemingway vein, two former

RAF bomber pilots are getting companionably drunk together not long after the end of the war, reminiscing about "jinking" on their bombing missions:

> "It would just be a gentle pressure with the ball of my foot upon the rudder-bar; a pressure so slight that I would hardly know that I was doing it, and it would throw the bombs on to a different house and onto different people. It is all up to me, the whole thing is up to me and each time that I go out I have to decide which ones shall be killed . . ."
>
> "I jinked once," I said, "ground-strafing I thought I'd kill the ones on the other side of the road instead."
>
> "Everybody jinks," he said. "Shall we have another drink?"

In "The Soldier," a story of 1948, a former soldier's growing paranoia/psychosis is signaled by a pathological growing numbness in his body: by degrees he is losing his capacity to feel sensation, even pain. Suffering from a kind of delayed shell shock—with which his wife is inexplicably unsympathetic—he becomes susceptible to hallucinations and sudden outbursts of rage:

> He moved his hand over to the left—and the moment the fingers touched the knob, something small but violent exploded inside his head and with it a surge of fury and outrage and fear. He opened the door, shut it quickly behind him and shouted: "Edna, are you there?"

Like numerous other calculating females in Dahl's stories, canny Edna saves her life by dissociating herself from her troubled husband, who seems headed for incarceration in a mental asylum at the story's end, like the similarly over-sensitive male protagonist of "The Sound Machine," an amateur scientist named Klausner who has invented an ingenious machine that will be his undoing:

> there is a whole world of sound about us all the time that we cannot hear: It is possible that up there in those high-pitched inaudible regions there is a new exciting music being made, so powerful that it would drive us mad if only our ears were tuned to hear the sound of it . . . This machine . . . is designed to pick up sound vibrations that are too high-pitched for reception by the human ear, and to convert them to a scale of audible tones, I tune it in, almost like a radio.

Since Klausner is "a frail, nervous, twitchy little man, a moth of a man, dreamy and distracted," we are not surprised when the sound machine picks up the "frightful, throatless shrieks" of roses being cut in the garden next door, and the terrible shriek of a tree into which an ax has been driven: "enormous and frightful and . . . it had made him feel sick with horror." Klausner too is led away: the inevitable fate for an individual who hasn't inured himself to the horrors of even ordinary life, like "normal" people.

One of Dahl's most gripping stories is the very brief "The Wish," in which a highly sensitive, imaginative, and lonely child fantasizes lurid dangers in the design of a carpet in his home—"The red parts are red-hot coals . . . the black parts are poisonous snakes"—which he has no choice but to walk on, with nightmare results as an initially playful notion blossoms into what appears to be a full-blown psychosis, or worse. (Are the poisonous snakes really alive?) Subtly rendered, poignantly convincing, "The Wish" is reminiscent of Conrad Aiken's classic tale of encroaching childhood madness, "Silent Snow, Secret Snow." A kindred tale of growing adult paranoia originating in childhood trauma is "Galloping Foxley," in which a London commuter in his early sixties begins to imagine that a fellow passenger on his train is an old public school prefect—"A 'boazer' we called it"—now in his sixties; as a boy, this Foxley had been a brutal sadist allowed by Repton school tradition to beat any of the "fags" in his residence:

> Anyone who has been properly beaten will tell you that the real pain does not come until about eight or ten seconds after the stroke [with a cane]. The stroke itself is merely a loud crack and a sort of blunt thud against your back side, numbing you completely (I'm told a bullet wound does the same). But later on . . . it feels as if someone is laying a red hot poker right across your naked buttocks and it is absolutely impossible for you to prevent yourself from reaching back and clutching it with your hands.

Rare among Dahl's stories, "Galloping Foxley" ends upon an unexpectedly muted, unmelodramatic note.[2]

In the aptly titled "Poison," one of Dahl's most brilliantly realized stories, an Englishman living in Bengal, India, is held thrall in his bed by what he believes to be a krait (a highly poisonous snake common to the region) coiled and sleeping on his stomach, beneath a sheet. The terrified man, unable to move for fear of waking the snake, is aided by a fellow Englishman, the narrator of the story, and by a local Indian doctor who behaves heroically only to be viciously insulted when the ordeal is over by the racist Englishman he'd helped: "You dirty little Hindu sewer rat!" This story, for most of its length an excruciating tale of suspense, exudes the air of a fable even as it must have made for painful reading at the time of its first publication, in the popular American magazine *Collier's*.

After these admirable early stories, in which Roald Dahl would seem to have invested much of his own, intimate experience, Dahl moves decisively away from prose fiction of an intensely inward, sympathetic kind: intimacy is rejected for distance, sympathy for an Olympian detachment, as if the writer were determined not to succumb to the dangers of over-sensitivity like his victim-characters, but to identify with their punitive and sadistic tormenters, like the prefect bully Foxley who goes unpunished for his cruelty. In *Someone Like You*, and in successive collections of stories, Dahl casts a very cold eye upon the objects of his satire who are divided about equally, to paraphrase that most savage of English satirists, Jonathan Swift, between "fools and knaves." Jeremy Treglown speaks of Dahl's admiration for Ian Fleming ("One of his heroes") and of Dahl's increasing focus upon situation, to the exclusion of character:

Critics have often commented on how pared-down Dahl's narrative style at its best can be, and it's interesting how much else he does without. Setting, climate, architecture, food, dress, voice—all are sketched briefly, and with the most familiar, even clichéd strokes, as if to clear the way for what really matters.

As Roald Dahl's books for children are often fueled by fantasies of tricks, pranks, revenge in various guises, so what "really matters" in Dahl's mature work is punishment: "Vengeance Is Mine, Inc.," a slapdash anecdotal tale ostensibly set in New York City, might well be the title for Dahl's collected stories. Like his younger contemporaries Muriel Spark and Patricia Highsmith, Dahl has a zest for blackly comic/sadistic situations in which characters, often hapless, are punished out of all proportion to their wrongdoings. In one of the more subtly crafted stories, the ironically titled "The Way Up to Heaven," first published in *The New Yorker* in 1954, an exasperatingly slow, doddering, self-absorbed old coot, seemingly so wealthy as to live in a "large six-storey house in New York City, on East Sixty-second Street, [with] four servants" and his own private elevator, is allowed, by his long-suffering wife, to remain trapped in the elevator as she leaves for six weeks in Europe to visit with her daughter:

The chauffeur, had he been watching [Mrs. Foster] closely, might have noticed that her face had turned absolutely white and that the whole expression had subtly altered. There was no longer that soft and rather silly look. A peculiar hardness had settled itself upon the features. The little mouth, usually so flabby, was now tight and thin, the eyes were bright, and the voice, when she spoke, carried a new air of authority.

"Hurry, driver, hurry!"

"Isn't your husband traveling with you?" the man asked, astonished.

"Certainly not . . . Don't sit there talking, man. *Get going*! I've got a plane to catch for Paris!"

In a mordantly funny coda that must have stirred visceral dread in male, upper-middle-class *New Yorker* readers of that pre-feminist era, the elderly liberated woman, returning from a highly enjoyable visit with her daughter, is pleased to discover when she re-enters the six-storey town house, a "faint and curious odor in the air that she had never smelled before."

In the frequently anthologized blackly humorous anecdotal tales "Lamb to the Slaughter" and "William and Mary," kindred long-suffering wives of annoying husbands exact lethal if improbable revenge: in "Lamb to the Slaughter," a revenge-tale of comic-book simplicity, a woman named Mary is told by her "senior policeman" husband that he intends to leave her; with a single swing of a frozen leg of lamb, she kills him; when his policeman-colleagues come to investigate, Mary roasts the lamb and serves it to the idiots who, eating, speculate on where the murder weapon might be:

"Personally, I think it's right here on the premises."

"Probably right under our noses . . ."

And in the other room, Mary Maloney began to giggle.

In the belabored revenge fantasy "William and Mary," another exasperated wife named Mary exacts a yet more ingenious revenge upon her husband, or upon his brain, which has been removed from his body following his "death" and kept alive by artificial means in a basin, at enormous expense. In a plot purloined from the popular science-fiction novel *Donovan's Brain* (1943) by Curt Siodmak, the egotistical William Pearl, reduced to what resembles a "great gray pulpy walnut," will be free to luxuriate in a purely intellectual world, "able to reflect upon the ways of the world with a detachment and a serenity that no man had ever attained before" linked to the outside world by a single, ghastly eye, the brain will even be able to peruse the London newspapers. But we know that William, or his brain, will not be treated with the wifely devotion William might have wished for, since Mary is perceived in broadly villainous strokes by a scientist-friend of her husband:

> What a queer little woman this was, he thought, with her large eyes and her sullen, resentful air. Her features, which must have been quite pleasant once, had now gone completely. The mouth was slack, the cheeks loose and flabby, and the whole face gave the impression of having slowly but surely sagged to pieces through years and years of joyless married life.

Mary's revenge too is one of comic-book simplicity: she will take her husband's brain away with her, and blow smoke rings into the permanently opened eye: "I just can't wait to get him home."

This is the art, if "art" is the appropriate term, of caricature that prefers to jab, stab, slash its subjects instead of attempting to present them with any degree of complexity or sympathy. Grotesque descriptions of flat, cartoon characters are Dahl's stock-in-trade, intended perhaps to be amusing but often merely peculiar, as in this thumbnail sketch of a mildly deranged gentleman named Mr. Botibol:

> He resembled, to an extraordinary degree, an asparagus. His long narrow stalk did not appear to have any shoulders at all; it merely tapered upwards, growing gradually narrower and narrower until it came to a kind of point at the top of the small bald head. He was tightly encased in a shiny blue double-breasted suit, and this . . . accentuated the illusion of a vegetable to a preposterous degree.

Elsewhere, in the jokey "Dip in the Pool," Mr. Botibol, or his namesake, is described as resembling a "bollard" with "skinny legs . . . covered in black hairs": his fate is to drown in the ocean as a senile old woman gazes on unperturbed. Dahl's females are particularly grotesque specimens, like Mrs. Ponsonby of "Nunc Dimittis" who is "so incredibly short and squat and stiff, [she looked as if] she had no legs at all above the knees," has a "salmon mouth" and fingers "like a bunch of small white snakes wriggling in her lap." The narrator of this sour little anecdote is an elderly bachelor—a "vicious, vengeful old man"— who takes revenge upon a woman friend for having gossiped about him by displaying a portrait of her part-naked, unattractive body to their mutual friends; that the poor woman wears a hefty brassiere ("an arrangement of black straps as skillfully and scientifically rigged as the supporting cables of a suspension bridge") and is "bow-legged, like a jockey" is presented as particularly shocking. (The portrait painter of "Nunc Dimittis" would seem to have been modeled upon Gustav Klimt, known to have painted his female subjects nude before clothing them in their elaborate fin-de-siècle finery.) Most notably, there is the formidable president of the Daughters of the American Revolution, yet another, presumably unrelated Mrs. Ponsonby:

> The door was opened by the most enormous female I had ever seen in my life. I have seen giant women in circuses. I have seen lady wrestlers and weight-lifters . . . But never had I seen a female so tall and broad and thick as this one. Nor so thoroughly repugnant . . . I was able to take most of it in—the metallic silver-blue hair with every strand glued into place, the brown pig-eyes, the long sharp nose sniffing for trouble, the curled lips, the prognathous jaw, the powder, the mascara, the scarlet lipstick and, most shattering of all, the massive shored-up bosom that projected like a balcony in front of her . . . And there she stood, the pneumatic giant, swathed from neck to ankles in the stars and stripes of the American flag.

It must be that such misogynist female portraits are self-portraits of the misogynist's malformed soul, they draw forth such quivering, barely containable loathing.[3]

As Jonathan Swift is the most obsessively scatological of English satirists, so Roald Dahl is the most obsessively sexual, in stories as casually lewd as "The Great Switcheroo" (two men, wholly ordinary husbands and fathers, plot to "switch" wives in the night, without the silly wives' knowing) or as doggedly protracted as "Bitch" (the womanizer Oswald Cornelius finances the development of a perfume with irresistible aphrodisiac powers, brand-name "Bitch") in which the very man who is revolted by massive Mrs. Ponsonby ends up having sex with her in what, one assumes, Dahl means to be a comic scene:

> I was standing naked in a rosy room and there was a funny feeling in my groin. I looked down and saw that my beloved sexual organ was three feet long and thick to match. It was still growing. It was lengthening and swelling at a tremendous rate ... Bigger and bigger grew my astonishing organ, and it went on growing, by God, until it had enveloped my entire body and absorbed it within itself. I was now a gigantic perpendicular penis, seven feet tall and handsome as they come.

In the breezy "Mrs. Bixby and the Colonel's Coat" the unnamed narrator, presumably speaking for the author, with the impassioned lunacy of Philip Wylie ranting about women—"Momism"—in the long-forgotten screed against women *Generation of Vipers* (1942), informs us:

> America is the land of opportunity for women. Already they own about eighty-five percent of the wealth of the nation. Soon they will have it all. Divorce has become a lucrative process ... Young men marry like mice, almost before they

reach the age of puberty, and a large proportion of them have at least two ex-wives on the payroll by the time they are thirty-six years old. To support these ladies in the manner to which they are accustomed, the men must work like slaves, which is of course precisely what they are.

Yet, from time to time, a clever man can exact a merciless punishment upon a woman, even when, as in "The Last Act," the woman has been a devoted wife to her late husband, after years of mourning at last daring to revive an old boyfriend's interest in her, with cataclysmic results:

> Then at last, Conrad put his tongue into one of her ears. The effect upon [Anna] was electric. It was as though a live two-hundred-volt plug had been pushed into an empty socket, and all the lights came on and the bones began to melt and the hot molten sap went running down into her limbs and she exploded into a frenzy . . . She flung her arms around Conrad's neck and started kissing him back with far more gusto than he had ever kissed her and although he looked at first as though he thought she was going to swallow him alive, he soon recovered his balance.

In this crude misogynist fable which Jeremy Treglown in his introduction concedes that Dahl "would have done better to have scrapped," the vengeful Conrad so humiliates Anna sexually, the poor woman is driven to commit suicide.

In the yet cruder misogynist fantasy "Georgy Porgy," a

priggish, sexually repressed minister is both repelled by and attracted to women:

> Provided they remained at a safe distance, I could watch them for hours on end with the same peculiar fascination you yourself might experience in watching a creature you couldn't bear to touch—an octopus, for example, or a long poisonous snake.

Recoiling from his childhood experience with a cartoon monster-mother, George conducts improbable experiments with white rats, determining that the female of the rat species is more sexually rapacious than the male, even when death by electrocution is involved; it's no surprise that he falls prey to a female parishioner with the ominous name Roach whose face is covered with a "pale carpet of fuzz" and whose enormous mouth, threatening a kiss, is "huge and wet and cavernous." Soon, in a parody-paroxysm of female sexual desire, Miss Roach begins to "grunt and snort like a hog"; crying, "Don't! Don't, Mummy!" George finds himself sucked into the woman's very mouth where, after a ludicrous struggle reminiscent of certain of the mock-heroic adventures of Swift's Lemuel Gulliver among the giant Brobdignagians, the virginal bachelor is swallowed: "I could feel the slow powerful pulsing of peristalsis dragging away at my ankles, pulling me down and down and down . . ."

Dahl's punished figures are not exclusively sexual victims: in "Taste," a nouveau riche wine connoisseur is insulted at his own dinner table by a "famous gourmet"; in "The Pig," as in a cautionary Grimms' fairy tale for greedy children, a young man who cares too much for food is led off to be butchered with other pigs strung up by their ankles: "taking Lexington gently by one ear with his left hand, [the slaughterer] raised his right hand and deftly slit open the boy's jugular vein with a knife."

Not all of Dahl's stories end so grimly, and not all of Dahl's satire is sadistic. The funniest story in the collection, and one in which no one gets killed or even humiliated, is "The Great Automatic Grammatizator," an eerily prescient fable of 1952 in which an aspiring young writer invents a computer-printing press to churn out ingeniously formulaic books:

> First, by depressing one of a series of master buttons, the writer made his primary decision: historical, satirical, philosophical, political, romantic, erotic, humorous or straight. Then, from the second row (the basic buttons), he chose his theme: army life, pioneer days, civil war, world war, racial problem, wild west, country life, childhood memories . . . The third row of buttons gave a choice of literary style: classical, whimsical, racy, Hemingway, Faulkner, Joyce, feminine, etc. The fourth row was for character, the fifth for wordage . . . ten long rows of pre-selector buttons.

Within a year, the machine has produced "at least one half of all the novels and stories published in the English language."

Except for writers of major stature, in whose lesser work there may be some archival, extra-literary, or morbid interest, the indiscriminate all-inclusiveness of a "collected stories" is not a good idea. What a dispiriting sight, a table of contents listing forty-eight short stories with no divisions into books and dates, as the author himself had intended! (No short story writer, like no poet, would simply toss a chronological arrangement of his work into a form so lacking in interior structure: individual collections of short stories and poems have beginnings, middles, and ends that have been judiciously pondered.) Though the advantage of a purely chronological arrangement of work is that the reader may perceive the development of a writer's style, his growth, and the prevailing themes that make his work distinctive, the disadvantage is that the reader may perceive the deterioration of the writer's style, his decline, and his reliance upon predictable themes. Of the forty-eight stories, scarcely more than one-third seem truly notable, and these come relatively early in Dahl's lengthy, forty-five-year career. The volume trails away in affable narrated anecdotal sketches, as if Dahl had lost interest in the craft of storytelling as he seems to have lost the sting of vengefulness. The last four or five stories might have been printed out by the Great Automatic Grammatizator or by "Georgy Porgy" who, after his nervous breakdown, seems to have become a writer-satirist whose final object of satire is writing itself:

> I find that writing is a most salutory occupation at a time like this, and I spend many hours a day playing with sentences. I regard each sentence as a little wheel, and my ambition lately has been to gather several hundred of them together at once and to fit them all end to end, with the cogs interlock-

ing, like gears, but each wheel a different size, each turning at a different speed. Now and then I try to put a really big one right next to a very small one in such a way that the big one, turning slowly, will make the small one spin so fast that it hums. Very tricky, that.

REVISITING NABOKOV'S *LOLITA*

Laughter is the primeval attitude toward life—an
attitude that survives only in artists and criminals.
—OSCAR WILDE

Like all classics, *Lolita* is a special case. An occasion for
enormous controversy—bitter denunciations, fulsome
praise—at the time of its publication in 1955, the novel has
acquired, over the decades, like such scandalous predecessors
as James Joyce's *Ulysses* and D. H. Lawrence's *Lady Chatter-
ley's Lover*, the patina of the lewd classic: far more people have
heard of it, and have an opinion about it, than have read it. Individuals with virtually no interest in literature, particularly the
fussily self-referential, relentlessly ornate Nabokovian manner,
know who Lolita was, or is; or imagine that they do. Humbert
Humbert, the narrator of *Lolita, or The Confession of a White
Widowed Male*, the hapless lover of the twelve-year-old American schoolgirl, provides a definition of the "Lolita" prototype:

Between the age limits of nine and fourteen there occur
maidens who, to certain bewitched travelers, twice or many

times older than they, reveal their true nature which is not human, but nymphic (that is, demoniac); and these chosen creatures I propose to designate as "nymphets."

(Is Humbert Humbert a pedophile? In fact, he gives little evidence of being attracted to girls as young as nine, fortunately; his erotic attractions are for older girls, who arouse his ardor as "little nymphs" or "nymphets," who seem to mimic adult sexuality while retaining a childlike innocence.) Nabokov makes clear by way of Humbert's background that the nymphet-prototype precedes the actual girl: as Humbert had been in love as a prepubescent boy with a girl named Annabel, whom the slangy, vulgar, so very American Lolita later embodies. We are meant to think that Humbert's (perverse, criminal) predilection for prepubescent girls is his fate, and not his choice.

Famously, Humbert confides in the reader, as to a panel of jurors, his most shocking revelation:

Frigid gentlewomen of the jury! I had thought that months, perhaps years, would elapse before I dared to reveal myself to Dolores Haze; but by six she was wide awake, and by six fifteen we were technically lovers. I am going to tell you something very strange: it was she who seduced me.

And, later, in trying to describe "that strange, awful, maddening world—nymphet love," Humbert confides:

I have but followed nature. I am nature's faithful hound. Why then this horror that I cannot shake off? Did I deprive her of her flower? Sensitive gentlewomen of the jury, I was not even her first lover.

Like Oscar Wilde, similarly torn between the "demonic" attractions of the flesh, in Wilde's case for young boys, and the propriety of a sternly judging society, Humbert Humbert experiences his predicament as so hopeless, the conflicts of his appetites so beyond remedy, he has no recourse but to turn to comedy for solace. *Lolita* is richly stocked with "realistic" details, for Nabokov had a sharp, shrewd eye, especially for human failings, but in essence *Lolita* is a blackly surreal comedy. Humbert Humbert is a comic character, forever trying to explain himself, excuse himself, and yet, in the next breath, incriminating himself further; after he has become Lolita's lover, and is legally her stepfather, he tries to seduce her into being a kind of accomplice of his in incorrigible sex-deviant fashion:

> In whatever town we stopped I would inquire, in my polite European way, anent the whereabouts of . . . local schools. I would park at a strategic point, with my vagrant schoolgirl beside me in the car, to watch the children leave school— always a pretty sight. This sort of thing began to bore my so easily bored Lolita . . . she would insult me and my desire to have her caress me while [schoolgirls] passed by in the sun.

Even in this outrageous confession, Humbert Humbert tries to seduce the reader into sympathizing with him: deviancy isn't a choice but a fate. Isn't it cruel of Lolita to insult *him*.

Lolita is a brilliantly nuanced portrait of a sex addict in thrall to his addiction even when the addiction has been and can be satisfied by someone close at hand; for always there is a yearning for the new, the not-yet-attained, the anonymous schoolgirls passing Humbert's car—bodies of "immortal daemons" disguised as female children that seem, for the moment, to have eclipsed Humbert's lust for Lolita. Humbert is a comic portrait of the very type for whom pornography has been invented and by whom, in the United States alone, it has become a billion-dollar industry for its addicts are continually yearning, continually sated and continually ravenous for more.

In his archly self-defensive afterword to the 1956 edition, Vladimir Nabokov speaks scornfully of those who attempt to read *Lolita* for its pornographic potential. One can argue that there is, at *Lolita*'s core, a soft-core/sentimental pornographic romance, but few readers intent upon pornography will have the patience to make their way through the author's Byzantine prose. (Reading *Lolita* for its erotic content is akin to reading Mary Shelley's *Frankenstein* for its horror content.) Especially, such readers will be deterred by the lengthy, increasingly improbable and forced melodrama-farce of Part II, in which a sinister double of Humbert Humbert named Clare Quilty appears to seduce Lolita away from her deranged stepfather. (In the impressively executed but not very sensuous 1962 film of *Lolita* directed by Stanley Kubrick, Clare Quilty is given a campy/clownish portrayal by Peter Sellers while James Mason is a sensitive but not very "demonic" Humbert Humbert.) *Lolita* is much-read and admired by undergraduate English majors with whom Nabokov's cutting, somewhat adolescent sarcasm strikes a chord: his Humbert Humbert is an adult, skewed version of J. D. Salinger's Holden Caulfield who, as we may recall, has a powerful emotional attachment to his younger sister, and feels a general revulsion for most grown-ups.

Scandalous in its time, *Lolita* has transcended the circumstances of its early controversy as it has transcended the circumstances of its time and place: late 1940s, early 1950s "repressed" America. Along with *Pale Fire*, Nabokov's yet more ambitious novel of 1962, *Lolita* is a feat of literary legerdemain, a shimmering cascade of brilliant passages set like jewels in an elegant tapestry. It is surely one of the most convincing portrayals in literature of, if not the human condition per se, the (fated) condition of the obsessive.

SHIRLEY JACKSON'S WITCHCRAFT: *WE HAVE ALWAYS LIVED IN THE CASTLE*

> We eat the year away. We eat the spring and the
> summer and the fall. We wait for something to
> grow and then we eat it.
>
> —SHIRLEY JACKSON, FROM *WE HAVE*
> *ALWAYS LIVED IN THE CASTLE*

Of the precocious children and adolescents of mid-twentieth-century American fiction—a dazzling lot that includes the tomboys Frankie of Carson McCullers's *The Member of the Wedding* (1946) and Scout of Harper Lee's *To Kill a Mockingbird* (1960), the murderous eight-year-old Rhoda Penmark of William March's *The Bad Seed* (1954), and the slightly older, disaffected Holden Caulfield of J. D. Salinger's *The Catcher in the Rye* (1951) and Esther Greenwood of Sylvia Plath's *The Bell Jar* (1963)—none is more memorable than eighteen-year-old "Merricat" of Shirley Jackson's masterpiece of Gothic suspense *We Have Always Lived in the Castle* (1962). At once feral child, sulky adolescent, and Cassandra-like seer, Merricat addresses the reader as an intimate:

My name is Mary Katherine Blackwood. I am eighteen years old, and I live with my sister Constance. I have often thought that with any luck at all I could have been born a werewolf, because the two middle fingers on both my hands are the same length, but I have had to be content with what I had. I dislike washing myself, and dogs, and noise. I like my sister Constance, and Richard Plantagenet, and *Amanita phalloides*, the death-cup mushroom. Everyone else in my family is dead.

Merricat speaks with a seductive and disturbing authority, never drawn to justifying her actions but only to recounting them. One might expect *We Have Always Lived in the Castle* to be a confession, of a kind—after all, one or another of the Blackwood sisters poisoned their entire family, six years before—but Merricat has nothing to confess, still less to regret; *We Have Always Lived in the Castle* is a romance with an improbable—magical—happy ending. As readers we are led to smile at Merricat's childish self-definition, as one who dislikes "washing myself"; it will be many pages before we come to realize the significance of *Amanita phalloides* and the wish to have been born a werewolf. In this deftly orchestrated opening, Merricat's wholly sympathetic creator/collaborator Shirley Jackson has struck every essential note of her Gothic tale of sexual repression and rhapsodic vengeance; as it unfolds in ways both inevitable and unexpected, *We Have Always Lived in the Castle* becomes a New England fairy tale of the more wicked variety, in which a "happy ending" is both ironic and literal, the consequence of unrepentant witchcraft and a terrible sacrifice—of others.

Like other, similarly isolated and estranged hyper-sensitive young-female protagonists of Shirley Jackson's fiction— Natalie of *Hangsaman* (1951), Elizabeth of *The Bird's Nest* (1954), Eleanor of *The Haunting of Hill House* (1959)— Merricat is socially maladroit, highly self-conscious and disdainful of others. She is "special"—her witchery appears to be self-invented, an expression of desperation and a yearning to stop time with no connection to satanic practices, still less to Satan. (Merricat is too willful a witch to align herself with a putative higher power, especially a masculine power.) Her voice is sharp, funny, compelling—and teasing. For more than one hundred pages Merricat taunts us with what she knows, and we don't know; her recounting of the tragic Blackwood family history is piecemeal, as in the tangled back-story there is an echo of Henry James's *The Turn of the Screw*—that masterwork of unreliable narration in which we are intimate witnesses to a naively repressed young woman's voyeuristic experience of sexual transgression and "exquisite pathos." Like the innocent pubescent-girl-protagonists of *The Member of the Wedding* and *To Kill a Mockingbird*, Merricat Blackwood appears to be a typical product of small town rural America—much of her time is spent outdoors, alone with her companion cat Jonas; she's a tomboy who wanders in the woods, unwashed and her hair uncombed; she's distrustful of adults, and of authority; despite being uneducated, she is shrewdly intelligent, and bookish. At times Merricat behaves as if mildly retarded, but only outwardly; inwardly, she's razor-sharp in her observations, and hyper-alert to threats to her well-being. (Like any damaged person Merricat most fears change in the unvarying rituals of her household.) A mysterious amalgam of the childlike and the treacherous, Merricat is "domesticated" by only one person, her older sister Constance.

> "Wear your boots if you wander today," Constance told me . . .
>> "I love you, Constance," I said.
>> "I love you too, silly Merricat."

There is a lovely lyricism to her observations when she's alone, and out-of-doors:

> The day outside was full of changing light, and Jonas danced in and out of shadows as he followed me . . . We were going down into the long field which today looked like an ocean, although I had never seen an ocean; the grass was moving in the breeze and the cloud shadows passed back and forth and the trees in the distance moved . . . I am walking on buried treasure, I thought, with the grass brushing against my hands and nothing around me but the reach of the long field with the grass blowing and the pine woods at the end; behind me was the house, and far off to my left, hidden by trees and almost out of sight, was the wire fence our father had built to keep people out.

Even in this pastoral setting Merricat is brought back forcibly to the prejudices of her upbringing: the Blackwoods' contempt for others.

If Merricat is mad, it's a "poetic" madness like the madness of the young heroine of *The Bird's Nest*, whose subdued personality harbors several selves, or the madness celebrated by Emily Dickinson—"Much Madness is divinest Sense—/To a discerning Eye—/Much sense—the starkest Madness—'Tis the Majority" [435]. Her condition suggests paranoid schizophrenia in which anything out of the ordinary is likely to be threatening and all things are signs and symbols to be deciphered—"All the omens spoke of change." Merricat is determined to deflect "change"—the threat to her household—through witchcraft, a kind of simple, sympathetic magic involving "safeguards": "the box of silver dollars I had buried by the creek, and the doll buried in the long field, and the book nailed to the tree in the pine woods; as long as they were where I had put them nothing could get in to harm us." Merricat—surely like her creator—is one for whom words are highly potent, as well:

On Sunday morning the change was one day nearer. I was resolute about not thinking my three magic words and would not let them into my mind, but the air of change was so strong that there was no avoiding it; change lay over the stairs and the kitchen and the garden like fog. I would not forget my magic words; they were MELODY GLOUCESTER PEGASUS, but I refused to let them into my mind.

By degrees we learn that there are many household tasks that Merricat isn't allowed to do, like help in the preparation of food or handle knives. Minor frustrations have a violent effect upon her: "I could not breathe; I was tied with wire, and my head was huge and going to explode . . . I had to content myself with smashing the milk pitcher which waited on the table; it had been our mother's, and I left the pieces on the floor so that Constance would see them." It's ironic that Merricat's aristocratic disdain of other people derives from her identification with her rich New England family—now nearly extinct—whom she seems to have hated violently when they were alive. It may have been her parents' disciplining of her that precipitated the family tragedy when, as Uncle Julian reminisces, Merricat was "a great child of twelve, sent to bed without her supper."

In the novel's opening, suspenseful chapter, Merricat must make her way from the Blackwood manor house at the edge of the village into town, as the intermediary between the remaining Blackwoods and the outer world: "Fridays and Tuesdays were terrible days, because I had to go into the village. Someone had to go to the library, and the grocery; Constance never went past her own garden, and Uncle Julian could not." Here is no Grover's Corners as in Thornton Wilder's sentimental classic of small town America, *Our Town*: this is a New England town of "dirty little houses on the main highway"—a place of unmitigated "ugliness" and "rot" where dwell individuals poised to "come at [Merricat] like a flock of taloned hawks—birds descending, striking, gashing with razor claws." Hostility toward the Blackwoods seems to have predated the Blackwood poisoning scandal:

> The people of the village have always hated us . . . The blight on the village never came from the Blackwoods; the villagers belonged here and the village was the only proper place for them.
>
> I always thought about rot when I came toward the row of stores; I thought about burning black painful rot that ate away from inside, hurting dreadfully. I wished it on the village.

Merricat's fantasies are childish, alarmingly sadistic: "I am walking on their bodies."—"I am going to put death in all their food and watch them die."—"I would have liked to come into the grocery some morning and see them all, even the Elberts and the children, lying there crying with the pain and dying. I would then help myself to groceries . . . stepping over their bodies, taking whatever I fancied from the shelves." Such unmitigated hatred, out of all proportion to any source within *We Have Always Lived in the Castle*, suggests a savage Swiftian indignation that passes beyond social satire of the kind written by Jackson's older contemporaries Sinclair Lewis and H. L. Mencken, into the realm of psychopathological caricature. (Jackson's difficulties with her fellow citizens in North Bennington, Vermont, are well documented in Judy Oppenheimer's harrowing biography *Private Demons*, 1988: the suggestion is that Jackson and her husband, the flamboyant "Jewish-intellectual" cultural critic Stanley Edgar Hyman aroused resentment, if not outright anti-Semitism, in their more conventional Christian neighbors.) The animosity of the villagers for the Blackwoods suggests the priggish racism of Jackson's subtly modulated short story "Flower Garden"—in which a newcomer to a New England village unwisely befriends a resident black man—and the barbaric behavior of the villagers of Jackson's most famous story "The Lottery" in which a yearly ritual of scapegoating and stoning to death is enacted by lottery. Here, in a place said to closely resemble the North Bennington of Shirley Jackson's day, a dirge-like tune of unknown origin prevails from generation to generation, unquestioned by the brainless local citizenry:

Lottery in June, corn be heavy soon.

In *We Have Always Lived in the Castle*, a jeering chant follows in Merricat's wake when she ventures into town:

Merricat, said Connie, would you like a cup of tea?
Oh, no, said Merricat, you'll poison me.

In the village, life is crude, cruel, noisy and ugly; in the Blackwood manor house, life is quiet, sequestered, governed by the daily custom and ritual of mealtimes, above all inward— "Almost all of our life was lived toward the back of the house, or the lawn and the garden where no one else ever came . . . The rooms we used together were the back ones." The Blackwood house isn't haunted in quite the way that Hill House is haunted ("No live organism can continue for long to exist sanely under conditions of absolute reality. Hill House, not sane, stood by itself against its hills, holding darkness within . . ."), but its former, now deceased inhabitants emerge in portentous times, in Merricat's sleep, calling her name—to warn her? To torment her? By degrees we discover the secret of the Blackwood house—the poisonings, by arsenic, six years before, of the entire family except Constance, then twenty-two years old, Merricat, then twelve, and their Uncle Julian. Constance, who'd prepared the meal that day, and took care to wash out the sugar bowl before police arrived, was accused of the poisonings, tried and acquitted, for lack of sufficient evidence; Merricat was sent away for the duration of the trial, then brought back to live with Constance and her uncle in their diminished household. (Julian, who has never recovered from the trauma of being poisoned, persists in believing that Merricat died in the "orphanage"—despite the fact that he and his niece inhabit the same house.) Merricat's uncle is preoccupied with writing up his account of the poisonings:

> In some ways, a piece of extraordinarily good fortune for me. I am a survivor of the most sensational poisoning case of the century. I have all the newspaper clippings. I knew the victims, the accused, intimately, as only a relative living in the house *could* know them. I have exhaustive notes on all that happened. I have never been well since.

Why no one seems to suspect—as the reader does, immediately—that the unstable Merricat, not the amiable Constance, is the poisoner is one of the curiosities of the novel, as it's a mystery why Constance is so indulgent of Merricat, who contributes nothing to the household. Certainly there's little subterfuge in Merricat's teasing of others, in alluding to various kinds of poisons; her tormenting of her cousin Charles contains a transparent threat:

> "The *Amanita phalloides*," I said to [Charles], "holds three different poisons. There is amanitin, which works slowly and is most potent. There is phalloidin, which acts at once, and there is phallin, which dissolves red corpuscles ... The symptoms begin with violent stomach pains, cold sweat, vomiting ... Death occurs between five and ten days after eating."

Constance's mild reproach: "Silly Merricat."

In much of Shirley Jackson's fiction food is fetishized to an extraordinary degree; ironic then, that the Blackwood family should be poisoned by one of their own, out of a family-heirloom sugar bowl. That the food-fetish has its erotic component is suggested by the means of poison—*Amanita phalloides*—and by the way Merricat so totally depends upon her older sister as a food provider, as if she were an unweaned infant and not a "great child" grown into an adult. Sexual attraction per se is virtually nonexistent in Jackson's fiction: the single sexual episode in all of her work appears to be a molestation of some kind, short of rape, that occurs in an early scene of *Hangsaman*—"Oh my dear God sweet Christ, Natalie thought, so sickened she nearly said it aloud, is he going to *touch* me?"—but the episode isn't described, and is never acknowledged by the afflicted young woman, who gradually succumbs to schizophrenia. Nowhere in Jackson's work is food more elaborately fetishized than in *We Have Always Lived in the Castle*, in which the three remaining members of a once-aristocratic family have virtually nothing to do but inhabit their blighted house and "eat the year away" in meals which the older sister prepares for them, three times a day, like clockwork; as in a Gothic parody of the comical self-portraits Shirley Jackson created for the women's magazine market in the 1950s, in such best-selling books as *Life Among the Savages* (1953) and *Raising Demons* (1956)—a housewife-mother's frustrations transformed, as by a deft twist of the wrist, into, not a grim account of disintegration and madness, still less the poisoning of her family, but lighthearted comedy. (It's ironic to note that Shirley Jackson died at the age of forty-nine, shortly after the publication of *We Have Always Lived in the Castle*, of amphetamine addiction, alcoholism and morbid obesity; negligent of her health for years, she is said to have spoken openly of not expecting to live to be fifty, and in the final months of her life suffered from agoraphobia so extreme she couldn't leave her squalid bedroom—as if in mimicry of the agoraphobic sisters of *We Have Always Lived in the Castle*.)

As Merricat has uneasily sensed, "change" is imminent, and will bring with it the invasion of the Blackwood household. Without having been invited, the sisters' boorish cousin Charles arrives, intent upon stealing their deceased father's money, which he believes to be in a safe; he dares to take Mr. Blackwood's position at the head of the dining room table—"He even *looks* like father," Constance says. Unwisely Charles threatens his young cousin Merricat: "I haven't quite decided what I'm going to do with you . . . But whatever I do, you'll remember it." It's a measure of Constance's desperation that though Charles is not a very attractive man, she appears drawn to him, as a way into a possible new life, a prospect terrifying to Merricat. Yet, the slightest wish on Constance's part for something other than her stultifying robot-life, and Merricat reacts threateningly, for the sisters' secret is the intimate bond between them, that sets them apart from all of the world. Throughout the novel there is the prevailing threat of the murderous Merricat whose fantasy life is obsessed with rituals of power, dominance, and revenge: "Bow your heads to our beloved Mary Katherine . . . or you will be dead."

The hideous arsenic deaths constitute the secret heart of *We Have Always Lived in the Castle*, as unspecified sexual acts appear to be at the heart of *The Turn of the Screw*: the taboo yet irresistible subject upon which all thinking, all speech, all actions turn. The sisters are linked forever by the deaths of their family, as in a quasi-spiritual-incestuous bond by which each holds the other in thrall. Food-shopping (by Merricat), food-preparation (by Constance), and food-consumption (by both) is the sacred, or erotic ritual that binds them, even after the house has been partly demolished by fire and they are living in its ruins:

"It is a very happy place, though." Constance was bringing breakfast to the table: scrambled eggs and toasted biscuits and blackberry jam she had made some golden summer. "We ought to bring in as much food as we can," she said . . .

"I will go on my winged horse and bring you cinnamon and thyme, emeralds and clove, cloth of gold and cabbages."

Witchcraft is a primitive attempt at science; an attempt to assert power by the powerless. Traditionally witchcraft, like voodoo, and spiritualism, has been the province of marginal individuals of whom most are women and girls. In Shirley Jackson's novel of multiple personalities, *The Bird's Nest*, the afflicted young heroine's psychiatrist—aptly named Dr. Wright—tries to explicate the bizarre psychic phenomena he has been trying to "cure":

> "Each life, I think . . . asks the devouring of other lives for its own continuance; the radical aspect of ritual sacrifice, the performance of a group, its great step ahead, was in organization; sharing the victim was so eminently practical. [*The Magic of Shirley Jackson*]

> The doctor spoke slowly, in a measured voice . . . : "The human creature at odds with its environment . . . must change either its own protective coloration, or the shape of the world in which it lives. Equipped with no magic device beyond . . . intelligence . . . the human creature finds it tempting to endeavor to control its surroundings through manipulated symbols of sorcery, arbitrarily chosen, and frequently ineffectual."

Shirley Jackson is rarely so explicit in her thematic intentions: it's as if her literary-critic/English professor husband Stanley Edgar Hyman were lecturing to her, in a manner that sounds like mild self-parody even as it helps to illuminate both the tangled *Bird's Nest* and the ruined *Castle.*

After Merricat sets a fire in the Blackwood house in the hope of expelling her detested cousin Charles, the yet more detested villagers swarm onto the private property. Some are firemen who seem sincere in their responsibility of putting out the fire but most want to see the Blackwood house destroyed: "Why not let it burn?"—"Let it burn!" The jeering rhyme is heard:

> Merricat, said Constance, would you like a cup of tea?
> Merricat, said Constance, would you like to go to sleep?
> O no, said Merricat, you'll poison me.

Radical change has swept upon the Blackwoods through the agency of Merricat, ironically. The fire she sets causes the death of Uncle Julian, the sisters are forced to flee into the woods, villagers enter the private residence and vandalize it. Yet, when the sisters return, in a tenderly elegiac scene, they discover that though most of the rooms are uninhabitable, all they require— a kitchen, primarily, where Constance can continue to prepare meals for Merricat—has been left intact. As if by magic the old house has been transformed: "Our house was a castle, turreted and open to the sky." Against all expectations the Blackwood sisters are happy in their private paradise "on the moon."

"I love you, Constance," I said.

"I love you too, Merricat," Constance said.

Constance has succumbed to Merricat entirely: the "good" sister has yielded to the "evil" sister. Constance even berates herself for being "wicked"—"I should never have reminded you of why they all died"—in this way acknowledging her complicity in the deaths. Now we understand why Constance never accused Merricat of the poisonings or made any attempt to defend herself against accusations that she was the murderer for, in her heart, she *was* and *is* the Blackwoods' murderer, and not Merricat; that is, not only Merricat. Her acknowledgment tacitly guarantees the sisters' permanent expulsion from the world of normal people—a world in which the psychologically damaged Merricat could not survive. *We Have Always Lived in the Castle* ends on an unexpectedly idyllic note like a fairy-tale romance in which lovers have found each other and even the villagers, repentant of their cruelty, pay the Blackwood sisters homage by bringing food-offerings to them, left at the ruins of their doorstep: "Sometimes they brought bacon, home-cured, or fruit, or their own preserves . . . Mostly they brought roasted chicken; sometimes a cake or a pie, frequently cookies, sometimes a potato salad or coleslaw . . . Sometimes pots of baked beans or macaroni." Here is the very Eros of food, an astonishing wish-fulfillment fantasy in which the agoraphobic is not pitied but revered, idolized; the destruction of her house isn't death to her, but a new life protected by magic: "My new magical safeguards were the lock on the front door, and the boards over the windows, and the barricades along the sides of the house." Repeatedly as in a rapture Merricat cries "Oh, Constance, we are so happy." The sisters' jokes are slyly food-oriented, of course:

"I wonder if I *could* eat a child if I had the chance."
"I doubt if I could cook one," said Constance.

"AS YOU ARE GROOVED, SO YOU ARE GRIEVED": THE ART AND THE CRAFT OF BERNARD MALAMUD

In this illuminating biography of Bernard Malamud by Philip Davis, the first full-length biography of Malamud to be published, a story is told how, when Malamud was in his late fifties, a Pulitzer Prize winner (for *The Fixer*, 1966) and twice National Book Award winner (for *The Magic Barrel*, 1959, and *The Fixer*), at the height of his reputation and yet assailed by self-doubt, Malamud remarked to a friend that he regretted not having known the love of several beautiful women. Knowing the writer's lifelong preoccupation with routines, schedules, and the devoting of every possible hour to his work, his companion replied that such love affairs would have taken up a good deal of Malamud's time: "Which of your books would you have given up for these loves?" Malamud was silent for a moment and then said, "None."

The Yeatsian conundrum—"perfection of the life, or of the work?"—carries with it an overtone of (unconscious?) megalomania: for who, counting even William Butler Yeats, is likely to achieve "perfection" in either life or work; rather more, the writer might hope to perform as brilliantly in both as he is capable, or simply to perform at all, with a modicum of success in both quarters. Yet, to the desperately ambitious Malamud, as he emerges in Philip Davis's sympathetic yet persuasively "objective" portrait of the artist, such paradoxical questions were of the utmost importance, for to Malamud writing was not merely "writing" but carried with it an element of the visionary and the magical:

> "The more I see of artists the more I think of the great talent in the frail self." How many "nebbishes"—weak, spineless people—look good, [Malamud said] because of "this marvelous book of magic in them." What Malamud wanted ... was to "look good as a man," to use some of his magical talent as an artist to "improve as a person." It "goes with the theory I have of the person as 'stuff': 'stuff'" was the raw material of one's life, and self-will could be deployed to shape that stuff and form it creatively not just in writing but in living ... "I think that art would be richer if the self were."

The writer Jay Cantor, a student in Malamud's writing class at Harvard in the mid-1960s, vividly recalls:

> Malamud was a short man, with a close-clipped greying mustache, wearing often a grey cloth cap and a somewhat grey and restrained manner. He was surrounded then, and always, by an air that was both melancholy and decisive, as if he were weighed down by the guidance of a special Talmud only he knew about that said he must move, speak, act, in a certain way, whether it gave him pleasure or not.

More comically, Malamud's daughter Janna Malamud Smith, in her unsparing and oddly tone-deaf memoir *My Father Is a Book* (2006)—surely the most chilling of titles!—recalls how, when the Malamuds were living in Oregon and Malamud was teaching at Oregon State University at Corvallis, then as now not the most distinguished of American universities, as a little girl she would overhear her father talking to himself while shaving: "Someday I'm going to win." There is a Woody Allen–esque irony to the fact that, when Malamud received the National Book Award for *The Magic Barrel*, he was at last "allowed" to teach literature at this university best known for its agricultural school. (Malamud soon quit Oregon and returned to the East, where he would teach intermittently at more prestigious Bennington College for much of his academic life.) And even Malamud's publisher, the gratingly corrosive Roger Straus (of Farrar, Straus and Giroux) would one day sneer at the possibility of a biography of Malamud: "I think it's ridiculous. There was nothing there; as a life it was unexciting. Saul Bellow was filet mignon, Malamud was hamburger." (In droll Yiddish it would sound better: with such friends, who needs enemies?)

Shallow-flashy Straus was mistaken: Bernard Malamud is indeed well worth a biography, and in Philip Davis, Professor of English at the University of Liverpool, he has been posthumously very lucky to have been granted an ideal biographer, who has more than fulfilled laudable aims: "To place the work above the life to show how the life worked very hard to turn itself into that achievement" and to "show serious readers all that it means to be a serious writer, possessed of an almost religious sense of vocation—in terms of both the uses of and the costs to an ordinary human life." [p. vii]

Born in Brooklyn in 1914, of Jewish immigrant parents, Malamud seems to have been obsessively preoccupied with memories of his arduous, impoverished background, as of the stoic example of his grocer-father, through his life. Long after Malamud had ascended to the literary aristocracy of his time— president of American PEN, member of the American Academy of Arts and Letters, recipient of countless awards and honorary doctorates, not least the author of an eccentric baseball novel, *The Natural*, made into a film starring Robert Redford—he gives evidence of being as "time-haunted" as he'd been as a boy whose father had fled Ukraine "amid a rising tide of anti-Semitism and pogroms" and whose mother died in a mental hospital when he was fifteen. (Malamud would one day remark to an interviewer that he had to find in a "second life" what he had lost in his "first life": "The death of my mother, while she was still young, had an influence on my writing and there is in my fiction a hunger for women that comes out in a conscious way.") Like many another child of immigrant parents, Malamud was determined to invent himself as an American; he distinguished himself as a student, attended Columbia University on a government loan and received a master's degree in English in 1942 (his thesis, on Thomas Hardy's reputation as a poet in American periodicals, seems to have been uninspired and pedestrian); he began writing fiction while teaching high school in Brooklyn, began to be published in the mid-1940s, and achieved his first notable successes in the 1950s when his remarkable short stories, one day to comprise *The Magic Barrel*, began to be published in such magazines as *Partisan Review* and *Harper's Bazaar*. Subsequent to his marriage to "an Italian beauty"—not without warning her: "Though I love you and shall love you more, most of my strength will be devoted to realizing myself as an artist"—and their move to faraway Oregon in 1949, Malamud began to publish frequently, and well; in *Discovery*, *The New Yorker*, the *Saturday Evening Post*, and *Playboy*; his early novels *The Natural* (1952) and *The Assistant* (1957) were acclaimed, and *The Magic Barrel*, the most impressive of Malamud's several story collections, quickly acquired the aura of a Jewish-American classic. (And how aptly titled, this gathering of stories that so brilliantly combine the gritty realism of contemporary urban settings with the fabulist "magic" of the Jewish storytelling tradition.) Malamud's third novel, *A New Life* (1961), set in an Oregon academic community very like Corvallis, with an idealistic but schlemiel-like protagonist named Levin, has an idiomatic ease and accessibility that distinguishes it from Malamud's more characteristic work, and certainly from *The Fixer*, a grimly compelling fable-like tale of virulent anti-Semitism in Tsarist Russia, as if Isaac Bashevis Singer and Franz Kafka had collaborated with Dostoyevsky to come up with the worst possible nightmare for a Jew, the accusation of having committed a ritual murder/sacrifice of a Christian child. (Yakov Bok's gradual emergence as a tragic hero is the substance of Malamud's novel, which was enormously difficult and exhausting for him to write over a period of several years: "Something in me has changed. I'm not the same man I was. I fear less and hate more."—a triumphant if treacherous epiphany for a Jew held captive in a Russian prison on lurid criminal charges.)

Beyond *The Fixer*, Malamud seems to have cast about for a comparably worthy subject: though he worked with his characteristic obsessiveness on the semi-autobiographical *Dubin's Lives* (1979), and on the fabulist/prophetic *God's Grace* (1982), it is Malamud's short stories that constitute the most memorable work of the last two decades of his life, notably the masterfully executed and compelling "My Son the Murderer," "Talking Horse," and the near novella-length "Man in the Drawer" from *Rembrandt's Hat* (1973). In 1982 *The Collected Stories of Bernard Malamud* was published to much critical acclaim and in 1989, three years after his death of a heart attack, Malamud's final, incomplete novel *The Ghosts* was published along with his previously uncollected stories.

In the prime of his career in the 1960s and early 1970s, Bernard Malamud was as highly regarded as his coeval Saul Bellow and his younger contemporary Philip Roth: an accidental triumvirate of terrifically talented Jewish-American writers ruefully described (by Bellow himself) as the "Jewish equivalent of the first-generation rag trade gone upmarket—the Hart, Schaffner, and Marx of literature." (Add to which, as in a Chagall fantasy, the transfigured Isaac Bashevis Singer, the most triumphantly "Jewish" of twentieth-century American writers, floats overhead.) Given the relative narrowness of Malamud's subject matter, the more subdued range of his writerly voice, and an aesthetic puritanism temperamentally at odds with the flamboyant self-displays of Bellow (*Herzog, Humboldt's Gift*) and Roth (*Portnoy's Complaint* etc.), it seems inevitable, if unfortunate, that Malamud should come to seem, in time, the least impressive of the four; Bellow's and Singer's Nobel Prizes (1976 and 1978 respectively) have given their work the imprimatur of international acclaim, and Roth's dazzling energies, that continue to this very hour, have given to Roth's work an air of improvident virtuosity utterly foreign to Malamud's more journeyman-like career. In the preface to this biography Philip Davis notes that he was invited to undertake the project by the Malamud family out of their concern "that (Malamud's) name was fading, his readership and literary standing in danger of decline."

In the preface, too, Davis quotes the notorious remarks of Sigmund Freud on the futility of the biographical enterprise:

> Anyone turning biographer has committed himself to lies, concealment, to hypocrisy, to flattery, and even to hiding his own lack of understanding, for biographical truth is not to be had, and even if it were it couldn't be useful.

So irrational an outburst provokes one to wonder what Freud was desperate to conceal from biographers, and whether he succeeded; in the case of Philip Davis's life of Malamud, it would seem that the subject, Malamud-as-a-writer, was both enigmatic to observers (like Frank Alpine of *The Assistant*, "he could see outside but no one could see in") and yet in his letters, drafts, and notes to himself, Malamud is tireless in his self-scrutiny, as if eager to be understood. Unsparing of what he perceives to be his limitations, Malamud yet takes pride in his hard-won accomplishments. Davis speaks of Malamud's commitment to "the human sentence"—prose that has been shaped through countless revisions: "The sentence as object—treat it like a piece of sculpture." The biography is a virtual treasure trove of writerly *pensées*, many of a quality to set beside those of Virginia Woolf gathered by Leonard Woolf in *A Writer's Diary*. Here emerges Bernard Malamud as a tireless craftsman trusting not to rushes of inspiration but to "labor":

> If you think of me at my desk, you can't be wrong—today, tomorrow, next month, possibly even a year from now. I sometimes wonder when there is time to live although somehow I do.

> When I can't add or develop, I refine or twist. Can you see that in my work?

> Rewriting tends to be pleasurable, in particular the enjoyment of finding new opportunities in old sentences, twisting, tying, looping structure tighter, finding pegs to tie onto that were apparently not there before, deepening meanings, strengthening logicality in order to infiltrate the apparently illogical the apparently absurd, the absurdly believable.

> Today I worked in mosaics, sentences previously noted, and put together in many hours . . . Today I invented sunshine; I invented it in the book and the sky of the dark day broke.

> I would start the story, writing each paragraph over and over until I was satisfied, before I went on to the next. Some writers can write a quick first draft—I can't. I can't stand rereading a first draft, so I had to make each paragraph as good as

it could possibly be at the time. Then when I had the whole story down, I found I could revise with ease.

Work slowly . . . Don't push tomorrow in today.

I love magic and the imagination is magic.

I have not given up the hero—I simply use heroic qualities in small men.

I don't know how not to work.

Art is a free man's prison.

Some are born whole, others must seek this blessed state in a struggle to achieve order.

I (succeed) in afterthought. I connect revisions with reformation.

My gift is to create what might be deeply felt.

One thing about writing, you have to create a rhythm for it . . . Having a bad time at the beginning is almost necessary, it's nothing more than the struggle to create and it's continually a struggle except that if you keep it right the struggle can become a dance. This week I'm dancing; I hope you are.

[Reading Hemingway as a young man] I was like the body of a cello which Hemingway drew his bow across. Hemingway was vibrating with the thing unsaid, which ultimately became death.

When you feel a sudden shaft of light in yourself after reading a story, you must ask yourself what did it and then you can do it.

As you are grooved, so you are grieved. One is conditioned early in family life to an interpretation of the world. And the grieving is that no matter how much happiness or success you collect, you cannot obliterate your early experience—diminished perhaps, it stays with you.

Most biographies trudge along the surface of a life, amassing and presenting facts, like rubble on a shovel, in which a very few precious gems might be visible; this pioneering biography of Bernard Malamud presents gem-like aphorisms like those quoted above, and insights and observations of the biographer's, on virtually every page. It is rare that a biographer succeeds in evoking, with a novelist's skill, such compassion for his (flawed, human) subject; yet more rare, that a biographer succeeds in so drawing the reader into the shimmering world he has constructed out of a small infinity of letters, drafts, notes, manuscripts, printed texts, interview transcripts, etc., that the barrier between reader and subject becomes near-transparent.

"LARGE AND STARTLING FIGURES": THE FICTION OF FLANNERY O'CONNOR

Flannery: A Life of Flannery O'Connor
by Brad Gooch

> Writers who see by the light of their Christian
> faith will have, in these times, the sharpest eye
> for the grotesque, for the perverse, and for the
> unacceptable ... To the hard of hearing you shout,
> and for the almost-blind you draw large and
> startling figures.
>
> —FLANNERY O'CONNOR, "THE FICTION
> WRITER AND HIS COUNTRY,"
> *MYSTERY AND MANNERS*

> Whenever I'm asked why Southern writers
> particularly have a penchant for writing
> about freaks, I say it is because we can still
> recognize one.
>
> —FLANNERY O'CONNOR, "SOME ASPECTS
> OF THE GROTESQUE IN SOUTHERN
> FICTION," *MYSTERY AND MANNERS*

Short stories, for all the dazzling diversity of the genre,
are of two general types: those that yield their meanings

subtly, quietly, nuanced and delicate and without melodrama as the unfolding of miniature blossoms in Japanese chrysanthemum tea, and those that explode like firecrackers in the reader's face. Flannery O'Connor (1925–1964) came of age in a time when subtlety and "atmosphere" in short stories were fashionable—as in the finely wrought, understated stories of such classic predecessors as Anton Chekhov, Henry James, James Joyce and such American contemporaries as Katherine Anne Porter, Eudora Welty, Peter Taylor, and Jean Stafford—but O'Connor's plain-spoken, blunt, comic-cartoonish and flagrantly melodramatic short stories were anything but fashionable. The novelty of her "acidly comic tales with moral and religious messages"—in Brad Gooch's aptly chosen words—lay in its frontal assault upon the reader's sensibility: these were not refined *New Yorker* stories of the era in which nothing happens except inwardly, but stories in which something happens of irreversible magnitude, often death by violent means. An escaped convict called The Misfit offhandedly slaughters a Southern family in back-country Georgia ("A Good Man Is Hard to Find")—a conniving old woman marries off her retarded daughter to a sinister one-armed tramp named Shiftlet, who immediately abandons the girl and drives off with the old woman's car ("The Life You Save May Be Your Own")—an embittered young woman who has changed her name from Joy to Hulga, crippled by the loss of a leg (in a "hunting accident" when she was ten), is seduced by a hypocritical young Bible salesman who steals her wooden leg ("Good Country People")—boy-arsonists set fire to a wooded property out of pure meanness, like latter-day prophets "dancing in a fiery fur-

nace" ("A Circle in the Fire")—a widowed property owner
who imagines herself superior to her tenant-farmers is gored
to death by their runaway bull ("Greenleaf")—a mentally dis-
turbed girl reading a textbook called *Human Development* in a
doctor's waiting room suddenly throws the book at the head of
a garrulous middle-class woman who imagines herself superior
to "poor-white trash" ("Revelation"). In the novella-length
Wise Blood (1952), O'Connor's first book publication, the fanatic Hazel Motes proclaims himself a prophet of the "Church
without Christ" and does penance for his sins by gouging out
an eye—in O'Connor's second, kindred novel *The Violent Bear
It Away* (1960), the fanatic young Francis Marion Tarwater
drowns an idiot cousin while baptizing him, is drugged and
raped by a sexual predator, revives and lurches off, like Yeats's
rough beast awakened, "toward the dark city, where the children of God lay sleeping."

     In the 1950s, when Flannery O'Connor first began to pub-
lish such idiosyncratic and mordantly comic fiction as *Wise
Blood* and the story collection *A Good Man Is Hard to Find*
(1955), the seemingly reclusive young writer from Milledgeville, Georgia—in Brad Gooch's description a "sleepy community at the dead center of Georgia" of which O'Connor said
dryly, "We have a girls' college here, but the lacy atmosphere
is fortunately destroyed by a reformatory, an insane asylum,
and a military school"—was perceived as a younger cousin
of such showier, more renowned and best-selling Southern
Gothic contemporaries as Carson McCullers and Truman
Capote.[1] In the wake of the more robust tall-tale Gothicism
of William Faulkner and Erskine Caldwell, with its encoded

social/political significance, and unambiguous heterosexuality, the extreme, effete, self-consciously grotesque and sexually ambiguous fiction of McCullers and Capote attracted a good deal of quasi-literary media attention: recall the simperingly effeminate dust jacket photo of Truman Capote for his debut novel *Other Voices, Other Rooms* (1948), and the scandalous quasi-literary life of the precocious McCullers who published her first, widely acclaimed novel *The Heart Is a Lonely Hunter* (1940) at the age of twenty-three, and by the age of thirty, given to alcoholic excess and a disastrous private life, was a burnt-out case despite the considerable achievement of *The Member of the Wedding* (1946). How ironic that during their turbulent, highly publicized lifetimes McCullers and Capote were far more famous than Flannery O'Connor, of whose invalided private life little was known, or might be said to be worth knowing; as O'Connor observed to a friend, "As for biographies, there won't be any biographies of me because, for only one reason, lives spent between the house and the chicken yard do not make exciting copy."

Through her radically truncated career, O'Connor's outwardly sensational, quirkily "Christian" fiction aroused mixed critical responses and modest sales; yet, though she was to die of lupus at the young age of thirty-nine, leaving behind a relatively small body of work, her reputation has steadily increased in the intervening years, while those of McCullers and Capote have dramatically shrunk. Having long exhausted his talent by the time of his alcohol- and drug-related death in 1984, at the age of sixty, Capote is now most regarded for his "non-fiction novel" *In Cold Blood*, atypical among his work;

McCullers may be remembered as a precociously but unevenly gifted writer of fiction for young adults whose work has failed to transcend its time and place. In such anthologies as *The Best American Short Stories of the Twentieth Century* edited by John Updike, Flannery O'Connor is included with one of her most frequently reprinted stories, "Greenleaf," while McCullers and Capote are missing altogether. Indeed, no postwar/ posthumous literary reputation of the twentieth century, with the notable exception of Sylvia Plath, has grown more rapidly and dramatically than that of O'Connor whose relatively small body of work has acquired a canonical status since her death in 1964.[2]

All this, in the face of O'Connor's unfashionable religious sensibility, in a mid-twentieth-century secular/materialist literary culture indifferent if not inhospitable to conservative Christian belief of the kind that seems to have shaped every aspect of the author's life. It's instructive to learn, for instance, in Gooch's meticulously detailed account of O'Connor's parochial-school background in Savannah, Atlanta, and her similarly circumscribed girlhood in Milledgeville, that O'Connor was born to an "Old Catholic" family with social pretensions on the mother, Regina's, side: a lifelong tug-of-war seems to have been enacted between the (quietly, slyly) rebellious Flannery and (stubborn, self-righteous and unflagging) Regina whose effort to mold her daughter into "the perfect Southern little girl" were doomed to failure. Instructive, too, to learn that the precociously gifted O'Connor thought of herself as "ancient" while still a child; the great trauma of her girlhood was her father Edward's death, from lupus, when O'Connor was fifteen, an event perceived by the stricken girl as a sign of God's grace equivalent to "a bullet in the side." "I can with one eye squinting take it all as a blessing." In retrospect, the title *Wise Blood* acquires a painfully ironic significance: O'Connor was destined to die of the incurable disease inherited from her father as if there were, in a cosmology of an unfathomable and mysterious cruelty condoned by the inscrutable God of the Roman Catholic faith, a "wisdom" in this tainted blood. In O'Connor's more transparent religious stories, that read like eccentric comic-strip parables—"The Enduring Chill," "Revelation," "Parker's Back," "The Artificial Nigger"[3]—meaning is suggested in blunt forceful images, as in the religious sonnets of John Donne or the metaphysical love-poems of the self-doubting Jesuit Gerard Manley Hopkins; these stories can be read, if not fully grasped, without recourse to Catholic dogma. (In his persuasive essay on O'Connor's work in *Sewanee Review*, 1962, "Flannery O'Connor's Devil," John Hawkes suggests that despite O'Connor's professed concern for morality, "the driving force of the immoral creative process transforms the author's objective Catholic knowledge of the devil into an authorial attitude in itself in some measure diabolical." [*The Art and Vision of Flannery O'Connor*, by Robert H. Brinkmeyer, Jr.] Of course, O'Connor herself denied such an attitude—*her* devil wasn't a merely literary devil but the "objective" Devil of Catholic theology.

In the primly didactic, earnestly school-girlish and forth-right essays and letters posthumously published under the titles *Mystery and Manners* (1969) and *Flannery O'Connor: Spiritual Writings* (2003), O'Connor speaks at length and repeatedly of her identity as a writer—"I write the way I do because (not though) I am a Catholic" (*Spiritual Writings*)—"The universe of the Catholic fiction writer is one that is founded on the theological truths of the Faith, but particularly on three of them which are basic—the Fall, the Redemption, and the Judgment. These are doctrines that the modern secular world does not believe in" (*Spiritual Writings*). O'Connor never suggests the slightest ambiguity concerning the supernatural underpinnings of her work—its calculatedly "incarnational" aspect ("The Nature and Aim of Fiction") [*Mystery and Manners*]—and her role as a writer possessed of an "anagogical vision"—"the kind of vision that is able to see different levels of reality in one image or situation." (*Mystery and Manners*). It isn't surprising that O'Connor might casually identify herself as a "thirteenth-century" Roman Catholic or that she cherishes the didactic possibilities of her art:

> The medieval commentators on Scripture found three kinds of meaning in the literal level of the sacred text: one they called allegorical, in which one fact pointed to another; one they called topical, or moral, which had to do with what should be done; and one they called anagogical, which had to do with the Divine life and our participation in it . . . I think it is this enlarged view of the human scene that the fiction writer has to cultivate if he is ever going to write stories that have any chance of becoming a permanent part of our literature.
>
> "The Nature and Aim of Fiction"

Writing fiction empowered by such a vision has no analogue within the secular universe—only the mystically committed writer could imagine that her writerly efforts might aid in her very salvation.

For instance, O'Connor offered this modest assessment of the elliptically autobiographical *The Violent Bear It Away*: "The book is a very minor hymn to the Eucharist." [*The Habit of Being*, ed. Sally Fitzgerald]. Yet more modestly, O'Connor seems to have thought of her writing as "an adjunct to her Roman Catholic faith" [*Flannery O'Connor, A Life* by Jean W. Cash], and spoke often in letters of the inspiration she drew from reading specifically Catholic writers (Lord Acton, John Henry Newman, Philip Hughes, Pierre Teilhard de Chardin and the "lofty lucent prose of Thomas Aquinas"); "I read theology," O'Connor boasted, "because it makes my writing bolder." By temperament and training puritanical, if not virulently anti-sexual, O'Connor was drawn to the writings of the eminent French Catholic novelist François Mauriac whose books addressed "the irreconcilability of sexual passion with the world of pure spirit"; in her mid-twenties, as a graduate writing student in the Iowa Writers' Workshop, O'Connor was so timid about sexual matters that she worried that an obscure "seduction" passage in one of her Workshop stories was "liable to corrupt anybody that read it and me too." (O'Connor's solution was to seek advice from an Iowa City priest who told her, commendably, that she "didn't need to write for fifteen-year-old girls"—though there is no evidence in O'Connor's fiction that she ever did write about anything remotely sexual, let alone salacious or obscene. The closest is the implied pederast rape scene at the end of *The Violent Bear It Away*.) Religious belief seems to be irrevocably fused, in O'Connor's imagination, with extreme sexual repression characteristic of the 1950s—like one of her fanatic adolescent preachers O'Connor was given to denouncing the "fornication" of New York City without having any firsthand experience of the city and to have impressed Elizabeth Hardwick, in 1949, when they'd met at Yaddo, as "like some quiet, puritanical convent girl from the harsh provinces of Canada . . . A plain sort of young, unmarried girl, a little bit sickly. And she had a very small-town Southern accent . . . whiney. She whined. She was amusing." Gooch includes a somewhat caddish account by a Harcourt, Brace textbook salesman named Erik Langkjaer who in 1954 forged a romantic sort of friendship with O'Connor which seems to have involved mostly long, intimate drives into the Georgia countryside.

> "I may not have been in love," [Langkjaer recounts in an interview] "but I was very much aware that she was a woman, and so I felt that I'd like to kiss her . . . She may have been surprised that I suggested the kiss, but she was certainly prepared to accept it."

> Yet, for [Langkjaer], the kiss felt odd. Remarkably inexperienced for a woman of her age [near-thirty], Flannery's passivity alarmed him. "As our lips touched I had a feeling that her mouth lacked resilience, as if she had no real muscle tension in her mouth, a result being that my own lips touched her teeth rather than lips, and this gave me an un-

happy feeling of a sort of *memento mori*, and so the kissing stopped."

(As O'Connor's earlier infatuation with the young, attractive, charismatic poet Robert Lowell, whom she'd encountered in a manic state at the Yaddo writers' colony, in 1948, remained unrequited, so O'Connor's relationship with Langkjaer must have been terribly disappointing to her, if not devastating, when, not long after this clumsy encounter, Langkjaer fell in love with a Danish woman whom he eventually married.) O'Connor's reaction to Langkjaer's abrupt departure from her life—the writer's inspired revenge on her erstwhile "material"—can be gauged by the brilliantly acidulous short story "Good Country People," clearly modeled after O'Connor's thwarted romance, in which a crudely manipulative Bible salesman kisses the one-legged philosophy Ph.D. Joy/Hulga prior to running off with her wooden leg:

he put his hand on her back again and drew her against him without a word and kissed her heavily.

The kiss, which had more pressure than feeling behind it, produced that extra surge of adrenalin in the girl that enables one to carry a packed trunk out of a burning house, but in her, the power went at once to the brain. Even before he released her, her mind, clear and detached and ironic anyway, was regarding him from a great distance, with amusement but with pity. She had never been kissed before but she was pleased to discover that it was an unexceptional experience and all a matter of the mind's control.

As Nietzsche tersely observed: "A joke is an epitaph on the death of a feeling." So sorrow in love might be transformed, through the corrosive alchemy of art, into something that, if a sour sort of compensation, can lay claim at least to a kind of quasi-permanence.

More touching than O'Connor's relationship with Langkjaer, and far more crucial to her emotional life, was O'Connor's close friendship of many years with an ardent admirer of her fiction named Betty Hester who'd been "dishonorably discharged" from the military for something called "sexual indiscretion"; Gooch is gentlemanly and tactful in suggesting that O'Connor herself may have been attracted to Hester, as to another intimate friend of this period, the "irrepressible" Maryat Lee, in ways other than merely Platonic. To the Atlanta novelist and critic Greg Johnson, to whom Betty Hester wrote more than forty years after O'Connor's death, Hester said, "As you must sense, I did love her *very*, very much—and, God knows, *do*." Yet with what prissy didacticism O'Connor declares herself homophobic: "As for lesbianism I regard that as any other form of uncleanness. Purity is the twentieth-century's dirty word but it is the most mysterious of the virtues."

In this engaging, sympathetic and yet intellectually scrupulous biography of O'Connor—something of a virtuoso performance, for a biographer whose previous sympathetic subject was the extravagantly and unapologetically "impure" Frank O'Hara[4]—Brad Gooch provides the ideal biographical commentary: his voice is never obtrusive, yet we feel his judgment throughout; his allegiance to his subject is never in doubt, yet we sense his critical detachment, especially in his tracing of

the ways in which "Flannery"—as Gooch calls O'Connor—
seems to have mapped out a strategy of survival for herself.
The most poignant sections of *Flannery* are the later chapters
when, trapped in her mother's house in the back-country Georgia she'd once hoped to flee, forced to remain a child as a consequence of her crippling illness, O'Connor bravely strove to
redeem her situation through her art and through every outward gesture of her intractable faith—including even a visit to
Lourdes in 1958. (Though no one visits Lourdes without the
implicit hope of experiencing a miracle, O'Connor cast herself
as something of an "accidental pilgrim" who joked that she
was "one of those people who could die for his religion sooner
than take a bath for it"—meaning an immersion in "holy water.") Even as her lupus steadily worsened, O'Connor remained
an unfailingly devout Catholic waking each morning, early,
"as soon as the first chicken cackles," with a ritual reading of
prayers from a breviary before being driven into Milledgeville
by Regina to attend 7:15 A.M. mass at Sacred Heart Church;
her writing life was compressed into just a few hours, but
these hours were precious to her, under the protection of her
mother. On her very deathbed O'Connor was determined to
work—"My my I do like to work . . . I et up that one hour like
it was filet mignon." O'Connor's childlike dependence upon
her formidable mother—the model, as Gooch suggests, for a
striking number of older, garrulous, smugly self-centered and
self-righteous Southern women in O'Connor's fiction[5]—was
paralleled by her childlike dependence upon religious ritual
and custom, an unswerving faith in the literal—i.e., not merely
"symbolic"—Eucharist, believed by Catholics to be the actual

blood and body of their savior Jesus Christ. To believe in such seeming illogic is the test of a Catholic's faith, characterized by O'Connor as submission to the mystery at the core of our spiritual beings:

> If the writer believes that our life is and will remain essentially mysterious, if he looks upon us as beings existing in a created order to whose laws we freely respond, then what he sees on the surface will be of interest to him only as he can go through it to the experience of mystery itself. His kind of fiction will always be pushing its own limits outward toward the limits of mystery. ["Some Aspects of the Grotesque in Southern Fiction"]

Only in the final years of her life did O'Connor come to feel dissatisfaction with her "large and startling figures" as a mode of artistic expression, as Gooch poignantly draws a parallel between the physical exhaustion of her worsening lupus and her sense of the limitations of her art. In a letter to a Catholic nun O'Connor asks for the woman's prayers:

> I've been writing eighteen years and I've reached the point where I can't do again what I know I can do well, and the larger things that I need to do now, I doubt my capacity for doing.

Rarely did O'Connor complain, still less protest her fate: "I expect anything that happens." If she claims, with what sounds like commingled wonder and rage, "I have never been

anywhere but sick," quickly she modifies her statement by
adding, aphoristically: "In a sense sickness is a place more instructive than a long trip to Europe, and it's a place where
there's no company, where nobody can follow ... Success is
almost as isolating and nothing points out vanity as well."
Like many invalids with a predilection for the "spiritual"—the
"mystical"—O'Connor seems to have made a connection, as
Gooch suggests a kind of "magical thinking," between her lupus and her writing:

> I was five years writing (*Wise Blood*) and up to the last was
> sure it was a failure and didn't work. When it was almost
> finished I came down with (lupus) and began to take cor-
> tisone in large doses and cortisone makes you think night
> and day until I suppose the mind dies of exhaustion if you
> are not rescued ... The large doses of ACTH send you off in
> a rocket and are scarcely less disagreeable than the disease.

Writing of the fanatic preacher Hazel Motes, under the spell of
her medication, O'Connor conceived the notion that

> I would eventually become paralyzed and was going blind
> and ... in the book I had spelled out my own course, or that
> in the illness I had spelled out the book.

In the fall of such physical dissolution, how comforting the
promises of the Holy Roman Catholic Church—

> As I understand it, the Church teaches that our resurrected
> bodies will be intact as to personality, that is, intact with all

the contradictions beautiful to you, except the contradiction of sin . . . for when all you see will be God, all you want will be God. [O'Connor, letter, December 16, 1955]

O'Connor managed a brave public persona, when addressing mostly Southern college audiences by way of "talks" about fiction writing, interviews and essays; it was her habit to assume a defensive pride in what others might define as limitations—"I am a Catholic peculiarly possessed of the modern consciousness, that thing that Jung describes as unhistorical, solitary and guilty"—as in her unapologetic allegiance to her place of birth and her parochial upbringing: "I'm pleased to be a member of my particular family and to live in Baldwin County, Georgia, in the sovereign state of Georgia, and to see what I can see from here" (see *Conversations with Flannery O'Connor*, edited by Rosemary M. Magee). (As Brad Gooch notes, at this time in the early 1950s Georgia was ranked highest in the nation "in the rate of lynchings and other murders.") Asked if she would like to meet James Baldwin whose first novel, *Go Tell It on the Mountain* (1952), had been published at about the time of *Wise Blood*, O'Connor replied coolly and very carefully: "No I can't see James Baldwin in Georgia. It would cause the greatest trouble and disturbance and disunion . . . I observe the traditions of the society I feed on—it's only fair. Might as well expect a mule to fly as me to see James Baldwin in Georgia." As O'Connor's grasp of communism was naively reductive—"On one side we see communism . . . against God, against Christ, against the Bible"—so O'Connor's grasp of the civil rights movement was startlingly crude and cruel in its Olympian disdain: "I say a plague on everybody's house as far as the race business goes." Yet several of O'Connor's later stories—"The Displaced Person," "Everything That Rises Must Converge," and "The Enduring Chill"—contain striking portraits of black, i.e. "Negro," characters presented with as much, or more, sympathy than their white neighbors, and in the fragment "Why Do the Heathen Rage?" a black servant named Roosevelt is the only individual who responds sensitively, with tears, to the spectacle of his employer crippled by a stroke. Like William Faulkner—who famously said that, if need be, in the threat of integration imposed by the federal government in the 1950s, he would take up arms and fight on the side of his (white, racist) Mississippi neighbors—O'Connor seems to have been something of a "cultural racist" in her private life but in her "incarnational" art, a writer who transcended the limitations of her time, her place, and her being.

Is the art of caricature a lesser or secondary art, set beside what we might call the art of complexity or subtlety? Is "cartoon" art invariably inferior to "realist" art? The caricaturist has the advantage of being cruel, crude, reductive, and often very funny; as the "realist" struggles to establish the *trompe l'oeil* of verisimilitude, without which the art of realism has little power to persuade, the caricaturist wields a hammer, or an ax, or sprays the target with machine-gun fire, transmuting what might be rage—the *savage indignation* of Jonathan Swift, for instance—into devastating humor. The most elevated psychological realism—the excessively mannered novels of Henry James, Virginia Woolf, and James Joyce—takes as its natural subject the *humanness* of its characters; the caricaturist has no interest in *humanness* except to mock it, and to make us laugh. Satire is the weapon of rectitude, a way of meting out punishment. Satire regrets nothing, and revels in unfairness in its depiction of what Flannery O'Connor called "large and startling figures."

Though O'Connor usually masked her disapproval of a wide range of threatening twentieth-century–isms—secularism, atheism, liberalism, Marxism—in comic tones, it's clear from the vehemence with which she frequently spoke in her letters as from the ways in which her fiction punishes her hapless characters that Christianity wasn't, for O'Connor, primarily a religion of charitable feelings, forgiveness, and "love" but rather a phenomenon requiring the disciplined interpretations of the Roman Catholic Church: "The Church is the only thing that is going to make the terrible world we are coming to endurable; the only thing that makes the Church endurable is that it is somehow the body of Christ and on this we are fed." It isn't surprising to learn that O'Connor began her career as a creative artist by drawing cartoons in mockery of human fatuousness and frailty nor that her earliest efforts were satirical pieces; her first "book," written at the age of ten and assembled by her proud father Edward, was titled "My Relitives." O'Connor observed with typical acerbic insight: "I come from a family where the only emotion respectable to show is irritation. In some this tendency produces hives, in others literature, in me both."

We can define the author's lifelong and variegated *irritation* in this context—Catholic, conservative, anti-liberal and

anti-"progressive"—as a folksy variant of the fear and loathing of the strong by the weak which Nietzsche defined in
On the Genealogy of Morals as *ressentiment*—the "imaginary
revenge" of puritanically repressive Christians against their
more pagan adversaries: "Whereas all noble morality grows
out of a triumphant affirmation of oneself, slave morality immediately says No to what comes from outside, to what is different, to what is not oneself: and *this* No is its creative deed."
Revulsion for the strong—the "normal"—by the weak—the
"invalided"—can't account for the genius of O'Connor's prose
fiction but provides a way of comprehending its messianic zeal.

Not the shimmering multi-dimensionality of Modernism but the two-dimensionality of cartoon art is at the heart
of the work of O'Connor, whose unshakable absolutist faith
provided her with a rationale with which to mock both her
secular and bigoted-Christian contemporaries in a succession
of brilliantly orchestrated short stories that read like parables
of human folly confronted by mortality: " 'She would of been a
good woman' "—the murderous Misfit says of an annoyingly
garrulous Southern woman at the conclusion of O'Connor's
"A Good Man Is Hard to Find"—" 'if it had been somebody
there to shoot her every minute of her life.' "

BOXING: HISTORY, ART, CULTURE

Boxing: A Cultural History
by Kasia Boddy

Every talent must unfold itself in fighting.
—FRIEDRICH NIETZSCHE,
"HOMER'S CONTEST"

In the brilliant and unsettling fragment "Homer's Contest," found among Nietzsche's unpublished writings after his death in 1900, the philosopher returns to obsessive themes originally explored in his first book, *The Birth of Tragedy Out of the Spirit of Music* (1872): namely, that contrary to the reigning morality of his time—a Protestant-Christian morality, at least officially—it is not "natural" not to fight; it is not "natural" not to fight to the death, in the service of "allowing . . . hatred to flow forth fully"; indeed, a "noble culture" is one that, like the ancient Greek culture, arises from "the altar of the expiation of murder." Far from being barbaric, the stylized Greek, or Homeric, contest gives a crucial ritualistic form to mankind's most murderous instincts, in this way containing the horror of anarchic violence: not brutality per se but the brutality of chaos is the true horror of humankind. In the Homeric world—the world of stylized art—we encounter "artistic deception" of a kind, that renders such horror bearable. But

> what do we behold when, no longer led and protected by the hand of Homer, we stride back into the pre-Homeric world? Only night and terror and an imagination accustomed to the horror. What kind of earthly existence do these revolting, theogonic myths reflect? A life ruled only by children of Night: strife, lust, deceit, old age, and death.

Out of the struggle with mankind's most brutish instincts there evolves a ritualistic appropriation of uncontrolled violence, whether the competition—the "contest"—is athletic, aesthetic, pedagogic; as the youths of Athens were educated through contests with one another, so their teachers and trainers were also engaged in contests with their peers. Where nineteenth-century sentiment disapproves of the "personal fight" in an artist, the Greek, in Nietzsche's interpretation, knows the artist *"only as engaged in a personal fight."* Orators, philosophers, sophists, dramatists as well as athletes and warriors must claim, as in these (imagined) words of Plato: "Look, I too can do what my great rivals can do; indeed, I can do it better than they . . . Only the contest made me a poet, a sophist, an orator." To remove the "contest" from Greek life is to "immediately look into that pre-Homeric abyss of a terrifying savagery of hatred and the lust to annihilate." Without the expulsion of the basest emotions in competition, "the Hellenic city, like the Hellenic man, degenerates."

Though Kasia Boddy's ambitious *Boxing: A Cultural History* frequently blurs the lines between boxing and fighting, her interest in the mythic underpinnings of this oldest and most controversial of "sports" is not extensive. Her introduction begins with a disappointingly literal (and dubious) statement:

> The symbolism of boxing does not allow for ambiguity; it is, as amateur middleweight Albert Camus put it, "utterly Manichean." The rites of boxing "simplify everything. Good and evil, the winner and the loser."

And, at her conclusion, a quote attributed to Sonny Liston: "It's always the same story—the good guy versus the bad guy." (Liston, who fought exclusively for money, whether in the effort of winning or in the expediency of losing, was invariably the "bad guy" in the Caucasian press, but acquired a darkly glamorous outlaw status elsewhere; one of his devotees, if not his avatar, is ex-heavyweight champion Mike Tyson.) Yet Boddy's own close readings of the careers of John L. Sullivan, Jack Johnson, Jack Dempsey, Joe Louis, Muhammad Ali among others, and such spectacular boxing matches as Joe Louis–Max Schmeling I and II, Muhammad Ali–Joe Frazier I, II, III. Muhammad Ali–George Foreman, challenge the simplicity of such statements. The most cursory examination of boxing as a phenomenon of social/ethnic/racial significance reveals that far from being bluntly "Manichean," boxing has always been steeped in ambiguity: "good" and "evil"/"bad" are hardly absolutes, but entirely matters of perspective. There can be no single "meaning" of any boxing match and it is impossible to completely decode the significance of the greatest and most iconic matches, that have come to acquire with time the aura of legend. Of athletic contests, boxing has always been the sport that isn't "played": one plays games, but boxing isn't a game so much as a mimicry of a tragic human action layered in irony, mystery, and the unspeakable or obscene; the most mesmerizing fights are those that repel as they attract, as if the spectator were being forced to participate in the violation of a sacred taboo. The roots of boxing would seem to be near-identical to those roots of ancient Greek tragedy that so fascinated Nietzsche as the noblest dramatization of man's essential divided and murderous soul.

At nearly five hundred densely packed pages, this investigation into "the intricate conceptual and iconographic constructions" that surround boxing has the heft of a work twice its length—the equivalent, in book form, of the old-style championship boxing matches that ran to as long as thirty rounds, often in the broiling sun. Despite the author's disclaimer of being "highly selective" in assembling her heterogeneous material, *Boxing: A Cultural History* would seem to include everything that has ever been written, depicted, or in any way recorded about boxing no matter how obscure, whimsical, or trivial; a treasure trove for boxing historians and *aficionados*, that might evoke vertigo in less committed readers. By immersing herself so indiscriminately in her subject, Boddy seems to be suggesting that boxing is so foundational and magnetic a presence in Western culture that its metaphors, however random and scattered, are of sufficient significance to be noted, though the critic acknowledges no especially personal experience with or interest in her subject other than its rich possibilities for critical appropriation. Still, this is not an objection: in theory, we can imagine a work of insightful scholarship about the cultural history of music, for instance, by a critic who has never really listened to music, or a definitive ornithological work by an individual who has never seen a live bird. I found most of *Boxing: A Cultural History* fascinating if exhausting: for where else within a single volume could one locate pages of plot summaries of Hollywood boxing films from the classic (James Cagney's *Winner Take All*, 1932) to the forgotten and forgettable (*Never Come Morning*, 1942); where else such a gathering of boxing pictures, from reproductions of classic works of art by Théodore Géricault, Thomas Eakins, John Sloan, George Bellows to numerous crude cartoons, a witty little drawing of Jack Dempsey by Djuna Barnes, and "Sturdy Young Bodies and Stout Young Hearts," a promotional postcard of Father Flanagan's Boys' Home in Nebraska in the 1930s. It is instructive to be informed that "the first report of a prize fight in literature" is included in the account of the funeral games for Patroklus in Homer's *The Iliad*, and that the story of Dares in Virgil's *Aeneid* (19 B.C.) is "one of the first fight stories in which the restraining referee is the hero"; in *The Odyssey*, in the confrontation of Odysseus with the duplicitous suitors of his wife Penelope, we have the "first instance of spectators as villains in a boxing story: unwilling to fight themselves, but vicariously enjoying the risks someone else will run, and gambling on the outcome." In the *Memoirs* (1816) of the British pugilist Daniel Mendoza we have what is possibly the "first ghost-written" sports autobiography; the "first boxing match recorded in a newspaper, *The Protestant Mercury*, took place in 1681, in the presence of the Duke of Albermarle," the first boxing film was made in August 1894 ("six rounds of a minute each between minor [American] prize-fighters Mike Leonard and Jack Cushing"). It's a novelty fact, or factoid, that fight fixing began at the ninety-eighth Olympics, according to Pausanias's *Guide to Greece* (170 A.D.) and that Ernest Hemingway's 1927 story "The Killers" is one of the first stories to "explore the relationship between boxing and organized crime"; the first "boxing kangaroo" was exhibited in London in 1892. It is unsurprising perhaps but not uninteresting to learn that many early British boxers were also butchers and that the most vocal of the early Dadaists, Tristan Tzara, issued the manifesto in 1918: "Every man must shout and use his fists ... there is great destructive, negative work to be done."

More instructive perhaps is the revelation that nineteenth-century British poets, in particular the hyper-macho Byron, were enthralled by the "Fancy" (an insider upscale term for boxing); poor doomed John Clare in his Northampton madhouse was seen "shadow-boxing in his cell, crying out 'I'm Jones the Sailor Boy,' and 'I'm Tom Spring' " while the more genteel William Wordsworth "enjoyed a rare immunity to 'boximania.' " Like a magnet that draws all objects to it, Boddy's boxing-as-metaphor proliferates alarmingly, prevailing through poetry of widely varying merit from the time of Sophocles ("Whoever challenges Eros to a match/Like a boxer fist-to-fist, he is out of his wits") to the "proletarian" Horace Gregory in "Dempsey, Dempsey" of 1935 ("I can't get up, I'm dead, my legs/are dead, see, I'm no good,/they got me and

I'm out,/down for the count./I've quit, quit again,/only God save Dempsey, make him get up again,/Dempsey, Dempsey") and our most celebrated precursor of rap music Cassius Clay/ Muhammad Ali ("It started twenty years past./The greatest of all was born at last.") And it is illuminating to learn the degree to which boxing, "or street-fighting with pretensions to boxing" as well as "linguistic pugnacity" are predominant themes in James Joyce's *Ulysses*: "While parodying its postures and patois, Joyce relished the dramatic possibilities of boxing." Indeed, as Boddy's masterwork of bricolage sweeps on there comes to be something wonderfully Joycean—oceanic, indefatigable, just slightly deranged—in the very quantity of data Kasia Boddy has amassed. One thinks of those notorious miles-long fishing nets of the Pacific so fine-meshed as to catch everything and anything in its path.

Of all athletic "contests" it is likely that none predates boxing, or pugilism. Highly stylized images of "boxing boys" on Eastern Mediterranean pottery date back to the late Bronze Age and allusions to such combat extend through the "classical golden age"—in the earliest of Greek works, Homer's *The Iliad* and *The Odyssey* (eighth century B.C.) athletic games are described that allegedly occurred at the time of the Trojan War (circa 1200 B.C.), like the funeral games for Anchises staged in Virgil's *The Aeneid* (19 B.C.), in which the compelling tale of Dares is recounted ("Dares had youth on his side and speed of foot. Entellus had the reach and the weight, but his legs were going . . . Like hailstones from a dark cloud rattling down on roofs, Entellus battered Dares with a shower of blows from both hands and sent him spinning." In her concise opening chapter "The Classical Golden Age," Boddy notes that boxing was crucial to the great Panhellenic festivals of ancient Greece—the Olympian, the Pythian, the Nemean, and the Isthmian. (The most prestigious games, the Olympic, began in 776 B.C., and boxing was introduced in 688 B.C.) From the start, there seemed to be the fear that boxing might degrade its audience as well as its participants: women were confined to the back rows of such events, or banned altogether; in one of Lucilius's sneering epigrams, not respect for the veteran pugilist is portrayed but cruel contempt: "Having such a mug, Olympicus, go not to a fountain nor look in any transparent water, for you, like Narcissus, seeing your face clearly, will die, hating yourself to the death." The predominant image of Boddy's first chapter is the famous fourth-century statue of a battered boxer, *The Pugilist at Rest*, a sculpture of surpassing if brutal beauty that, many centuries later, would be evoked in Thom Jones's most powerful work of fiction, *The Pugilist at Rest* (1993):

> The statue depicts a muscular athlete approaching his middle age . . . (He) is sitting on a rock with his forearms balanced on his thighs . . . There is a slight look of befuddlement on his face, but there is no trace of fear . . . Beside the deformities on his noble face, there is also the suggestion of weariness and philosophical resignation.

It is in the classical era, Boddy argues, with its mixture of savagery and "philosophy," that the "inextricable mixture in pugilism of high decorum and low cunning, of beauty and damage, of rhetoric and bodily fluids" that will recur through subsequent centuries is first sounded.

By the time of the English Golden Age of boxing—approximately 1780 to Queen Victoria's accession in 1837—boxing's Greek origins had long been forgotten. Prize-fighting—"the Fancy"—flourished as "a truly *British* art"—"an antidote to '*foreign Effeminacy*' " in alliance with gambling, another fancy of the times. British aristocrats, including the Prince of Wales, patronized the sport and writers as various as Pierce Egan (*Boxiana; or Sketches of Ancient and Modern Pugilism*; *Life in London*, 1821), Washington Irving (*Tales of a Traveller*, 1824), Thomas DeQuincy (articles in *Blackwood's*), Byron (*Don Juan*, notably canto 11), John Hamilton Reynolds (*The Fancy*, 1820), William Hazlitt ("Jack Tars," 1826; "The Fight," 1822) were inspired to write about it, often with dazzling results. Both William Hogarth and Théodore Géricault depicted boxing scenes of exceptional interest. "The spectre of effeminacy was constantly evoked," Boddy says, in the "rhetoric of nationalist masculinity." Yet "effeminacy" would triumph by the time of Victoria's reign when the Fancy sharply plummeted in popularity as a consequence of scandals and the withdrawal of aristocratic patronage. In the new, Victorian era, middle-class Protestant values held sway, repelled by the "unruly sport favored by an alliance of the working and upper classes (the 'bawling, hustling, and smashing Populace' and the 'great broad-shouldered Barbarians,' as Matthew Arnold put it)" as Boddy suggests. From this time onward, though boxing/fighting—"fistic phraseology"—would figure prominently in several of Charles Dickens's novels, and in occasional work by A. Conan Doyle (reputedly an excellent amateur boxer himself) and other British writers, the disreputable sport's center of gravity would shift triumphantly to America, where it remains to the present time.

From the bare-knuckle era of John L. Sullivan, whose highly publicized reign as heavyweight champion lasted a remarkable decade—1882 to 1892—American boxing was both a marginal sport and big business: it scarcely mattered that, at the start, prize-fighting was "outlawed"—there were fights almost nightly in the New York City area, as in numerous communities in the United States. (See George Bellows's powerful paintings *Club Night* (1907), *Both Members of This Club* (1909), *Stag at Sharkey's* (1909), Goyaesque visions of private boxing clubs like scenes out of hell.) In 1920, boxing was finally legalized, and properly licensed, in the New York area, but its association with gambling, corrupt politicians and criminals flourished. Part of the glamour of prize-fighting has always been its seeming defiance of middle-class Protestant mores and the loathed civilizing "influence" of women; watching other men fight has always been, for men, as for some women, an ecstatic experience not unlike a Dionysian orgy in which large crowds of individuals, likely to be anonymous to one another, are raised to a fever-pitch of bonding. Boddy notes how a "steady stream of middle-class men" in pursuit of the "strenuous" life sparred and worked out in boxing clubs in the late nineteenth and early twentieth centuries; how such artists as the notable Thomas Eakins were drawn to boxing as a screen or scrim of sorts for the artist's fascination with the young male body. In Eakins's case:

> Eakins was uninterested in painting boxers exchanging blows . . . [He] wanted to show that the artist could find heroism and beauty in male semi-nudity without having recourse to Rome . . . While [his] chiseled white body evokes classical sculpture, [the young boxer's] tanned face, neck and hands remind us that he is a working-class American boy.

Bellows's struggling boxers of the early 1900s lack all homoerotic allure; they are desperate creatures intent upon "winning"—whatever paltry purse, or meager round of applause. In Bellows's most famous painting, *Dempsey and Firpo* (1924), however, painted when boxing was not only legalized but something of an upper-middle-class spectacle attended by elegantly dressed men and women, the pasty-pale "Dempsey" bears little resemblance to photographs of the actual, dark-tanned and more muscular Jack Dempsey, and the clumsy Argentinian giant Firpo—the much-hyped "Wild Bull of the Pampas"—has a sculpted and serene look utterly alien to the actual Firpo who, by this time in the historic fight, had been knocked down by Dempsey a remarkable seven times. (These were the days when referees did not too quickly intervene in male havoc!) In fact, Bellows had not even seen the championship fight firsthand but painted it from other sources, giving the scene a highly stylized and synthetic air that makes of its ostensible violence a mere aesthetic *frisson*. Bellows seems to be suggesting that, as the violent brawl becomes ever more commodified—and merchandised—it has come to resemble any other sort of American entertainment, and its practitioners more resemble mannequins than actual boxers. In Boddy's words, "The 1920s are often recalled as a golden age of sport, but it was an age of mass consumption rather than mass participation ... Worse still was listening to the radio ('sport at two removes')." And there was the imminent, yet more voracious age of television which would transform boxing forever by drawing audiences away from local arenas, centralizing (first in New York's Madison Square Garden, then in Las Vegas) what had been essentially a neighborhood sport, and in this way providing for gamblers, and for organized crime, an irresistible source of income. (How ideal television was for boxing: just two near-naked athletes generally in prime physical condition, dramatic opportunities for close-ups, three-minute rounds separated by one-minute intermissions custom-designed for advertisements; what ideal circumstances for betting, and for bribing!) Boddy is especially good in her close analysis of mid-century American *boxiana*, domesticated and exploited in a way very unlike the *boxiana* of Pierce Egan's Fancy: as soon as boxing matches become a Friday-night staple on network television, the savage, sordid underpinnings of the sport faded in public consciousness, and the public was left to admire a sequence of highly promoted though often genuinely talented and idiosyncratic boxing champions.

Boxing has always been dominated by the heavyweight division, as the heavyweight division is dominated by the champion and his highest-ranked contenders; so long as the heavyweight champion is a considerable macho figure, espe-

cially if he happens to be handsome, charismatic, and controversial, boxing can be a highly lucrative sport—at least for
managers and promoters, if not always for boxers. Boddy succinctly discusses the leading heavyweight champions in terms
of their cultural significance: swaggering John L. Sullivan, "the
Boston Strong boy," the very embodiment of Irish-American
machismo, who didn't become simply a celebrity during his
ten-year reign, but "a screen onto which a wide variety of feelings and attitudes could be projected"; his more suave succes-
sor "Gentleman Jim" Corbett (heavyweight reign 1892–1897)
who ended his career after retirement by staging boxing exhi-
bitions and appearing in a number of plays—"Why a fighter
can't be careful about his appearance I don't understand"; the
controversial Jack Johnson, our first black American heavyweight (1908–1915), whose astonishing dancer-like boxing
skills revolutionized the sport and whose yet more astonishing defiance of wholesale white racism would set the tone for
Cassius Clay/Muhammad Ali five decades to come; and "The
Manassa Mauler" Jack Dempsey (1919–1926) whose brilliant
manager Jack Kearnes parlayed his boxer's considerable but
limited skills to unprecedented box-office bonanzas like the
heavily promoted "Battle of the Century"—with the French
lightweight champion Georges Carpentier in 1921, whom
Dempsey beat handily in four rounds—the first million-dollar
gate in ring history.

A talismanic figure to this day, as a champion, Dempsey
fought relatively few contenders. He was shameless about elud-
ing the reputedly best boxer of his era, "The Black Menace"
Harry Wills, in 1925; if Dempsey had been a contemporary

of Jack Johnson, he would never have stepped into the ring with the more skilled black boxer, and the great Jack Johnson's name would be but a footnote in American boxing history. In an era of white racism, Dempsey was one of the tribe. Yet, as Boddy points out, like Joe Louis in a very different way, Jack Dempsey became an iconic figure throughout the thirties and beyond "both to those who identified with his losses and failures, and those who felt that they too could one day be champion if only they worked hard enough."

Divided into nine chapters of different lengths and strategies—among them " 'Fighting, Rightly Understood,' " "Like Any Other Profession," "Sport of the Future," "Save Me, Joe Louis; Save Me, Jack Dempsey"—and a conclusion crammed with enough information and ideas to fuel an entirely new book, *Boxing: A Cultural History* must have been a considerable challenge to organize. Obliged to be a history of *culture* and not simply of *boxing*, this prodigious book begins to stagger under the weight of its Sargasso Sea of materials, at about midway, in Chapters 5 and 6. Though the chronological history of boxing is in itself enormously appealing, Boddy's methodology requires her to frequently interrupt it with so much cultural detritus that the story becomes quickly snarled, even to one who is familiar with it; references to Jack Dempsey abound, but we drift far from the core individual, and we're likely to feel mildly cheated here, as elsewhere when Boddy "covers" such great fights as Louis–Schmeling II, Muhammad Ali–Joe Frazier I, II, III and Muhammad Ali–Foreman—by the relatively scant space spent on *boxing* set beside countless pages of cultural inquiry into, for instance,

boxing posters advertising Hollywood fight films, lengthy ex-
egeses of such texts as Budd Schulberg's novel *The Harder
They Fall*, the maelstrom of Black Muslim propaganda and
Caucasian America reaction surrounding Muhammad Ali in
the tumultuous 1960s. Certainly it is interesting, to a degree,
to see to what extent contemporary American culture has been
saturated with boxing/fighting references, but the instinct to
"fight" is after all a primary human instinct, and might well
have manifested itself in any number of other ways apart
from boxing. Skilled though Boddy is in literary analysis and
paraphrase, so many "examples" of boxing/fighting in culture
quickly come to seem numbing, as in this (shortened) excerpt
from Jack London's *Martin Eden* in which seemingly sophisticated men revert to the Zolaesque "animal machine":

> Then they fell upon each other, like young bulls, in all the
> glory of youth, with naked fists, and with hatred, with de-
> sire to hurt, to maim, to destroy. All the painful, thousand
> years' of gains of man in his upward climb through creation
> were lost . . . Martin and CheeseFace were two savages, of
> the stone age . . .

It's hardly surprising that Jack London's male protagonists
revert to "savagery"—in this and every other work of fiction by
the author of the American classic *The Call of the Wild* (1903);
such is the inevitable trajectory of their fate. London lacked
an imagination beyond the grimly determinist "naturalism" of
his time; his "plots" could run in but one direction, like hur-
tling locomotives. His obsessive themes touch only tangentially

upon the tradition, discipline, and culture of boxing, which is a very different matter from mere savagery, as observers of boxing are frequently required to explain. Boddy concedes, "The boxing ring is only one of many settings in which the validity of naturalist ideas can be tested and observed" but "naturalism" per se can be applied to an infinite variety of human, if not sub-human activities, always drawing the same very few conclusions: life is nasty, brutish, and short.

In her rather too freewheeling association of boxing with mere fighting, which prevails throughout the book, Boddy needs to distinguish more responsibly between the "savage" and "instinctual"—that is, the "untrained" and "unstudied" nature of brute fighting—and what boxing *is*: a not-natural, not-unreflective, not-brainless but assiduously trained and reflective tradition somewhere between a "sport" and an "art" that places far more emphasis than most viewers could guess upon the stratagems of self-defense including indefatigably practiced footwork. To watch a boxer seriously training (as I'd once watched the twenty-year-old heavyweight contender Mike Tyson at his Catskill camp preparatory to Tyson's defeat of Trevor Berbick in November 1986), is to realize firsthand how *contrary to nature* boxing actually is; how one might argue that when practiced on the highest levels, the discipline of boxing bears more relationship to a shrewdly cerebral contest like chess than to anything like street-fighting, and boxing's essential establishment of a mysterious and often profound bond between boxers—all the more brotherly for its being baptized in blood—is a crucial component in boxing culture which is largely invisible to the "public" eye.

Boddy's methodology as a cultural critic reduces what was once *living* to its *symbolic representations*. To some extent this is the natural process of criticism, analysis, quantification. It is the external—"public"—nature of boxing that engages her, the deciphering of large public texts in which individuals figure as mere hieroglyphics:

> Today much of the visual representation of boxing capital-
> izes on, or interrogates, the symbolic resonance of specific
> individuals, objects and events. Certain fights have a particu-
> larly powerful resonance or aura—a "uniqueness" that can
> only be understood by saying "I was there," or "I remember
> where I was when it happened."

But how does this distinguish boxing from any other pub-lic event? Woodstock or Altamont, the Red Sox winning the World Series, a "historic" event seen "live" on television? Cul-tural criticism quickly reaches a point of saturation at which all iconographies are equal: those that are "real" (an actual boxing match) and those that are "fiction" (Sylvester Stallone's fairy-tale *Rocky* franchise); those that begin with historic "per-sons" (Muhammad Ali, Marilyn Monroe) but are transmog-rified by art, or a process to which the term "art" is applied (Andy Warhol's 1977 lithograph *Muhammad Ali: Hand on Chin,** Andy Warhol's 1964 lithograph *Blue Marilyn*). Where the critic's predominant focus is a theory of media manipula-tion, the subject itself may be irrelevant:

---

* Warhol found Ali "boring but very handsome."

The story of boxing (and indeed of most sports) from the early nineteenth-century onward has been one of gradual transformation into mass-market entertainment. Each new technological development (film, radio and television) has brought a larger audience to individual contests.

True of boxing but perhaps truer of football, basketball, pop music and national politics. And it might be argued that with the demise of Friday night boxing matches in the 1960s, there are far fewer fights, and fewer boxers involved in the sport; millions of viewers may watch pay-per-view to see a much-hyped championship fight broadcast in Las Vegas, but audiences for boxing overall may well be declining, with the rise of so many competing sports.

What is the most valuable about *Boxing: A Cultural History* isn't its ideas so much as its wonderfully heterogeneous gathering of specifics. To read Boddy's book is to confront dozens—hundreds?—of inspired mini-essays. One has to do with the transformation of dashing young Cassius Clay/Muhammad Ali as a "Muslim Saint Sebastian" in 1966—the "White Liberal Hope"—through the deification of Ali in such films as *When We Were Kings* (1996) and his transformation into a sort of "New Age spiritual guru." Succumbing to the neurological disorder Parkinson's disease "merely added poignancy to his story" as Boddy observes: in 2005, Ali was awarded the Presidential Medal of Freedom by George W. Bush. (He who'd once been, in the prime of his life, a member of the Nation of Islam and an unabashed black racist!) Another illuminating digression, in a chapter already crammed to bursting, is the wittily titled "Two Nice Jewish Boys in the Age of Ali"—the "nice Jewish boys" being Bob Dylan and Norman Mailer.

Nearing the end of her massive book, like a valiant boxer staggering with exhaustion in the twelfth, final round of a championship fight, Boddy simply stops and tell us: "My aim [has been] less to offer a comprehensive survey than to propose further lines of inquiry: . . . dialectical, iconographic, and naturalist." To the very end she is searching still for the mysterious essence of boxing, which, as Nietzsche would have perceived, is a far deeper and more "sacred" human activity than its mass-market appropriation can suggest:

> To accept that the "essence" or "basic fact" of boxing is "the fact of meat and body hitting meat and bone" is to reject, or at least downplay, the intricate conceptual and iconographic constructions that surround it.

Boddy quotes Carlo Rotella: "It takes constant effort to keep the slippery, naked, near-formless fact of hitting swaddled in layers of sense and form."

This is a problem, if it is a problem, exclusively for the critic; the boxer knows a deeper truth, as Mike Tyson once said: "Other than boxing, everything is so boring."

II.

CONTEMPORARIES

REMEMBERING JOHN UPDIKE

The New Yorker
"Book Bench," January 28, 2009

John was a slightly older classmate in a vast high school populated by not-prosperous rural youths in some netherland of the 1950s. Of course, John was president of this class; no doubt, I was secretary. I've been reading John's work since I became an adult and can only content myself with the prospect of his new, so sadly posthumously published *Endpoint and Other Poems* and *My Father's Tears and Other Stories* and rereading the newly reissued *The Maples: Stories* as well as rereading his work through the remainder of my life. I think there must be a story or two, and even one of his more slender novels, which, unaccountably, I have not yet read. My students love "Friends from Philadelphia," which was John's first published story in *The New Yorker*. What a seemingly artless little gem! My students are stunned by it and by the fact that John wrote it when he was hardly older than they are.

We had met a number of times—my (late) husband Raymond Smith and I visited John and Martha in Beverly Farms, Massachusetts, on several very nice occasions. John was always gracious, warmly funny, kind, and bemused—and of course very bright, informed, and ardent when it came to literature. When he gave a brilliant talk and reading at Princeton some years ago I was honored to introduce him to a large, packed auditorium. I teach his lovely stories each semester—John's language is luminous, sparkling, and glinting, with a steely sort of humor. Think of an iridescent butterfly of surpassing beauty that yet—if you persist in examining it—will yield a considerable sting. I could never gauge how serious John was about his Christian faith—or, rather, the Christian faith—though some sense of the sacred seems to suffuse his work in its most ordinary, even vulgar moments, at which Updike was a master at transcribing. "Snow makes white shadows, there behind the yews, dissolving to the sun's slant kiss, and pools itself across the lawn as if to say *Give me another hour, then I'll go*" ("Endpoint"). I will miss John terribly, as we all will.

HOMER & LANGLEY

by E. L. Doctorow

Of archetypal domestic horrors that haunt Americans—
an unnerving panoply of tabloid possibilities that includes the post-partum-depressed mother who drowns her
children, the deranged father who slaughters his family and
then himself, the formerly tractable teenager who becomes a
drug addict, a serial killer, a goth practitioner of satanic rites,
an Ivy League dropout—none is more terrifying than the
agoraphobic-recluse-hoarder: the individual, usually though
not invariably elderly, who has retreated into his dwelling-
place as into a burrow, creates of his household a labyrinth
of stacked newspapers and magazines, "collectibles" and
trash, very often raw garbage, and very often domestic pets—
dogs, cats—that, allowed to breed haphazardly, make of the
dwelling-place a worse sinkhole of squalor. Few of us can
imagine ourselves involved in deranged acts of violence but all
too many of us can imagine ourselves the hapless victims of
our possessions—paralyzed by things we're unable to sort out
and discard, trapped by our own affluence, crushed, smothered, annihilated beneath tons of trash as in a grim allegory of

Consumerism's shadow-side. How else to explain our ongo-ing fascination with the Collyer brothers, Langley and Homer, whose decaying bodies were discovered in March 1947 amid more than one hundred tons of trash in the Collyer family brownstone on once-fashionable Fifth Avenue at 128th Street, and who were the subjects of a high-profile series of articles for the *New York Times* and, in 1954, a Book-of-the-Month Club best seller titled *My Brother's Keeper* by Marcia Davenport. (Davenport's novel, derided by literary critics for its tabloid melodrama, remains warmly recalled by readers well into the twenty-first century, as passionate testimonies on Amazon at-test.) Once merely eccentric bachelor-brothers from a highly respectable Manhattan family who came to tragic ends, the Collyer brothers have become mythopoetic, larger than life. Once merely sensational, their story has become a kind of cau-tionary tale as memorable as any of Grimms' fairy tales.

E. L. Doctorow, a writer of dazzling gifts and seemingly boundless imaginative energy, our great chronicler of Ameri-can mythopoetics in such brilliantly and variously executed novels as *The Book of Daniel* (1971), *Ragtime* (1975), *Loon Lake* (1980), *Billy Bathgate* (1989), *The Waterworks* (1994), *World's Fair* (1985), and more recently *City of God* (2000) and *The March* (2005) has turned his attention to the Collyer legend in his new, eleventh novel *Homer & Langley*. In con-trast to the ambitious and multi-faceted *The March*, a chron-icle of the Union Army's notorious march through Georgia and South Carolina under the generalship of Sherman, in the closing months of the Civil War, *Homer & Langley* is a sub-dued, contemplative and resolutely unsensational account of the brothers' fatally imbricated lives. Told in the form of a first-person narrative by the elderly Homer—"the blind brother"—it's addressed to a French woman journalist whom Homer has encountered on the street, and with whom he becomes naively infatuated, in the final months of his life, though he scarcely knows "Jacqueline Roux" and will never encounter her a second time; it's a *Bildungsroman* in which virtually nothing happens to the protagonist except that, with the passing of years, and the diminution of his hearing as well as his blindness, Homer succumbs ever more passively to his elder brother Langley's paranoid fantasies and predilection for compulsive hoarding—"It was as if the times blew through our house like a wind."

Protected by a modicum of inherited wealth from needing to engage in any crucial way with the outside world, the Collyer brothers age without maturing. As a young man, Homer is a promising pianist enrolled at the West End Conservatory of Music; his blindness is no handicap in the Collyers' social circle but rather an attribute—"[My] helplessness was very alluring to a woman trained since birth, herself, to be helpless. It made her feel strong, in command, it could bring out her sense of pity . . . She could express herself, give herself to her pent-up feelings, as she could not safely do with a normal fellow." Homer has a thwarted love affair with a Hungarian housemaid who is accused—by Langley—of being a thief; both brothers fall in love with a pious young Catholic girl who enters a religious order and, years later, is one of four nuns raped and shot to death in a "remote Central American village"—a revelation that provokes the already misanthropic Langley to permanently close the shutters of their house. Langley, the more troubled brother, attends Columbia University for a while but becomes permanently disabled—his lungs ruined by mustard gas and his soul gutted by the "monstrousness" of the world—as a soldier in World War I.

The brothers' characters are of less interest than the narrative uses to which their reclusive lives are put by Doctorow in his signature sleight-of-hand melding of private and public lives: during Prohibition, the brothers visit speakeasies, and become acquainted with gangsters; during the Great Depression, they open their brownstone to "tea dances" at which Homer plays piano; in the 1960s they mingle with hippies at an antiwar rally in Manhattan and allow a commune of hippies to "crash" with them for a month—Homer has a final love affair, hardly more than a few sexual encounters, with the flower child Lissey whose youthful body is attractive to him even as her ideas seem "silly." It's in these sections in which, as in Doctorow's most widely read novel *Ragtime*, "real" people cavort with "historical figures," that *Homer & Langley* is most buoyant and entertaining. But with the departure of the hippies from their already cluttered brownstone, the brothers' "abandonment of the outer world" becomes irreversible.

As in the much-lauded 1975 documentary film *Grey Gardens*, which depicts the lives of the two Edith Beales in their squalid East Hampton mansion, the appeal of the Collyer brothers' story lies in its lurid setting. Doctorow notes, following the bizarre inventory first published in the *New York Times* in 1947, not only the countless stacks—tons!—of newspapers "[that] had, like some slow flow of lava, brimmed out of (Langley's) study" [p. 76] but also a complete Model T automobile, reconstructed in the dining room, in the hope of generating electric energy from the motor; many thousands of books spilling out of the brownstone's original library owned by the Collyers' physician-father, now long deceased; broken furniture, records, phonographs and turntables; children's toys, gas masks . . .

> The house by this time in our lives was a labyrinth of hazardous pathways, full of obstructions and many dead ends. With enough light someone could make his way through the zigzagging corridors of newspaper bales, or find passage by slipping sideways between piles of equipment—the guts of pianos, motors wrapped in their power cords, boxes of tools, paintings, car body parts, tires, staked chairs, tables on tables, headboards, barrels, collapsed stacks of books, antique lamps, dislodged pieces of our parents' furniture, rolled-up carpet, piles of clothing, bicycles . . . stacks of lumber, used tires, and odd pieces of furniture, a legless bureau, a bedspring, two Adirondack chairs . . . items stored in the expectation that someday we would find uses for them.

Yet there is a nightmare logic to the brothers' withdrawal to a suffocating safe haven where "our footsteps echoed, as if we were in a cave or an underground vault." There is something of the romance of rebellion in Langley—initially—his postwar bitterness transformed "into an iconoclastic life of the mind"— but as the brothers age and are obliged to live ever more primitively, in a dwelling bereft of electricity, heat, water and even, once they barricade the windows, daylight, the grubbiness and horror of their situation are impossible to ignore, even by the blind Homer:

> [I]n the minds of the [neighborhood] juvenile delinquents who'd begun to pelt our house Langley and I were not the eccentric recluses of a once well-to-do family ... we had metamorphosed, we were the ghosts who haunted the house we had once lived in.

As if foreseeing his and his brothers' lurid tabloid fate to come: "What could be more terrible than being turned into a mythic joke? How could we cope, once dead and gone, with no one available to reclaim our history?"

Historically, Homer Collyer (1881–1947) was the elder of the Collyer brothers; he didn't go blind until he was an adult, and had a degree in admiralty law, which he seems never to have used; Langley (1885–1947) claimed to have a degree in engineering from Columbia University—which claim was disputed by Columbia. In fictionalizing the brothers' story Doctorow alters the record in minor but significant ways: he updates the narrative by at least twenty years and makes of his Homer the younger and more sensitive brother, a concert pianist of musical ability but lacking confidence. The historical Langley wasn't a World War I veteran, still less a victim of gas warfare, but was the pianist of the family, not Homer; evidence would seem to suggest that Langley was severely psychotic. Doctorow's Langley is corrosively eloquent, a modern-day

Diogenes, or a prophet out of the Hebrew Bible; his cynicism suggests the later, embittered years of America's most popular and beloved writer Mark Twain. Here is Langley's Theory of Replacements:

> Everything in life gets replaced. We are our parents' replacements just as they were replacements of the previous generation. All the herds of bison they are slaughtering out west, you would think that was the end of them, but they won't all be slaughtered and the herds will fill back in with replacements that will be distinguished from the ones slaughtered ... (Time) advances through us as we replace ourselves to fill the slots.

Homer interprets his brother's theory as Langley's "bitterness of life or despair of it." In Doctorow's novel Langley's obsession with saving newspapers isn't a random symptom of psychosis but an intellectual if quixotic project reminiscent of the maniacal effort of Flaubert's deluded seekers after truth Bouvard and Pecuchet—a fanatic effort of

> counting and filing news stories according to category: invasions, wars, mass murders, auto, train, and plane wrecks, love scandals, church scandals, robberies, murders, lynchings, rapes, political misdoings with a subhead of crooked elections, police misdeeds, gangland rubouts, investment scams, strikes, tenement fires, trials civil, trials criminal, and so on. There was a separate category for natural disasters such as epidemics, earthquakes and hurricanes ... As he explained,

eventually . . . he would have enough statistical evidence to narrow his findings to the kinds of behavior that were, by their frequency, seminal human behavior . . . He wanted to fix American life in one edition that he called Collyer's eternally current dateless newspaper, the only newspaper anyone would ever need.

Unlike the brothers of Marcia Davenport's *My Brother's Keeper*, destroyed by female duplicity and manipulation, amid a romantic-melodramatic plot involving a beautiful Italian soprano and a tyrannical family matriarch, Doctorow's brothers eke out their lives as victims of their own stunted personalities. No single, significant drama defines their lives, only just the whimsical vicissitudes of fate. There is a Beckett-like bleakness to Homer's final lines, addressed to his remote muse Jacqueline Roux:

> There are moments when I cannot bear this unremitting consciousness. It knows only itself. The images of things are not the things in themselves . . . My memories pale as I prevail upon them again and again. They become more and more ghostly. I fear nothing so much as losing them altogether and having only my blank endless mind to live in . . . Jacqueline, for how many days have I been without food? There was a crash, the whole house shook. Where is Langley? Where is my brother?

The circumstances of the brothers' deaths were more sensational—and pathetic—than Doctorow indicates in *Homer*

& Langley: Langley was crawling through a newspaper tunnel to bring food to his blind, now-paralyzed brother when one of his own booby traps was triggered causing him to be crushed beneath tons of debris. Homer starved to death. Yet it was Homer's body that was found first, while Langley, believed still alive, was the object of a highly publicized citywide "manhunt" for several days until his body too was found amid the rubble, only a few feet from his brother's body. In *Homer & Langley* Doctorow has evoked an American folk-myth writ small, a touching and poignant double portrait of individuals whom social background and class privilege could not protect from extinction.

IN ROUGH COUNTRY I:
CORMAC McCARTHY

If God meant to interfere in the degeneracy of
mankind, would he not have done so by now?
—*BLOOD MERIDIAN*

Pascal's enigmatic remark in the *Pensées*, "Life is a dream a little less inconstant," would be a fitting epigraph for the novels of Cormac McCarthy that unfold with the exhausting intensity of fever dreams. From the dense Faulknerian landscapes of his early, East Tennessee fiction to the monumental Grand Guignol *Blood Meridian*; from the prose ballads of the *Border Trilogy* to the tightly plotted crime novel, *No Country for Old Men*, McCarthy's fiction has been characterized by compulsive and doomed quests, sadistic rites of masculinity, a frenzy of perpetual motion—on foot, on horseback, in cars and pickups. No one would mistake Cormac McCarthy's worlds as "real" except in the way that fever dreams are "real," a heightened and distilled gloss upon the human condition.

Born in Providence, Rhode Island, in 1933, Cormac McCarthy was brought to live in East Tennessee at the age of four and from there moved to El Paso, Texas, in 1974. By his own account, he attended the University of Tennessee in 1952 and was asked not to return because his grades were so poor.

Subsequently he drifted about the country, worked at odd jobs, enlisted in the U.S. Air Force for four years of which two were spent in Alaska; after his discharge, he returned to the University of Tennessee for four years but left without receiving a degree. McCarthy's first four novels, which won for him a small, admiring audience of literary-minded readers, are distinctly Southern-Gothic in tone, setting, characters, language; his fifth, the mock-epic *Blood Meridian*, set mostly in Mexico and California in the years 1849 to 1878, marks the author's dramatic reinvention of himself as a writer of the West: a visionary of vast, inhuman distances for whom the intensely personal psychology of the traditional realistic novel holds little interest.

Rare among writers, especially contemporary American writers, Cormac McCarthy seems to have written no autobiographical or memoirist fiction or essays. *Suttree* (1979), set along the banks of the Tennessee River at Knoxville, has the sprawl, heft, and gritty intimacy of autobiographical fiction in the mode of Jack Kerouac, but is not. McCarthy's most intelligent and sensitive protagonist so far has been John Grady Cole of *All the Pretty Horses* and *Cities of the Plain*, a stoic loner at the age of sixteen who plays chess with surprising skill, is an instinctive horseman, and, in other circumstances, would have studied to be a veterinarian, but John Grady is not representative of McCarthy's characters and shares no biographical background with the author. More generally, McCarthy's subjects are likely to be individuals driven by raw impulse and need, fanaticism rather than idealism, for whom formal education would have ended in grade school and who, if they carry a Bible with them like the nameless kid of *Blood Meridian*, "no word of it could he read."

In *The Orchard Keeper* and *Outer Dark* the dream-like opacity of Faulkner's prose is predominant. These are slow-moving novels in which back-country natives drift like somnambulists in tragic/farcical dramas beyond their comprehension, let alone control. The setting is the East Tennessee hill country in the vicinity of Maryville, near the author's childhood home. Very like their predecessors in Faulkner's fiction set in mythical rural Yoknapatawpha County, Mississippi, McCarthy's uneducated, inarticulate and impoverished characters struggle for survival with a modicum of dignity; though they may endure tragic fates, they lack the intellectual capacity for insight. In *The Orchard Keeper*, the elderly Ather Ownby, "keeper" of a long-decayed peach orchard, is an independent and sympathetic figure who winds up confined to a mental hospital after firing his shotgun at county police officers. His rebellious spirit has been quelled, he has little but banalities to offer to a neighbor who has come to visit him: "Most ever man loves peace, and none better than an old man." In *Outer Dark*, the hapless young mother Rinthy searches the Appalachian countryside for her lost baby, taken from her by her brother, the baby's father, and given to an itinerant tinker: a mix of Faulkner's Dewey Dell, of *As I Lay Dying*, who vainly seeks an abortion, and Lena Grove, of *Light in August*, who vainly seeks the man who has impregnated her, Rinthy makes her way on foot through an increasingly spooky landscape, but never finds her baby. *Outer Dark* is a more willfully obscure and self-consciously literary novel than *The Orchard Keeper*, burdened

by an excess of heavily Faulknerian prose in which even acts
of startling violence come muted and dreamlike, lacking an elemental credibility:

> The man took hold of the child and lifted it up. It was watch-
> ing the fire. Holme [Rinthy's brother] saw the blade wink in
> the light like a long cat's eye slant and malevolent and a
> dark smile erupted on the child's throat and went all broken
> down the front of it. The child made no sound. It hung there
> with its one eye glazing over like a wet stone and the black
> blood pumping down its naked belly.

Beyond even Faulknerian obliqueness, McCarthy has
eliminated all quotation marks from his prose so that his characters' speech isn't distinct from the narrative voice, in this way
adumbrating the curious texture of our dreams in which spoken language isn't heard so much as felt and dialogue is swallowed up in its surroundings. This manner of narration, which
some readers find distracting and pretentious, like McCarthy's
continuous use of (untranslated) Spanish in his later novels,
seems appropriate in these circumstances, and in any case will
persist through his career:

> The man had stretched out before the fire and was propped
> up on one elbow. He said: I wonder where a feller might find
> him a pair of bullhide boots like them you got.
>
> Holme's mouth was dust dry and the piece of meat
> seemed to have grown bigger. I don't know, he said.
>
> Don't know?

He turned the shirt again. He was very white and naked sitting there. They was give to me, he said.

Of McCarthy's four Tennessee-set novels, *Child of God* is the most memorable, a *tour de force* of masterfully sustained prose set pieces chronicling the life and abrupt death of a mountain man named Lester Ballard with a proclivity for collecting and enshrining dead bodies, predominantly those of attractive young females, in a cave to be discovered by Sevier County, Tennessee, officials only after his death:

> The bodies were covered with adipocere, a pale gray-cheesy mold common to corpses in damp places, and scallops of light fungus grew among them as they do on logs rotting in the forest. The chamber was filled with a sour smell, a faint reek of ammonia. The sheriff and the deputy made a noose from a rope and they slipped it around the upper body of the first corpse and drew it tight . . . Gray soapy clots of matter fell from the cadaver's chin. She ascended dangling. She sloughed in the weem of the noose. A gray rheum dripped.

Presumably based upon an actual case, or cases, of necrophiliac devotion in Appalachia, the legend of Lester Ballard is presented with dramatic brevity and an oblique sort of sympathy in a chorus of local voices:

> I don't know. They say he never was right after his daddy killed himself. They was just the one boy. The mother had run off . . . Me and Cecil Edwards was the ones cut him

down. He come in the store and told it like you'd tell it was rainin out. We went up there and walked in the barn and I seen his feet hanging. We just cut him down, let him fall on the floor. Just like cuttin down meat. He stood there and watched, never said nothin. He was about nine or ten year old at the time.

The narrator's voice suggests an eerie channeling of the "child of God" (that is, one who is "touched in the head"), Lester Ballard, if Ballard possessed the vocabulary to express his deepest yearnings: "Were there darker provinces of night he would have found them." Ballard's debased and choked voice in collusion with the author's skill at simile yields wonderful results on every page:

When Ballard came out onto the porch there was a thin man with a mouthful of marbles, articulating his goatbone underjaw laboriously, the original one having been shot away.

Ballard squatted on his heels in the yard opposite the visitor. They looked like constipated gargoyles.

Say you found that old gal up on the turnaround?

Ballard sniffed. What gal? he said.

Freed of the ponderous solemnity of Faulknerian stream-of-consciousness, McCarthy has found a way to dramatize Faulknerian themes in a voice brilliantly his own. Like a balloon the author's omniscient eye floats above the bleakly comic adventures of his mock-hero: "An assortment of cats taking the weak sun watched [Lester Ballard] go." Among the set pieces of *Child of God* are inspired riffs like outtakes from Erskine Caldwell's luridly exploitative *Tobacco Road* (1932) and *God's Little Acre* (1933), in which redneck Appalachians spawn swarms of dim-witted mammalian females as in a pornographic fever dream: the dump keeper's "gangling progeny" with "black hair hanging from their armpits" and "sluggard lids," named from a medical dictionary—"Urethra, Cerebella, Hernia Sue"—who move like cats and like cats in heat attract "swains" by the dozens. Ballard is attracted to the "long blonde flatshanked daughter that used to sit with her legs propped so that you could see her drawers. She laughed all the time." Yet it isn't Ballard but the omniscient narrative voice that presents such scenes:

> They fell pregnant one by one. [The dump keeper] beat them. The wife cried and cried. There were three births that summer. The house was filling up, both rooms, the trailer . . . The twelve year old began to swell. The air grew close. Grew rank and fetid. He found a pile of rags in a corner. Small lumps of yellow shit wrapped up and laid by. One day in the woods . . . he came across two figures humping away. He watched from behind a tree until he recognized one of his girls. He tried to creep up on them but the boy was wary and leaped up and was away through the woods hauling up his breeches as he went. The old man began to beat the girl with the stick he carried. She grabbed it. He over-balanced. They sprawled together in the leaves. Hot fishy reek of her freshened loins. Her peach drawers hung from a bush. The air about him grew electric. Next thing he knew his overalls

were about his knees and he was mounting her. Daddy quit, she said. Daddy. Ohhh.

Fleeing lawmen, Ballard finds himself trapped in an underground cave:

> In the morning when the light in the fissure dimly marked him out this drowsing captive looked so inculpate in the fastness of his hollow stone you might have said he was half right who thought himself so grievous a case against the gods.

Tragic farce, or farcical tragedy, *Child of God* is very likely McCarthy's most perfectly realized work of fiction for its dramatic compression and sustained stylistic bravura, avoiding the excesses of his later, more ambitious novels.

Blood Meridian, or, The Evening Redness in the West, McCarthy's fifth novel and the first set in the southwest borderlands to which he would lay a passionate literary claim, is the author's most challenging work of fiction, a nightmare chronicle of American marauders in Mexico in the 1850s rendered in voices grandiloquent and colloquial, ecstatic and debased, biblical and bombastic. Like William Gaddis's *The Recognitions* and Thomas Pynchon's *Gravity's Rainbow, Blood Meridian* is a highly idiosyncratic novel much admired by other writers, predominantly male writers, but difficult of access to a general reading audience, if not repellent. Admirers of *Blood Meridian* invariably dislike and disparage McCarthy's "accessible" best-selling *Border Trilogy*, as if these novels were a betrayal of the solemn rites of macho sadism and impacted fury of *Blood Meridian*[1] for which the ideal cover art would be a Hieronymus Bosch rendering of some scenes of Zane Grey.

Yet *Blood Meridian* and the *Border Trilogy* are counterpoised: the one a furious debunking of the legendary West, the other a subdued, humane, and subtle exploration of the tangled roots of such legends of the West as they abide in the human heart. Where *Blood Meridian* scorns any idealism except the jeremiad—"War is god"—the interlinked novels of the *Border Trilogy* testify to the quixotic idealism that celebrates friendship, brotherhood, loyalty, the integrity of the cowboy-worker as one whose life is bound up with animals in a harsh, exhausting, and dangerous environment: "I love this life," says Billy Parham of *Cities of the Plain*. After the phantasmagoria of *Blood Meridian*, the domestic realism of much of the *Border Trilogy* comes as a natural corrective.

All these novels of McCarthy's memorialize the southwestern landscape and its skies and weather, obsessively. In all, men and boys on horseback are in continual, often repetitive movement. "They rode on" is a mantra persistent as a clatter of hoofbeats. Often, whether in nineteenth-century Mexico or twentieth-century Texas, men may camp "in the ruins of an older culture deep in the stone mountains" oblivious of the history of such indigenous native ruins as they are of what such ruins might suggest of their own mortality. In the most romantic of the novels, *All the Pretty Horses*, sixteen-year-old John Grady Cole rides on his grandfather's ranch beneath a sun "blood red and elliptic," along an old Comanche trail:

At the hour he'd always choose when the shadows were long and the ancient road was shaped before him in the rose and canted light like a dream of the past where the painted ponies and the riders of that lost nation came down out of the north with their faces chalked and their long hair plaited and each armed for war which was their life . . . all of them pledged in blood and redeemable in blood only.

In *Blood Meridian* the adolescent romance-fantasy of Native American savages on the warpath erupts into an apocalyptic reality experienced by a crew of American mercenaries hired by a Mexican governor to scalp Indians at $100 a head:

A legion of horribles, hundreds in number, half naked or clad in costumes attic or biblical or wardrobed out of a fevered dream with the skins of animals and prior owners, coats of slain dragoons, frogged and braided cavalry jackets, one in a stove pipe hat and one with an umbrella and one in white stockings and a bloodstained weddingveil . . . death hilarious, all howling in a barbarous tongue and riding down upon them like a horde from a hell more horrible yet than the brimstone land of christian reckoning, screeching and yammering and clothed in smoke . . .

. . . they had circled the company and cut their ranks in two and then rising up again like funhouse figures, some with nightmare faces painted on their breasts, riding down the unhorsed Saxons and spearing and clubbing them and leaping from their mounts with knives . . . and stripping the clothes from the dead and seizing them up by the hair and passing their blades about the skulls of the living and the dead alike and snatching aloft the bloody wigs and hacking and chopping at the naked bodies, ripping off limbs, heads, gutting the strange white torsos and holding up great hand-fuls of viscera, genitals, some of the savages so slathered up with gore they might have rolled in it like dogs and some who fell upon the dying and sodomized them with loud cries to their fellows.

McCarthy's scenes of ecstatic violence are interlarded through *Blood Meridian* with a periodicity the reader will find effective or numbing depending upon his predilection for fantasy vio-lence beyond even the biblical Book of Revelation or the most lurid of comic books.

Where *Child of God* is a horror story writ small, depicted with masterly restraint, *Blood Meridian* is an epic accumu-lation of horrors, powerful in the way of Homer's *Iliad*; its strategy isn't ellipsis or indirection but an artillery barrage through hundreds of pages of wayward, unpredictable, brain-less violence. The "degeneracy of mankind" is McCarthy's great subject, infinitely demonstrable and as timely in our era of jingoist American aggression as it would have been in the decade following the end of the Vietnam War debacle, when *Blood Meridian* was published. Early on in the novel, a U.S. army captain broods over the "loss" of Mexican territory in the recent (1846 to 1848) war:

We fought for it. Lost friends and brothers down there. And then by God if we didn't give it back. Back to a bunch of barbarians that even the most biased in their favor will admit have no least notion on God's earth of honor or justice or the meaning of a republican government . . .

The captain leaned back and folded his arms. What we are dealing with, he said, is a race of degenerates. A mongrel race, little better than niggers. And maybe no better. There is no government in Mexico. Hell, there's no God in Mexico . . . We are dealing with a people manifestly incapable of governing themselves. And do you know what happens with people who cannot govern themselves? That's right. Others come in to govern for them . . .

We are to be the instruments of liberation in a dark and troubled land.

Soon, the nameless kid from Tennessee, eerily adumbrating Cormac McCarthy's migration westward, has signed up with a renegade band of Americans to embark upon, in a Mennonite prophet's words, "War of a madman's making onto a foreign land."

Though "the kid" is the closest to a sympathetic protagonist in *Blood Meridian*, McCarthy makes no effort to characterize him in any but a rudimentary way. We are not meant to identify with him, only just to perceive him, the youngest among a crew of psychopath-killers, as an unreflective participant in a series of violent, often demonic and deranged episodes that soon begin to repeat themselves. Countless men seem to be killed, yet the crew, led by a psychopath named Glanton, seems never to be depleted: "They rode on." *Blood Meridian* is coolly detached from any of its subjects, distanced and ironic

in the way of a classic Brechtian play; terrible things occur
but only as in fairy tales, bluntly summarized and soon forgotten:

> When Glanton and his chiefs swung back through the
> [Gileno Indian] village people were running out under the
> horses' hooves and the horses were plunging and some of
> the men were moving on foot among the huts with torches
> and dragging the victims out, slathered and dripping with
> blood, hacking at the dying and decapitating those who
> knelt for mercy . . . One of the Delawares emerged from the
> smoke with a naked infant dangling in each hand and squat-
> ted at a ring of midden stones and swung them by the heels
> each in turn and bashed their heads against the stones so
> that the brains burst forth through the fontanel in a bloody
> spew and the humans on fire came shrieking forth . . .

Among Glanton's crew, a black man named Jackson resolves
his feud with a white man named Jackson:

> The white man looked up drunkenly and the black stepped
> forward and with a single stroke swapt off his head.
> Two thick ropes of dark blood and two slender rose like
> snakes from the stump of his neck and arched hissing into
> the fire. The head rolled to the left and came to rest at the
> expriest's feet where it lay with eyes aghast.

Apache revenge for the Americans' atrocities:

They found the lost scouts hanging head downward from the limbs of a fireblacked paloverde tree. They were skewered through the cords of their heels with sharpened shuttles of green wood and they hung gray and naked above the dead ashes of the coals where they'd been roasted until their heads had charred and the brains bubbled in the skulls and steam sang from their noseholes. Their tongues were drawn out and held with sharpened sticks thrust through them and their torsos were sliced open with flints until the entrails hung down on their chests . . .

Animals, too, are prodigiously slaughtered in *Blood Meridian*, among them horses, dogs, puppies, even a dancing bear. Here, the Americans attack a Mexican mule team, unleashing an ecstatic gush of language beyond even Faulkner:

The riders pushed between them and the rock and methodically rode them from the escarpment, the animals dropping silently as martyrs, turning sedately in the empty air and exploding on the rocks below in startling bursts of blood and silver as the flasks broke open and the mercury loomed wobbling in the air in great sheets and lobes and small trembling satellites and all its forms grouping below and racing in the stone arroyos like the imbreachment of some ultimate alchemic work decocted from out the secret dark of the earth's heart, the fleeing stag of the ancients fugitive on the mountainside.

Among the mercenaries is an unlikely seer/prophet known as the judge. Initially a figure of uncanny eloquence as he is utterly without conscience, the judge would seem to be McCarthy's demented spokesman, interpreting what would otherwise be brute, brainless violence passing immediately into oblivion. The judge is a gigantic man nearly seven feet tall, bald, beardless, the "enormous dome of his head when he bared it blinding white and perfectly circumscribed so that it looked to have been painted." A figure out of some demonic mythology or cartoon Hades, the judge "shone like the moon so pale he was and not a hair to be seen anywhere on that vast corpus, not in any crevice nor in the great bores of his nose and not upon his chest nor in his ears nor any tuft at all above his eyes nor to the lids thereof." He carries a rifle inscribed *Et In Arcadia Ego*. He rescues an Apache child from a slaughter only to wantonly scalp him on the trail as, later, he rescues two orphaned puppies only to toss them into a river. Even on the war trail he pauses like a gentleman naturalist to "botanize" and take notes for demented sermons to be delivered between bouts of mayhem and murder:

The truth about the world ... is that anything is possible. Had you not seen it all from birth and thereby bled it of its strangeness it would appear to you for what it is, a hat trick in a medicine show, a fevered dream, a trance bepopulate with chimeras having neither antecedent nor precedent, an itinerant carnival, a migratory tentshow whose ultimate destination after many a pitch in many a muddy field is unspeakable and calamitous beyond reckoning.

The judge's constant theme is the "degeneracy of mankind" of which he would seem to be a prime example, preaching an ethic out of Thomas Hobbes in which "all trades are contained in that of war" and "war is the ultimate game because war is at last a forcing of the unity of existence. War is god." Improbably, the obese, often naked judge survives while most of his comrades are killed; the last we see of him, through the kid's eyes, is in 1878, in a tavern somewhere in Texas "among every sort of man" as their seeming exemplar. Prone to inflated rhetoric, as much buffoon as seer, the judge would seem to be a more deranged and far more malevolent Captain Ahab, or an unstoppered Kurtz (of Conrad's *Heart of Darkness*) whose succinct judgment "The horror! The horror!" has been replaced here by slews of verbiage and goofy behavior in the way of Marlon Brando's shamelessly campy performance in Coppola's *Apocalypse Now*, a reimagining of *Heart of Darkness* set in Vietnam during the Vietnam War. But where Conrad presents the "impenetrable darkness" of the debased Kurtz sparingly, McCarthy so frequently unleashes the judge upon the reader that over the sprawl of hundreds of pages he becomes increasingly a caricature:

> Towering over [the dancers] is the judge and he is naked dancing . . . huge and pale and hairless, like an enormous infant. He never sleeps, he says. He says he'll never die.

Cormac McCarthy's least known and surely most undervalued work is his five-act play *The Stonemason* (1994), a remarkable feat of ventriloquism in its intimate depiction of four generations of a close-knit black family, descendants of slaves, in Louisville, Kentucky, in the 1970s. With its enormous, commercially impractical cast (thirteen named characters in addition to numerous others) and lengthy, eloquent but undramatic monologues, *The Stonemason* would seem to have been written to be read and not performed.

Where *Blood Meridian* celebrates an unflinching and numbing nihilism, *The Stonemason* celebrates bonds of family love and responsibility. Like the *Border Trilogy*, it celebrates the integrity of work and the sometimes mystical bond between individuals (in McCarthy's work, exclusively men) linked by a common craft or trade: "You can't separate wisdom from the common experience and the common experience is just what the worker has in plenty." The play's narrator is a thirty-two-year-old black man, Ben Telfair, who'd originally planned to be a teacher but turned stonemason in emulation of his revered 101-year-old grandfather Papaw; it's a memory play, with elaborate stage directions intended to "give distance to events and place them in a completed past." Its central event is the death of the patriarch stonemason Papaw which seems to precipitate, as in a classic tragedy, the sudden disintegration of the Telfair family: the suicide of Ben's father, a stonemason not content to live within his financial means, and the heroin overdose death of Ben's nineteen-year-old nephew Soldier. Intelligently tender-hearted, realistic in language, characters, and story, *The Stonemason* more resembles a play by August Wilson than anything by Cormac McCarthy; it's a testament to the author's versatility if not his audacity.

Much of the play is comprised of beautifully composed

language turning upon Ben's idealization of Papaw and of the sacred vocation of stonemasonry. The play avoids a dramatic resolution but takes us through a period of mourning and regeneration as Ben, grieving for his losses, has a vision of his deceased grandfather that assures him "[Papaw] would guide me all my days and he would not fail me, not fail me, not ever fail me." Is this ending meant to be taken at face value, or ironically? *The Stonemason* would seem to be a play lacking a subtext, imagined without irony; its conflicts are open and reiterated. Admirer's of McCarthy's lurid grandiloquence and penchant for minutely described scenes of carnage would very likely be baffled by the naive and unquestioned idealism of *The Stonemason*:

> Grace I know is much like love and you cannot deserve it. It is freely given, without reason or equity. What could you do to deserve it? What?

And,

> For true masonry is not held together by cement but by gravity. That is to say, by the warp of the world. By the stuff of creation itself. The keystone that locks the arch is pressed in place by the thumb of God . . . For we invent nothing but what God has put to hand.

As *The Stonemason* is a rebuke of sorts to the "war god" of *Blood Meridian*, so the closely linked novels of the *Border Trilogy* are a tribute, in their warmly sympathetic depiction of the lives of young ranch hands in Texas and New Mexico in the 1950s, to such traditional values as friendship, loyalty, compassion, courage, physical endurance and (male) stoicism; though suffused with nostalgia for a way of life rapidly coming to an end in the Southwest in the decade following the end of World War II, for the most part the novels avoid sentimentality. (Why "sentimentality" need be avoided in serious literature, as it's rarely avoided by serious people in actual life, is another issue.) Where the prevailing atmosphere of *Blood Meridian* is apocalyptic and its structure operatic, erupting into arias of esoteric violence and inflated language at regular intervals, the prevailing atmosphere of the *Border Trilogy* is something like the common sense of (male) adult maturity as it collides with (male) adolescent passion and idealism. What erupts as drama, often as tragic drama, in the ballad-like tales of John Grady Cole (of *All the Pretty Horses* and *Cities of the Plain*) and his contemporary Billy Parham (of *The Crossing* and *Cities of the Plain*), is adolescent yearning, beautifully rendered by McCarthy in an infinity of ways through hundreds of pages of prose in homage to the West:

> There was an old horseskull in the brush and [John Grady Cole] squatted and picked it up and turned it in his hands. Frail and brittle. Bleached paper white. He squatted in the long light holding it . . .
>
> What he loved in horses was what he loved in men, the blood and the heat of the blood that ran them. All his rev-

erence and all his fondness and all the leanings of his life were for the ardenthearted and they would always be so and never be otherwise.

With this statement the novelist would seem to bare his own ardent heart, making vulnerable what in practitioners of literary irony is kept well hidden.

In a telling scene in *Cities of the Plain*, John Grady Cole on his way to town with "hair all slicked back like a muskrat" pauses for a conversation with an old ranch hand to whom he speaks with a touchingly filial courtesy. The old man tells John Grady a tale of barroom violence in Juarez, Mexico, in 1929.

> . . . Tales of the old west, he said.
>
> Yessir.
>
> Lots of people shot and killed.
>
> Why were they?
>
> Mr. Johnson passed the tips of his fingers across his jaw. Well, he said. I think these people mostly come from Tennessee and Kentucky. Edgefield district in South Carolina. Southern Missouri. They were mountain people. They come from mountain people in the old country. They always would shoot you. It wasn't just here. They kept comin west and about the time they got here was about the time Sam Colt invented the sixshooter and it was the first time these people could afford a gun you could carry around in your belt. That's all there ever was to it. It had nothin to do with the country at all. The west.

Nothing to do, in other words, with the "degeneracy of mankind" but only with the brainless predilection for violence in a specific historic/sociological context.

Through the more than one thousand pages of the *Border Trilogy* the essential conflict is between two distinct ways of life: the way of the wanderer-on-horseback and the way of settled, circumscribed life. The yearning to leave home and "light out for the Territory ahead of the rest" (in Huckleberry Finn's memorable final words) is perhaps the most powerful of yearnings in McCarthy's novels, far more convincing, for instance, than John Grady Cole's romantic infatuations with Mexican girls. Though for most Americans the vast, empty spaces of rural Texas and New Mexico would seem roomy enough, for the boy-heroes of McCarthy's fiction Mexico is the region of exotic adventure and mystery: "where the antique world clung to the stones and to the spores of living things and dwelt in the blood of man." The slickly villainous Mexican pimp Eduardo of *Cities of the Plain* gives the yearning a cruder interpretation:

> [Americans] drift down out of your leprous paradise seeking
> a thing now extinct among them. A thing for which perhaps
> they no longer even have a name. Being farmboys of course
> the first place they think to look of course is a whorehouse.

In fact there is nothing salacious nor even sexual in the interlocked tales of John Grady Cole and Billy Parham. Even as John Grady becomes a lover he remains in essence chastely stoic as the hero of a traditional boy's adventure story.

Initially, both John Grady and Billy, of Texas and New

Mexico respectively, are drawn to crossing the Mexican border on horseback as a means of escaping the increasingly somber facts of their lives (with the death of John Grady's grandfather, the family ranch will be sold and he must leave; both Billy Parham's parents are murdered) and of proving themselves as men. Though minutely grounded in the verisimilitude of ranch life and the *gravitas* of the physical world, which no one has more powerfully evoked than Cormac McCarthy, each novel attempts to link its boy-heroes with ballad or fairy-tale elements that some readers may find implausible, if not preposterous. The best way of appreciating McCarthy's achievement in the *Border Trilogy* is simply to suspend disbelief when the novels swerve into their mythic mode. For example, the first part of *The Crossing*, a tenderly observed love story of a kind between the teenaged Billy Parham and a pregnant female wolf he has trapped, and leads across the Mexican border with the intention of releasing her in the mountains, is an extraordinary piece of imaginative prose, like the novel's final pages in which Billy encounters a terribly crippled stray dog. Here is Billy's homage to the mysterious and beautiful predator he has had to kill, to end her suffering:

> He squatted over the wolf and touched her fur. He touched the cold and perfect teeth. The eye turned to the fire gave back no light and he closed it with his thumb and sat by her and put his hand upon her bloodied forehead and closed his own eyes that he could see her running in the mountains, running in the starlight ... Deer and hare and dove and ground-vole all richly empaneled on the air for her delight,

all nations of the possible world ordained by God of which she was one among and not separate from ... He took up her stiff head out of the leaves and held it or he reached to hold what cannot be held, what already ran among the mountains at once terrible and of a great beauty, like flowers that feed on flesh.

John Grady's "ardent heart" for horses is equally convincing, but far less convincing is the boy's predilection for falling disastrously in love with Mexican girls (highborn in *All the Pretty Horses*, an abused prostitute in *Cities of the Plain*) whom he naively wishes to marry. Not much of this is credible and virtually none of it is original, but the doomed boy-girl romance of *All the Pretty Horses* helped to make the novel McCarthy's breakthrough best seller. In the more skillfully composed *Cities of the Plain*, in essence a reprise of *All the Pretty Horses* in a darker tone, John Grady's second love affair, with a teen-aged prostitute both abused and saintly in the way of a Dostoyevskian girl of the streets, leads to their death in a brilliantly choreographed knife-fight sequence with Eduardo, stylized and ritualistic as a Japanese Noh play. Before he is killed by the American boy he hasn't taken altogether seriously, Eduardo pronounces this cultural judgment:

> In his dying perhaps the suitor will see that it was his hunger for mysteries that has undone him. Whores. Superstition. Finally death. For that is what has brought you here. That is what you were seeking ...
>
> Your kind cannot bear that the world be ordinary. That it

contain nothing save what stands before one. But the Mexican world is a world of adornment only and underneath it is very plain indeed. While your world—he passed the knife back and forth like a shuttle through a loom—your world totters upon an unspoken labyrinth of questions.

In McCarthy's later fiction such seemingly allegorical figures begin to intrude, as if the author had become impatient with the conventions of realism, like the later, pointedly didactic Tolstoy in his "moral fables" telling us what he wants us to think in an elevated vatic language. Dialogue gives way to rambling monologues, sermons, and homilies in the second half of *The Crossing*, as Billy Parham encounters strangers on his pilgrimage, each with a story to tell him. After the dramatic conclusion of *Cities of the Plain*, the author adds an anticlimactic epilogue in which a garrulous stranger appears to tell the now seventy-eight-year-old Billy Parham what life is all about.

This story like all stories has its beginning in a question. And those stories which speak to us with the greatest resonance have a way of turning upon the teller and erasing him and his motives from all memory. So the question of who is telling the story is very consiguiente.

It's as if the novelist were providing a gloss on his novel, or his notes to himself during its composition.

So long as McCarthy trusts to John Grady Cole and Billy Parham to embody truths they cannot perhaps articulate, the *Border* novels are works of surpassing emotional power and beauty; elegies to a vanishing, or vanished frontier world, in the decades following World War II. "The world will never be the same," the adolescent Billy is told by an older horseman in *The Crossing*, to which Billy replies, "I know it. It ain't now." By the end of the trilogy Billy has become an elderly homeless man, long since horseless and friendless, taken in by a family out of pity and given "a shed room off the kitchen that was much like the room he'd slept in as a boy."

As if we were forced to see Huckleberry Finn in his later years, a homeless drifter broken in body and spirit, for whom the romance of "setting off for the Territory" is long past.

A partial inventory of the macho artillery employed in McCarthy's ninth novel *No Country for Old Men* includes: a short-barreled Uzi with a twenty-five round clip; an AK-47 automatic; a short-barreled H & K machine pistol with a black nylon shoulderstrap; a short-barreled shotgun with a pistol stock and a twenty-round drum magazine; a Tec-9 with two extra magazines; a nickel-plated government .45 automatic pistol; a heavy-barreled .270 on a '98 Mauser action with a laminated stock of maple and walnut and a Unert1 telescopic sight; a stainless steel .357 revolver; a nine-millimeter Glock; a twelve-gauge Remington automatic with a plastic military stock and a parkerized finish fitted with a shop-made silencer "fully a foot long and big around as a beercan." Too many to count are undesignated pistols and shotguns, some of them short-barreled. There is a cattle gun acquired by a psychopath killer and put to cruel use:

[Chigurh] placed his hand on the man's head like a faith healer. The pneumatic hiss and click of the plunger sounded like a door closing. The man slid soundlessly to the ground, a round hole in his forehead from which the blood bubbled and ran down into his eyes carrying with it his slowly uncoupling world visible to see.

Llewelyn Moss, a former Vietnam War sniper, a Texan on the run from the psychopath, employs some of the weaponry in this arsenal but is "a strong believer in the shotgun." The sheriff of Comanche County, an older man named Bell, prefers old-fashioned police-issue Colts—"If that don't stop him you'd better throw the thing down and take off runnin' "—and the old Winchester model 97—"I like it that it's got a hammer." Men are judged by their prowess with firearms but also by the boots they choose to wear: "Nocona" for Moss; "expensive Lucchese crocodile" for a self-described hit man named Wells in the hire of a wealthy Houston businessman/drug smuggler; ostrich-skin boots for the psychopath Chigurh.

Not the Texas frontier of legend but contemporary rural Texas in the vicinity of Sanderson, near the Mexican border, is the setting for this fast-plotted action novel about heroin smugglers and the considerable collateral damage among the innocent and not-so-innocent in their wake. The novel takes its title from William Butler Yeats's "Sailing to Byzantium": "That is no country for old men. The young/In one another's arms, birds in the trees/—Those dying generations—at their song . . ." Yeats's country is Ireland, seemingly suffused with erotic energy; McCarthy's country is suffused with the malevolent Eros of male violence. Not horses or wolves but firearms and their effect upon human flesh is the object of desire in *No Country for Old Men*, which reads like a prose film by Quentin Tarrantino. With the exception of Sheriff Bell, the moral conscience of the novel, characters are sketchily and perfunctorily drawn as if on the run. At the center of the action is a psychopath who shoots his way through scenes invincible as a Terminator-like instrument of destruction and given to vatic utterances: "When I came into your life your life was over."

Shorn of the brooding lyricism and poetic descriptive passages that have become McCarthy's signature style, *No Country for Old Men* is a variant of one of the oldest of formula suspense tales: a man discovers a treasure, unwisely decides to take it and run, bringing upon himself and others a string of calamities ending with his death. Alfred Hitchcock coined the term "MacGuffin" to signify the arbitrary object of pursuit: someone has something (an icon, a secret formula, any variety of treasure) that others want, generating chase scenes, killings, suspense in Hitchcock's ingeniously contrived films. In *No Country for Old Men* the MacGuffin is drug money— "Two point four million. All used bills"—discovered by Moss in the aftermath of an apparent shoot-out by rival drug smugglers in the wilds north of the Mexican border, where Moss is hunting antelope. In addition to the money, Moss also takes some Mexican brown heroin and several firearms which in the course of his doomed adventure will be put to frequent use.

Thirty-six, married to a much younger woman, a naive

risk taker who puts both himself and his wife in jeopardy, Moss doesn't exist as much more than a function of the plot, a kind of puppet jerked about by the author. Since the predominant mode of narration in *No Country for Old Men* is detached, as in a screenplay, a documentation of physical actions, we follow Moss and his nemesis Chigurh, cutting from one to the other as in an action film, without being privy to their motives. (After several readings, I still can't understand why, having stolen the drug money and escaped safely, Moss decides to revisit the scene of the carnage to help the only surviving, badly wounded Mexican, rather than anonymously summon professional help for the man. Except to get himself sighted and pursued by drug dealers, and precipitate the plot, this isn't a very sensible decision.)

In essence, *No Country for Old Men* is a showcase for McCarthy's psychopath killer Anton Chigurh and the mayhem he perpetrates upon mostly unarmed and helpless individuals. There is no sexuality in McCarthy's fiction but only a minutely described, ecstatically evoked Eros of physical violence, repeatedly evoked in prose. As his almost exact contemporary John Updike has written with ecstatic tenderness of physical heterosexual love, so McCarthy writes of physical violence with an attentiveness found in no other serious writer except Sade:

> Chigurh shot [Wells] in the face. Everything that Wells had ever known or thought or loved drained slowly down the wall behind him. His mother's face, his First Communion, women he had known. The faces of men as they died on their knees before him. The body of a child dead in a road-

side ravine in another country. He lay half headless on the bed with his arms outflung, most of his right hand missing.

And, in the aftermath of a bloody street shoot-out:

> The man [he'd shot in the back] was lying in a spreading pool of blood. Help me, he said. Chigurh took the pistol from his waist. He looked into the man's eyes. The man looked away.
>
> Look at me, Chigurh said . . .
>
> He looked at Chigurh. He looked at the new day paling all about. Chigurh shot him through the forehead and then stood watching him. Watching the capillaries break up in his eyes. The light receding. Watching his own image degrade in that squandered world.

No match for Chigurh is the former Vietnam War sniper Moss, who takes "a couple of rounds in the face":

> There was no chock under Moss's neck and his head was turned to the side. One eye partly opened. He looked like a badman on a slab. They'd sponged the blood off of him but there were holes in his face and his teeth were shot out.

Like an invincible figure in a video game of murder and mayhem, Chigurh is flatly portrayed and not very convincing: "I have no enemies. I don't permit it." When he delivers most of the drug money to the unnamed Houston businessman/drug smuggler, instead of keeping it for himself, he explains that his rampage has been "simply to establish my bonafides. As some-one who is an expert in a difficult field."

All that keeps *No Country for Old Men* from being a skillfully executed but essentially meretricious thriller is the presence, increasingly rambling and hesitant as the novel proceeds, of the sheriff of Comanche County, one of the "old men" alluded to in the title. Dismissed as a "redneck sheriff in a hick town. In a hick state," Bell is intended as a moral compass amid the whirligig of amorality. He is courageous and well intentioned but ineffectual as a lawman, unable to stop Chigurh's rampage and hardly capable of identifying him. Where he hadn't had a single unsolved homicide in his jurisdiction in forty-one years, now he has nine unsolved homicides in a single week. The new breed of psychopath drug dealer/assassin is beyond Bell's power to control as the new Uzis and machine pistols are beyond the old-style Colts and Winchesters. It's possible that Cormac McCarthy, described in a recent interview as a "southern conservative,"[2] intends Bell's social-conservative predilections to speak for his own, explaining the high crime rate in Comanche County in this way: "It starts when you begin to overlook bad manners. Any time you quit hearin Sir and Mam the end is pretty much in sight . . . It reaches into ever strata." More pointedly,

> I think if you were Satan and you were settin around tryin to think up somethin that would just bring the human race to its knees what you would probably come up with is narcotics . . . [Satan] explains a lot of things that otherwise don't have no explanation.

Bell is evidently unfamiliar with the blood-drenched history of his state and its protracted border wars, so vigorously documented elsewhere in Cormac McCarthy. He's a man left behind by his era confronted with a moral void beyond even Satan: "What do you say to a man that by his own admission has no soul? Why would you say anything?"

Nowhere has Cormac McCarthy addressed this question more powerfully, and more succinctly, than in his post-Apocalyptic novel *The Road* (2006), the most widely acclaimed of his numerous works of fiction. Throughout this bleakly prophetic short novel with its affinities to such twentieth-century visionaries as Samuel Beckett and José Saramago, we are in the presence of a stripped-down humanity, *in extremis*; utterly vanished is the crude, jocular, tall-tale black humor of McCarthy's earlier novels, and McCarthy's sense of a community of individuals bonded by common loss, or threat of loss, as in the elegiac *Border Trilogy* and the besieged Comanche County of *No Country for Old Men*. Throughout the novel McCarthy evokes an air of antiquity: though we are presumably in a future time, we are more truly in the past, before history: this is the Hades of Homer, the Inferno of Dante. In the way of Bosch, Dürer, and Goya, and in the mode of the most malevolently inventive contemporary doomsday filmmaker— like George Miller, creator of the *Mad Max* series—McCarthy exults in the depiction of human corpses amid his desiccated landscape, and in the suggestion of violent, grotesque deaths: mummified bodies are sighted in doorways and in vehicles, garishly displayed on pikes, or posed like waxworks dummies in a vast and unspeakable allegory. In a little clearing is a "black thing skewered over coals"—a "charred human infant headless and gutted and blackening on the spit." In this hell, McCarthy's protagonist is shrewd enough to know that he must always be able to see behind him—he has affixed a rearview motorcycle mirror to the shopping cart in which he pushes his belongings, in the kind of small but painstakingly defining detail that makes Cormac McCarthy so vivid a writer. What would be an abstract and perhaps over-familiar doomsday polemic in the imagination of another writer is an emotionally gripping tale in McCarthy's.

The Road is quintessential McCarthy: a variant upon a picaresque adventure tale. Where in the *Border Trilogy* the boys' quests began as romantic pilgrimages, however bleakly the last novel, *Cities of the Plain*, ends, and there is a youthful vigor to the prose suggestive of ceaseless, restless, exuberant motion—usually on horseback—*The Road* is a work of numbing bleakness, pessimism; the journey is on foot, very slow, haphazard, less an adventure than an unmitigated ordeal. An unnamed father and his son—Everyman, Everyboy—are embarked upon a journey with no destination other than the hope of escaping the impending Appalachian winter by taking back roads along the southern coast. Here is a return to McCarthy's eastern Tennessee roots—though in tone very like the rough country of McCarthy's West. Civilization has been destroyed in what seems to have been an instantaneous flash of nuclear energy—ash sifts down from overcast skies, most wildlife has become extinct, and other surviving *Homo sapiens*, observed with great caution and horror, have reverted to barbarism in graphic visual imagery of the kind scattered through *Blood Meridian*:

> Shapes of dried blood in the stubble grass and gray coils of viscera where the slain had been field-dressed and hauled away. The wall beyond held a frieze of human heads, all faced alike, dried and caved with their taut grins and shrunken eyes . . . The heads not truncheoned shapeless had been flayed of their skins and the raw skulls painted and signed across the forehead in a scrawl and one white bone skull had the plate sutures etched carefully in ink.

As McCarthy has never shown the slightest interest in politics or history—even his most realistic novel, *Suttree*, takes place in a topical vacuum—so in this parable of human folly and its tragic aftermath there is no explanation of why war was waged, and by whom; if in fact the devastation is global, as we are led to assume; from this point onward, history itself is extinct. It's as if the demons of *Blood Meridian*—the men who "settled" the West by imposing their barbarism upon an exquisitely beautiful nature—have triumphed. McCarthy's vision is Manichean: there are "good" people and there are "evil" people—the former at the mercy of the latter. Horribly, in *The Road*, evil people are devouring good people in orgies of desperate cannibalism.

This monochromatic vision would be unbearable except for McCarthy's beautifully rendered "poetic" prose. Here is an

incantatory voice that makes of devastation—doom itself—
something rich and strange, as in the late poetry of T. S. Eliot:

> They stood on the far shore of a river and called to him.
> Tattered gods slouching in their rags across the waste. Trek-
> king the dried floor of a mineral sea where it lay cracked and
> broken like a fallen plate. Paths of feral fire in the coagulated
> sands. The figures faded in the distance. He woke and lay in
> the dark.

And in the richly evocative final passage of the novel:

> Once there were brook trout in the streams in the moun-
> tains. You could see them standing in the amber current
> where the white edges of their fins wimpled softly in the
> flow. They smelled of moss in your hand. Polished and mus-
> cular and forsional. On their backs were vermiculate pat-
> terns that were maps of the world in its becoming. Maps and
> mazes. Of a thing which could not be put back. Not be made
> right again. In the deep glens where they lived all things were
> older than man and they hummed of mystery.

As usual McCarthy's perspective is coolly omniscient: his narrative voice seems to hover just above individuals like the
questing father and his son, without entering into them fully.
We see through the father's anxious eyes—we share his anxious thoughts—but we are simultaneously distinct from him
and are aware at all times that he's a (fictitious, allegorical)

character in a tale. Admirers of McCarthy's more varied prose may miss the flashes of his droll, deformed wit, always evident amid the excesses of *Blood Meridian*, the novel that most resembles *The Road*; McCarthy's favored theme is male barbarism, in contrast to the brotherly sentiment of the boy-heroes of the *Border Trilogy*, or the tender feelings Billy Parham has for the (female) wolf in *The Crossing*—the (female) wolf as the boy-hero's *anima*. In *The Road*, it's significant that there is no maternal figure: McCarthy has disposed of the mother, as a suicide. (McCarthy's female portraits are flat as cartoon figures set beside his men. The wife in *The Road* speaks as no woman in recorded history is ever likely to have spoken—"I am done with my own whorish heart and I have been for a long time." No word more inexorably male than *whorish*!) Only a father remains—only *the father*—pushing the possessions of his depleted family in a shopping cart—an ironic, disfigured artifact of a lost consumer culture—armed with a revolver containing only two bullets. It's significant—and alarmingly timely—that father and son are wearing masks to protect them from the befouled air. Their primary tasks are to scavenge food and to stay out of sight of other people. In the course of the journey the boy begins to perceive that the father, intent upon his and his son's survival, is gradually changing into a savage like the others. One is reminded of Faulkner's terse summation of the Negro housekeeper of the afflicted house of the Compsons, in *The Sound and the Fury*: "They endured." (As if the singular Dilsey were in fact multiple, emblematic.)

The Road is McCarthy's most lyric novel as it is his most horrific and perhaps his most personal: there is an acknowledgment of human love here missing in McCarthy's more characteristic work. Who could have imagined, given the lurid and zestful black humor of *Child of God* and *Blood Meridian*, and the celebration of unfettered bachelorhood of the *Border Trilogy*, that in later years Cormac McCarthy would write so feelingly about parental love for a child? Of course the child is a boy as the parent who has been courageous enough to survive to protect him is male. In McCarthy's Manichean/Old Testament cosmology, the female has yet to be born.

IN ROUGH COUNTRY II:
ANNIE PROULX

Fine Just the Way It Is
Wyoming Stories 3
by Annie Proulx

> She realized that every ranch she passed had lost
> a boy, lost them early and late, boys smiling, sure
> in their risks, healthy, tipped out of the current of
> life by liquor and acceleration, rodeo smashups,
> bad horses, deep irrigation ditches, high trestles,
> tractor rollovers and unsecured truck doors.
> Her boy, too. This was the waiting darkness that
> surrounded ranch boys, the dangerous growing up
> that cancelled their favored status. The trip along
> the road was a roll call of grief.
>
> —ANNIE PROULX,
>
> FROM "TITS-UP IN A DITCH"

Like a flash flood rushing along a normally meandering stream, Annie Proulx's most characteristic short stories move with a deceptive sort of sinister casualness, before the point of impact, and of disaster—but "disaster" for Proulx, as for her kinsman-contemporary Cormac McCarthy whose quasi-mystical western territory is to the south (New Mexico, Texas, Mexico) of Proulx's photo-realist Wyoming territory, is likely to be tersely and ironically noted, as the fall of a sparrow might be noted, one more event in the hard implacable heart of Nature. In Proulx's words:

> For me, the story falls out of a place, its geology and climate, the flora, fauna, prevailing winds, the weather. I am not people-centric, and I'm appalled at what human beings have done to the planet.*

And:

> I took rurality as my ground ... The landscapes [of Wyoming and Newfoundland] are different, but the economic situations and the beliefs of the people ... are quite similar, because they are all commanded by powers in urban centers. But because [the people] can't see who's making the rules and the economic strategies that govern them, they continue to believe in the independent rural life, which is deliciously ironic and very sad. [*Guardian* interview, December 11, 2004]

Through a sequence of vividly imagined and boldly idiosyncratic works of fiction—*Heart Songs and Other Stories* (1988), *Postcards* (1992), *The Shipping News* (1993), *Accordion Crimes* (1996), *Close Range: Wyoming Stories* (1999),

---

* *Guardian* interview, December 11, 2004, with Aida Edemariam.

That Old Ace in the Hole (2002), *Bad Dirt: Wyoming Stories 2* (2004)—Proulx has explored rural America *in extremis* with an admirable passion and patience for research of all kinds, both scholarly and reportorial. As she acknowledges in the front matter of *Close Range*, she is "an aficionado of local histories [who has] for years collected memoirs and accounts of regional lives and events in many parts of North America"; for her Texas/Oklahoma panhandle epic *Ace in the Hole*, Proulx allegedly spent three years of travel gathering information, of which in the end she could use but a relatively small portion; researching *The Shipping News*, by her account she fell asleep for two years reading *The Dictionary of Newfoundland English*. Lacking the Old Testament-prophet vehemence that permeates Cormac McCarthy's similarly elegiac work, but suffused with a similar aesthetic wonderment for the physical terrain of the West and the big skies above—both Proulx and McCarthy are tireless, if not relentless in their exacting depiction of Ansel Adams–like scenery—Proulx often laces her grimly naturalistic tales with flashes of bawdy humor, even an appealing goofiness, as if to suggest that, from the Olympian perspective of the Rockies, the mishaps, follies, and even the tragedies of humankind are of minuscule significance in a world in which "demons [are] sprinkled throughout . . . like croutons in a salad."

With the publication of this new collection of Wyoming stories, Proulx has now three volumes of Western tales of which the most famous—and the masterwork—remains the long, lyric, tenderly erotic "Brokeback Mountain" (originally published in *The New Yorker* in 1997) from the first volume *Close*

Range. This initial collection of Wyoming tales is perhaps the most substantial of the three volumes as well as containing, in its hardcover edition, poetically evocative watercolors of Western scenes by the artist William Matthews. Having moved to rural Wyoming in her early sixties, in 1994, after having lived for most of her life in small towns in New England, Proulx assimilated her vast new territory in much the same way that Cormac McCarthy, moving west from his longtime home in Tennessee, in 1976, assimilated his new Southwestern territory, as a landscape both historical and symbolic: a terrain of great physical beauty dwarfing the merely "human" in ways to evoke the allegorical Yukon tales of Jack London and the North African desert tales of Paul Bowles. Already in her fifties when she first began publishing short stories in magazines like *Gray's Sporting Journal, Harrowsmith*, and *Ploughshares*, and fifty-eight when she came to literary prominence with *The Shipping News*, Proulx is far less oracular than Cormac McCarthy, predisposed to vernacular speech and characters sketched in the broad, blunt strokes of such old-fashioned comics as "Dick Tracy," "Little Orphan Annie," and "Krazy Kat" in which caricature is the norm and the grotesque is signaled by "funny" names in abundance; we know that we are not in the rarefied literary territory of post-Jamesian, post-Chekhovian, post-Joycean fiction when we encounter such rural specimens as Pake Bitts, Diamond Felts and his rodeo sidekick Leecil Bewd, Dirt Sheets, Sutton Muddyman, Roany Hamp (female), Creel Zmundzinski, Reverend Jefford J. Pecker, Orion Horncrackle, Plato Bucklew, Gay G. Brawls, Georgina Crawshaw, Deb Sipple (male), Fiesta Punch, Budgel Wolfscale, Condor Figg, Hard

Winter Ulph, Chad Grills, Chay Sump, Queeda Dorgan, Sink Gartrell, Mizpah Fur, Hi Alcorn, Antip Bewley, Fenk Fipps and his friend Wacky Lipe, Fong Saucer, Bracelet Quean (male), Pastor Alf Crashbee, and numerous others whose hard-luck fates seem predestined in their names as in Proulx's thumbnail sketches that leap from the page like crude comical Weegee portraits:

> The terrain of [Car] Scrope himself consisted of a big, close-cropped head, platinum-blond mustache, a ruined back from a pneumatic drill ride on the back of a . . . tatter-eared pinto . . . feet wrecked from a lifetime in tight cowboy boots, and simian arms . . . His features, a chiseled small mouth, watercolored eyes, had a pinched look, but the muscled shoulders and deep chest advertised a masculine strength that had, over the years, attracted not a few women . . . [He] ate, in addition to large quantities of beef and pork, junk food from plastic sacks which set off itchy rashes and produced bowel movements containing long orange strands as though he had swallowed and digested a fox. ["Pair a Spurs"]

As Proulx observes in the tongue-in-cheek endings of two tall tales included in *Close Range*, "When you live a long way out you make your own fun" ("55 Miles to the Gas Pump") and "If you believe that you'll believe anything" ("People in Hell Just Want a Drink of Water").

Proulx's more sympathetically and realistically imagined stories, however, transcend caricature and are frequently moving, and memorable: characters may be foolish, hardly more than puppets or ants seen from the ironist's distance, but the prose in which they are rendered is likely to be sinewy, supple, tensely impacted and "poetic" in the best sense of the word. In a grimly powerful tale aptly titled "The Mud Below" from *Close Range*, a doomed young bull rider lives for "the turbulent ride [that gives him] the indescribable rush, shot him mainline with crazy-ass elation":

> Rodeo night in a hot little Okie town and Diamond Felts was inside a metal chute a long way from the scratch on Wyoming dirt he named as home, sitting on the back of bull 82N, a loose-skinned brindle Brahma-cross described in the program as Little Kisses . . . He kept his butt cocked to one side, his feet up on the chute rails so the bull couldn't grind his leg, brad him up, so that if he got thrashed he could get over the top in a hurry.

When the end comes for the bull rider, it comes quickly:

> In the sixth second the bull stopped dead, then shifted everything the other way and immediately back again and he was lost, flying to the left into his hand and over the animal's shoulder, his eye catching the wet glare of the bull, but his hand stayed upside down and jammed. He was hung up and good . . . The bull was crazy to get rid of him and the clanging bell. Diamond was jerked high off the ground with every lunge, snapped like a towel . . . The animal spun so rapidly its shape seemed to the watchers like mottled streaks

of paint, the rider a paint rag . . . His arm was being pulled from its socket. It went on and on. This time he was going to die before shouting strangers.

In fact, Diamond Felts doesn't die just then: he survives, if barely, to consider how "it was all a hard, fast ride that ended in the mud."

Close Range is bracketed by "The Mud Below" and the equally poignant and powerful "Brokeback Mountain," whose cowboy-lover protagonists

> were raised on small, poor ranches in opposite corners of the state, Jack Twist in Lightning Flat up on the Montana border, Ennis del Mar from around Sage, near the Utah line, both high school dropout country boys with no prospects, brought up to hard work and privation, both rough-mannered, rough-spoken, inured to the stoic life.

Herding and watching over sheep in a remote mountainside setting, Jack Twist and Ennis del Mar, seemingly "straight" boys, begin to have sexual relations as if by chance, and opportunity; no word tender as "love" will ever pass between them, but their lives are forever altered, their subsequent marriages blighted. The reader's intimacy with the young lovers on their mountainside tending sheep is rudely interrupted by Proulx's sudden switch of perspective:

> They never talked about the sex, let it happen, at first only in the tent at night, then in full daylight with the hot sun

striking down, and at evening in the fire glow, quick, rough, laughing and snorting, no lack of noises, but saying not a god-damn word except once Ennis said, "I'm not no queer," and Jack jumped in with, "Me neither . . ." There were only two of them on the mountain flying in the euphoric, bitter air, looking down on the hawk's back and the crawling lights of vehicles on the plain below . . . They believed themselves invisible, not knowing Joe Aguirre [their supervisor at Farm and Ranch Employment] had watched them through his 10x42 binoculars for ten minutes one day.

In Wyoming, as in most of America in the 1960s and 1970s, it would not have been likely that two male lovers could be tolerated, nor even feel that living together outright might be an option for them; Jack Twist and Ennis del Mar part, and come together in secret, and part again through the years until the mysterious death of Jack Twist that might have been an accident, or an act of savage homophobia, and the brooding Ennis del Mar is left to consider the significance of discovering, in the closet of his dead lover's boyhood room, his own shirt hanging inside a bloodied shirt of Jack's:

the pair like two skins, one inside the other, two in one. He pressed his face into the fabric and breathed in slowly through his mouth and nose, hoping for the faintest smoke and mountain sage and salty stink of Jack but there was no real scent, only the memory of it, the imagined power of Brokeback Mountain of which nothing was left but what he held in his hands.

Bad Dirt, more explicitly concerned with socio-economic changes wrought in rural Wyoming during the postwar fifties—"the Eisenhower era of interstate highway construction that changed Wyoming forever by letting in the outside" is characterized by saga-like narrations broken up among numerous protagonists, most of them seen at a bemused distance, as through a rifle scope ("By the weary age of thirty, [Deb Sipple] had been married twice, and it hadn't taken permanently either time despite the fact that he had small feet and a big pecker") and by breezily jocular tall tales like "The Hellhole" (in which Wyoming Game & Fish Warden Creel Zmundzinski discovers a sulfurous sinkhole into which poachers in the state forest can be manipulated into falling—"a fiery red tube about three feet across that resembled an enormous blowtorch-heated pipe. With a shriek the preacher disappeared. The whole thing had happened in less than five seconds"—and "Florida Rental" in which a woman besieged by her rancher-neighbor's voracious grazing cattle arranges to rent Florida alligators from a relative to scare them off. It's as if Proulx is determined not to draw too close to her characters, nearly all of whom are luckless and doomed, yet there is a quick sympathetic portrait of a woman named Suzzy New who has made a bad marriage to a rancher in "What Kind of Furniture Would Jesus Pick?":

All her life she had heard and felt the Wyoming wind and took it for granted. There had even been a day when she was a young girl standing by the road waiting for the school bus when a spring wind, fresh and warm and perfumed with pine resin, had caused a bolt of wild happiness to surge through her, its liveliness promising glinting chances. She had loved the wind that day. But out at [her husband's] ranch it was different and she became aware of moving air's erratic, inimical character. The house lay directly in line with a gap in the encircling hills to the northwest, and through this notch the prevailing wind poured, falling on the house with ferocity . . . When she put her head down and went out to the truck, it yanked at her clothing, shot up her sleeves, whisked her hair into raveled fright wigs.

With a similar sympathy for her young protagonist in "Them Old Cowboy Songs" in *Fine Just the Way It Is*, Proulx evokes the forlorn and lonely life of the "cowboy"—not the romance of Hollywood westerns but the drudgery of rural hired labor:

For Archie the work was the usual ranch hand's luck—hard, dirty, long and dull. There was no time for anything but saddle up, ride, rope, cut, herd, unsaddle, eat, sleep and do it again. On the clear, dry nights coyote voices seemed to emanate from single points in straight lines, the calls crisscrossing like taut wires. When cloud cover moved in, the howls spread out in a different geometry, overlapping like concentric circles from a handful of pebbles thrown into water. But most often the wind surging over the plain sanded the cries into a kind of coyote dust fractioned into particles of sound.

Archie's young wife Rose, giving birth unassisted in the couple's wilderness cabin, wakes from a bloody stupor

glued to the bed and at the slightest movement [feeling] a hot surge she knew was blood. She got up on her elbows and saw the clotted child, stiff and gray, the barley-rope cord and the afterbirth. She did not weep but, filled with an ancient rage, got away from the tiny corpse, knelt on the floor ignoring the hot blood seeping from her and rolled the infant up in the stiffening sheet. It was a bulky mass, and she felt the loss of the sheet as another tragedy . . . Clenching the knot of the dish towel in her teeth, she crawled out the door and toward the sandy soil near the river where, still on hands and knees, still spouting blood, she dug a shallow hole . . . and laid the child in it . . . It took more than an hour to follow her blood trail back to the cabin.

The bloody sheet lay bunched on the floor and the bare mattress showed a black stain like the map of South America. She lay on the floor, for the bed was miles away, a cliff only birds could reach . . . Barrel Mountain, bringing darkness, squashed its bulk against the window and owls crashed through, wings like iron bars. Struggling through the syrup of subconsciousness in the last hour she heard the coyotes outside and knew what they were doing.

It isn't clear whether Archie survives a terrible Wyoming winter but Rose is found dead at the cabin, rumored to have been luridly "raped and murdered and mutilated by Utes." The story's wisdom is simple frontier logic: "Some lived and some died, and that's how it was." It's only to those who haven't been listening closely that "Them Old Cowboy Songs" sound sentimental.

Though in most of her fiction Annie Proulx has focused on the hardscrabble lives of men, two of the more fully realized stories in *Fine Just the Way It Is* are told from the perspective of young women. In "Testimony of the Donkey" a young couple are similarly "suffused with euphoria" for the wilderness: "They had shown each other their lapsarian atavistic tastes, their need for the forest, for the difficult and solitary, for what [Catlin's] father called 'the eternal verities' " . . . Each is fiercely independent, obsessive:

> The real focus of their lives was neither work nor clutching love, but wilderness travel. As many days and weeks as they could manage they spent hiking the Big Horns, the Wind Rivers, exploring old logging roads, digging around ancient mining claims. Marc had a hundred plans. He wanted to canoe the Boundary Waters, to kayak down the Labrador coast, to fish in Peru. They snowboarded the Wasatch, followed wolf packs in Yellowstone's backcountry. They spent long weekends in Utah's Canyonlands, in Wyoming's Red Desert Haystacks looking for fossils. The rough country was their emotional center.

Casting off her lover, and in defiance of the Wyoming Forest Service which has closed the trail she intends to take, reckless Catlin persists in hiking alone in the Old Bison range; the reader waits for the inevitable to happen, an accident that leaves Catlin pinned by a heavy rock, helpless as she sinks into hallucination and lethargy, dying of thirst:

> Her entire body, her fingernails, her inner ears, the ends of her greasy hair, screamed for water. She bore holes in the sky looking for more rain . . .
>
> By morning the temporary jolt of strength and clarity was gone. She felt as though electricity was shooting up through the rock and into her torso . . . Apparitions swarmed from the snowbanks above, fountains and dervishes, streaming spigots, a helicopter with a waterslide, a crowd of garishly dressed people reaching down, extending their hands to her. All day a dessicating hot wind blew and made her nearly blind.

Reduced to sheer appetite and terror, poor Catlin who'd imagined herself so independent tries to call out her spurned lover's name—"but 'Marc' came out as a guttural roar, '*Maaaa* . . . ,' a thick and frightening primeval sound."

"Tits-Up in a Ditch"—the provocative title refers to a cow that has wandered off to die in a ditch, in this contorted position—is the final story of *Fine Just the Way It Is*, and the most ambitious and sympathetic. Narrated in an intentionally flat, repetitive prose shorn of the metaphor-laden language for which Proulx is known, the forty-two-page story is an extended elegy reminiscent of "Brokeback Mountain" in the bleakness of its characters' lives and the implacable nature of their losses, including those losses of which they are scarcely aware. The young female protagonist is Dakotah Lister whose rebellious teenaged mother has run away, leaving the fatherless Dakotah for her embittered grandparents to bring up on their run-down "trash" ranch: "Since [pioneer times] the country had become trammeled and gnawed, stippled with cattle, coal mines, oil wells and gas rigs, striated with pipelines. The road to the ranch had been named Sixteen Mile, though no one knew what that distance signified."

Dakotah's grandfather Verl Lister, like many another rural male in Proulx's Wyoming, once aspired to be a rodeo performer—

> a bareback rider who suffered falls, hyperextensions and breaks that had bloomed into arthritis and aches as he aged. A trampling had broken his pelvis and legs so that now he walked with the slinking crouch of a bagpipe player. [His wife Bonita] could not fault him for ancient injuries, and remembered him as the straight-backed, curly-headed young man with beautiful eyes sitting on his horse, back straight as a metal fence post.

—now a sort of macho-invalid on his deteriorating ranch close by the far more prosperous Match Ranch owned by villainous Wyatt Match—"a sharp-horned archconservative with a hard little smile like a diamond chip"—whose consuming vision is "maintaining the romantic heritage of the nineteenth-century ranch, Wyoming's golden time." Neither Verl Lister nor Wyatt Match is much more than a caricature sketched in broad slashing strokes, but Dakotah acquires a measure of depth and dignity as the story develops, despite her passivity and barely average intelligence; seemingly by chance Dakotah becomes involved with a high school classmate named Sash Hicks who marries her, impregnates her, breaks up with her and runs off to join the U.S. Army, leaving her to raise their infant son alone. Proulx's unembellished account of the young couple's failed marriage has the summary tone of the heavily ironic "Job History" of *Close Range*, in which a similarly luckless young married couple of an earlier generation try desperately to make a living in a rapidly changing rural Wyoming.

With naive idealism—imagining that she might study to become a "medic" of some sort—Dakotah herself enlists in the U.S. Army, but scores low on tests and winds up in the Military Police where, with seeming inevitability, given the grim contours and chute-like possibilities of Proulx's cosmology, she is seriously injured in an explosion at a checkpoint in Iraq, where she has been assigned the task of searching Iraqi women. Shipped back home with a prosthetic right arm, Dakotah discovers that her infant son has been killed in a vehicular accident caused by her ignorant grandfather Verl and that her husband Sash—from whom she was never divorced—has been shipped back to Wyoming too, in far worse shape than Dakotah:

> Sash Hicks had disintegrated, both legs blown off at midthigh, the left side of his face a mass of shiny scar tissue, the left ear and eye gone . . . He had suffered brain damage. But Dakotah recognized him, old Billy the Kid shot up by Pat Garrett. More than ever he looked like the antique outlaw.

In fact, in an ironic gender reversal, it isn't the disillusioned Dakotah but the damaged young veteran Sash Hicks who winds up—to use Wyoming's crudely poetic figure of speech—"tits-up in a ditch."

So too with much of the "old"—"rural"—Wyoming, Proulx suggests. In virtually every story in these three Wyoming volumes there is an acknowledgment, sometimes explicit, more often implicit, that—as the owner of the Harp Ranch concedes, in "What Kind of Furniture Would Jesus Pick?"—"the old world was gone." Young people flee their parents' ranches, preferring to live urban lives; ranch hands and "cowboys" are scarce, as able-bodied men prefer to work out of state, for more money; the once-Wyoming "paradise" is now

> [a] vast junkyard field of refineries, disturbed land, uranium mines, coal mines, trona mines, pump jacks and drilling rigs, clear-cuts, tank farms, contaminated rivers, pipelines, methanol-processing plants, ruinous dams, the Amoco mess, railroads, all disguised by the deceptively empty landscape.

All that remains of the glory days of the nineteenth century are theme-park ranches for tourists and hokey Wild West celebrations like the "Rodeo Days" parade in "What Kind of Furniture Would Jesus Pick?" in which a motley assortment of locals march as "pioneers," teenaged boys dress as "Indians," costumed "cowboys" trot past on horseback twirling six-shooters, and not a single rancher is represented: "It was all pioneers, outlaws, Indians, and gas."

Fine just the way it is is a smug expression used with dogmatic frequency by Wyoming residents like the archconservative rancher Wyatt Match, meaning that Wyoming is "fine" as it is, without the intrusion of despised outsiders like federal politicians and policy makers and anti-cattle/anti-beef agitators who want an end to the open-range grazing that has proven to be ruinous to the ecology of the West; ironically, *fine just the way it is* also happens to be a phrase used, in Proulx's satiric story "I've Always Loved This Place," by Charon, in reference to his own habitat, Hades.

ENCHANTED! SALMAN RUSHDIE

The Enchantress of Florence
by Salman Rushdie

> A graceful fool . . . or perhaps no fool at all.
> Perhaps someone to be reckoned with. If he had
> a fault, it was that of ostentation, of seeking to be
> not only himself but a performance of himself.
> —SALMAN RUSHDIE, FROM *THE*
> *ENCHANTRESS OF FLORENCE*

In Salman Rushdie's *Fury* (2001), a novel of Swiftian dyspepsia published the very week of 9/11, the fifty-five-year-old misanthropic Professor Malik Solanka, "retired historian of ideas," has enjoyed an unexpected popular success for having created a BBC-TV series called "The Adventures of Little Brain" in which a doll called "Little Brain"—handcrafted by Solanka himself—interviews a series of "Great Minds" dolls in a familiar history-of-philosophy format. "Little Brain" is a sassy, spiky-haired Candide who, in contemporary talk-show fashion, goads her interviewees into surprising revelations:

the favorite fiction writer of the seventeenth-century heretic Baruch Spinoza turned out to be P. G. Wodehouse, an

astonishing coincidence, because of course the favorite philosopher of the immortal shimmying butler Reginald Jeeves
was Spinoza . . . The Iberian Arab thinker Averroës, like his
Jewish counterpart Maimonides, was a huge Yankees fan . . .

In deep disgust with his contemporaries, especially his fellow
academicians at King's College, Cambridge, Solanka becomes
entranced by the possibility of seeing the world "miniaturized":

> It was a trick of the mind to see human life made small,
> reduced to doll size . . . A little modesty about the scale of
> human endeavor was to be desired. Once you had thrown
> that switch in your head, the hard thing was to see in the old
> way. Small was beautiful.

As Jonathan Swift demonstrates in the savage comedy of
Gulliver's Travels, "humanity" is but a matter of scale: rendered as dolls, miniaturized like the Lilliputians of Gulliver's
first voyage, we are reduced not only in size but in stature; our
ideals, our suffering, our most grievous quarrels are revealed as
ridiculous, and our "Great Minds" become comic characters to
be exploited by the media. When Swift's Gulliver ventures into
the land of the Brobdignagians, he is revulsed by the giants'
physical ugliness even as, a doll-like Lilliputian in their eyes,
his race is condemned by the King of Brobdignag in the most
pitiless Swiftian terms:

> I cannot but conclude the Bulk of your Natives, to be the
> most pernicious Race of little odious Vermin that Na-

ture ever suffered to crawl upon the Surface of the Earth. [*Gulliver's Travels*, "A Voyage to Brobdingnag,"]

Set primarily in New York City—a city "boiling" with money where the very harness bells on the horse-drawn carriages in Central Park jingle like "cash in hand"—*Fury* exudes an air of personal grievance and rage that seems disproportionate to Solanka's experience as a professor, historian, husband, father, minor celebrity; virtually everyone Solanka has known or encounters is despicable, given to embittered ranting monologues in confirmation of Solanka's conviction that "life is fury."

> Fury—sexual, Oedipal, political, magical, brutal—drives us to our finest delights and coarsest depths. Out of *furia* comes creation, inspiration, originality, passion, but also violence, pain, pure unafraid destruction, the giving and receiving of blows from which we never recover.

Typically in a novel by Salman Rushdie, the protagonist falls in love with a *femme fatale* (here, named "Neela Mahendra") so ravishingly beautiful that strangers stagger up to her to gape at her; he becomes "deeply enmeshed in her web . . . The queen webspyder, mistress of the whole webspyder posse, had him in her net." Soon, however, Solanka discovers that "this beautiful, accursed girl" is "an incarnation of a Fury"—

> one of the three deadly sisters, the scourges of mankind. Fury was their divine nature and boiling human wrath their

favorite food. He could have persuaded himself that behind her low whispers, beneath her unfailingly even tempered tones, he could hear the Erinyes' shrieks.

Greeted with a mixed critical reception in 2001, *Fury* is best appreciated as a machine-gun volley of Swiftian indignation, at its highest pitch fueled by a powerful charge of self-loathing like a *cri de coeur* from the beleaguered author whose life as a private citizen ended with nightmare abruptness on February 14, 1989, when the Iranian Ayatollah Khomeini issued a *fatwa*, or death sentence for Rushdie's alleged blasphemy in his pyrotechnic-Postmodernist surreal black comedy *The Satanic Verses* (1988); one feels the author speaking through the beleaguered Solanka in terror of the Erinyes—the Furies of ancient Athens—"Serpent-haired, dog-headed, bat-winged" hounding him for the remainder of his life.

Where the strategy of *Fury* is to miniaturize by way of corrosive satire, the strategy of Rushdie's new, tenth novel *The Enchantress of Florence*, an elaborately allegorized "romance-adventure" set in fifteenth- and sixteenth-century Florence and in Fatehpur Sikri, the capital city of India's Mughal empire, is to inflate in the more genial, disingenuous way of fables, fairy tales, *The Thousand and One Nights* as narrated by the archetypal storyteller Scheherazade. Because *The Enchantress of Florence* is simultaneously a postmodernist work of prose fiction, highly self-conscious and stylized, variously influenced by predecessor metafictionists John Barth (*Giles Goat-Boy, Chimera*), Italo Calvino (*Invisible Cities, If on a Winter's Night a Traveler*), Gabriel García Márquez (*One Hundred Years of*

Solitude, The Autumn of the Patriarch), among others, the inflation of Rushdie's characters and the story in which they participate is presented in comic-epic terms; here is a "historical novel" that is also an artful parody of the genre, by a master storyteller not unlike his audacious protagonist Niccolò Vespucci who mesmerizes the despotic Mughal emperor with his storytelling skills: the magician-charlatan-imposter-artist who is "not only himself but a performance of himself as well."

Rushdie's storyteller-hero is by no means an ordinary individual, even a somewhat extraordinary individual: this bold traveler from the West—we will learn, in time, that he is one Ago Vespucci of Florence, who has renamed himself Niccolò Vespucci after his closest boyhood friend Niccolò "il Machia" (Machiavelli)—rides in a bullock-cart standing up "like a god" when we first see him; his hair is a "dirty yellow" yet flows down around his face "like the golden water of the lake." The Western traveler to exotic India has an "overly pretty face"— in fact, the traveler is "certainly beautiful, and knew that his looks had a power of their own." Somehow, he has acquired seven languages: Italian, Spanish, Arabic, Persian, Russian, English, and Portuguese; he has been "driven out of his door by stories of wonder, and by one in particular, a story which could make his fortune or else cost him his life." As in the oldest and most enduring of young-male-quest tales, the youthful traveler seeks an audience with the ruler of the strange new land he is visiting; the ruler will be a patriarch, an older man likely to be tyrannical, yet drawn to the young man for his very brashness and cunning; if the young man seeks a father, the older man seeks a son: it is inevitable that the Mughal emperor whom the traveler encounters, Akbar the Great (1542–1605), will have sons who have disappointed him, and will long for a young man he can trust:

> That young man will not be my son but I will make him more than a son. I will make him my hammer and my anvil. I will make him my beauty and my truth. He will stand upon my palm and fill the sky.

As soon as Akbar meets the yellow-haired traveler—who gives his name as "Mogor dell'Amore"—he succumbs to the youth's charms, despite his suspicion that the traveler may be a charlatan: "How handsome this young man was, how sure of himself, how proud. And there was something in him that could not be seen: a secret that made him more interesting than a hundred courtiers." As Rushdie presents Akbar, the emperor is both a brooding philosopher-king who questions the tradition into which he has been born—"*Maybe there was no true religion* . . . He wanted to be able to say, it is man at the center of things, not god"—and something of a buffoon, a comically inflated mega-mythic figure:

> The emperor AbulFath Jalaluddin Muhammad, King of Kings, known since his childhood as Akbar, meaning "the great," and latterly, in spite of the tautology of it, as Akbar the Great, the great great one, great in his greatness, doubly great, so great that the repetition in his title was not only appropriate but necessary in order to express the gloriousness

of his glory—the Grand Mughal, the dusty, battle-weary, victorious, pensive, incipiently overweight, disenchanted, mustachioed, poetic, oversexed and absolute emperor, who seemed altogether too magnificent, too world-encompassing, and, in sum, too *much* to be a single human personage.

Much of *The Enchantress of Florence* is couched in such playful tongue-in-cheek bombast, echoing, at far greater length and with far more literary ambition, the comedy of Rushdie's charming book for children *Haroun and the Sea of Stories* (1990), in which folk and fairy tales are genially mocked. ("Here's another Princess Rescue Story I'm getting mixed up in," Haroun thought . . . "I wonder if this one will go wrong, too.") It isn't clear when we are to take Akbar seriously and when Rushdie is inviting the reader to laugh at him:

> The emperor's eyes were slanted and large and gazed upon infinity as a dreamy young lady might . . . His lips were full and pushed forward in a womanly pout. But in spite of these girlish accents he was a mighty specimen of a man, huge and strong. As a boy he had killed a tigress with his bare hands . . . [He was] a Muslim vegetarian, a warrior who wanted only peace, a philosopher-king: a contradiction in terms. Such was the greatest ruler the land had ever known.

Though he insists that he is not a tyrant and that he believes that "in the House of God all voices are free to speak as they choose" yet Akbar executes the grandson of an old enemy:

Then with a cry—*Allahu Akbar*, God is great, or, just possibly, Akbar is God—he chopped off the pompous little twerp's cheeky, didactic, and therefore suddenly unnecessary, head . . . He was not only a barbarian philosopher and a crybaby killer, but also an egotist addicted to obsequiousness and sycophancy who nevertheless longed for a different world . . .

What Akbar longs for is the exotic West: which comes to him in the guise of the yellow-haired "Mogor dell'Amore" with a tale to tell so tangled ("This was his way: to move toward his goal indirectly, with many detours and divagations") it will require hundreds of pages of Rushdie's challenging prose.

As the yellow-haired traveler and the emperor are so exaggerated as to suggest comic-book figures, so too are Rushdie's female enchantresses exaggerated to the point of burlesque. Of his numerous queens and mistresses Akbar's favorite is Jodha, who doesn't exist at all except as the emperor's sexual fantasy—"A woman without a past, separate from history, or, rather, possessing only such history as he had been pleased to bestow upon her." Here is Akbar's ideal—"mirror"—female.

She was adept at the seven types of unguiculation, which is to say the art of using the nails to enhance the act of love . . . She had marked him with the Three Deep Marks, which were scratches made with the first three fingers of her right hand upon his back, his chest, and on his testicles as well: something to remember her by . . . She could perform the Hopping of the Hare, marking the areolas around his nipples without touching him anywhere else on his body. And no living woman was as skilled as she at the Peacock's Foot.

But to Akbar's anima-self is given the insight about which *The Enchantress of Florence* is constructed, that Western Europe is enthralled by India, as India is enthralled by Western Europe:

> This place, Sikri, was a fairyland to them, just as their England and Portugal, their Holland and France were beyond [Jodha's] ability to comprehend. The world was not all one thing. "We are their dream," she told the emperor, "and they are ours."

And:

> The lands of the West were exotic and surreal to a degree incomprehensible to the humdrum people of the East.

At the court of Akbar it is even fantasized that Queen Elizabeth of England is "nothing less than the Western mirror of the emperor himself":

> She was Akbar in female form, and he, the Shahanshah, the king of kings, could be said to be an Eastern Elizabeth, mustachioed, nonvirginal, but in the essence of their greatness they were the same.

As the credulous Akbar becomes immediately infatuated with the yellow-haired Western traveler so he becomes infatuated with the traveler's (fraudulent) representation of the "faraway redhead queen," he sends Elizabeth love letters which are never answered declaring his "megalomaniac fantasies of creating a joint global empire that united the eastern and western hemispheres." In one of those post-modernist flash-forwards intended to break the storyteller's spell and to remind us as with a nudge in the ribs *This is just fiction, a tall tale being told by a veteran performer* the bemused omniscient narrator allows us a glimpse of the future:

> Near the end of his long reign, many years after the time of the charlatan Mogor dell'Amore had passed, the aging emperor nostalgically remembered that strange affair of [the Queen of England] . . . When the emperor learned the truth he understood all over again how daring a sorcerer he had encountered . . . By then, however, the knowledge was of no use to him, except to remind him of what he should never have forgotten, that witchcraft requires no potions, familiar spirits, or magic wands. Language upon a silvered tongue affords enchantment enough.[1]

"Witchcraft" is usually associated with females: in Rushdie's fevered cosmology these are invariably *femmes fatales* of the species to which the spectacularly beautiful webspyder Neela Mahendra of *Fury* belongs. Rushdie wryly mocks what are clearly his own obsessions: the yellow-haired traveler recalls having fallen in love with a Florentine prostitute who was born with only one breast which, "by way of compensation, was the most beautiful breast in the city, which was to say . . . in all the known world." Another legendary Florentine beauty is Simonetta Cattaneo who possesses "a pale, fair beauty so intense that no man could look at her without falling into a state of molten adoration, nor could any woman, and the same went for most of the city's cats and dogs." Qara Koz, the "Hidden Princess," said to be a descendent of Genghis Khan and preposterously claimed by the yellow-haired traveler to be his mother, is yet more beautiful, a goddess of beauty, whether in her Mughal identity as "Lady Dark Eyes" or as the "Enchantress of Florence"; this paragon of enchantment first appears in a magic mirror owned by the sinister Medici family, as a vision of unearthly beauty, "a visitor from another world"; she is meant "for palaces, and kings"; when she and her "mirror-self" servant are first glimpsed in Florence, brought back by the (Florentine) warrior-hero Argalia, it's "as if the Madonna had materialized":

> *l'ammaliatrice Angelica*, the so-called enchantress of Florence, brought men running from the fields, and women from their kitchens . . . Woodcutters came from the forests and the butcher Gabburra's son ran out from the slaughterhouse with bloody hands and potters left their kilns . . . [T]heir faces shone with the light of revelation, as though in those early days of their unveiling they were capable of sucking light in from the eyes of all who looked upon them and then flinging it out again as their own personal brilliance, with mesmeric, fantasy-inducing effects.

And, yet more fantastical:

> Within moments of her coming she had been taken to the
> city's heart as its special face, its new symbol of itself, the
> incarnation in human form of that unsurpassable loveliness
> which the city itself possessed. The Dark Lady of Florence.

Somehow, this Mughal princess who has, so far as the reader
is allowed to know, never been educated, has learned to speak
perfect Florentine Italian, in the modest effort, as her lover Argalia announces to all of Florence:

> [Qara Koz] comes here of her own free will, in the hope of
> forging a union between the great cultures of Europe and
> the East, knowing that she has much to learn from us and
> believing, too, that she has much to teach.

This declaration comes out of nowhere for there has been no
previous hint that Qara Koz, or the macho warrior-hero Argalia, has the slightest interest or awareness of anything like the
"great cultures" of the world: their tales have been *Arabian
Nights* in tone, affably improbable and very far from intellectual. Yet the claim has been made by the yellow-haired traveler
who spins out his story at the Mughal court:

> When the great warrior Argalia met the immortal beauty
> Qara Koz . . . a story began which would regenerate all
> men's belief—your belief, grand Mughal . . . in the undying

power and extraordinary capacity of the human heart for love.

"Love" seems a paltry word to describe the stunned adoration everyone in Rushdie's novel feels for Qara Koz who, even when she is beyond the zenith of her powers of enchantment, as she begins to lose her youth—she's twenty-six, and had begun her career as a sexual enchantress at seventeen—commands this sort of authority from the macho seafaring adventurer Andrea Doria:

> [the princess's] face was illumined by an unearthly light, so that she reminded Andrea Doria of Christ himself, the Nazarene performing His miracles, Christ multiplying loaves and fishes or raising Lazarus from the dead . . . Her powers were failing but she intended to exercise them one last time as they had never been exercised before, and force the history of the world into the course she required it to take. She would enchant the middle passage into being by the sheer force of her sorcery and her will . . . [Andrea Doria] fell to his knees before her . . . He thought of Christ in Gethsemane and how He must have looked to His disciples as He prepared Himself to die.

Where the enchantress Neela Mahendra of *Fury* is exposed as a man-eating Erinye, the Mughal princess Qara Koz is revealed as Christ the Savior. From the deconstructionist post-modernist perspective perhaps all myths are equally possible, as all myths are absurd? (In *Haroun and the Sea of Stories* Haroun's compulsively storytelling father Rashid confesses: "What to do, son . . . Storytelling is the only work I know."

No contemporary writer has so fetishized femaleness as Salman Rushdie, with unflagging zeal, idealism, and irony, in fiction after fiction: Rushdie's portrait in *The Enchantress of Florence* of the great Mughal painter Dashwanth would seem to be a self-portrait of the artist so heedlessly infatuated with his subject that he loses his soul to it and disappears into the artwork:

> [Dashwanth] was working on what would turn out to be the final picture of the so-called *Qara-Koz-Nama*, the Adventures of Lady Black Eyes . . . In spite of the almost constant scrutiny of his peers he had somehow managed to vanish. He was never seen again, not in the Mughal court, nor anywhere in Sikri, not anywhere in all the land of Hindustan.

Eventually, Dashwanth is discovered beneath a border of the portrait, miniaturized, in two dimensions, "crouching down like a little toad . . . Instead of bringing a fantasy woman to life, Dashwanth had turned himself into an imaginary being, driven . . . by the overwhelming force of love."

By the novel's end the "barren" Mughal princess has been absorbed into the emperor Akbar's *khayal*, "his god-like omnipotent fancy" having taken the place of his fantasy-queen Jodha. Even the most extraordinary female in the history of mankind is finally just a man's fancy, as Qara Koz has been the author's:

"I have come home after all," she told [Akbar]. "You have allowed me to return, and so here I am, at my journey's end. And now, Shelter of the World, I am yours."

Until you're not, the Universal Ruler thought. *My love, until you're not.*

How wonderfully ironic, and appropriate, that in the final lines of Rushdie's ingeniously constructed post-modernist "romance" the fevered sex-spell is finally broken: male omnipotence out-trumps the most powerful female sorcery, in time.

Amid this exotic *Arabian Nights* romance of hidden princesses, lonely emperors and brash young travelers from the West is a second romance, almost entirely separate from the first, a highly eroticized male romance involving the storyteller Vespucci's boyhood friends in Florence in the later years of the fifteenth century, one of whom is destined to become the celebrated and controversial author of *The Prince*: "In the beginning there were three friends, Antonino Argalia, Niccolò 'il Machia,' and Ago Vespucci." This story-opening is repeated several times through the hundreds of pages of *The Enchantress of Florence* as the story moves away from Florence, then returns; and moves away, and returns; and finally moves away again, to vanish into the Mughal emperor's all-absorbing *khayal*. Since the storyteller is Ago Vespucci (who has renamed himself "Niccolò") it's within his power to shift his scene at will, to evoke the past, or the future, to challenge the reader's capacity to keep characters straight by frequently renaming them, and to gleefully, tirelessly digress—how like Haroun's

storyteller father the "Shah of Blah" for whom "straight an-
swers were beyond [his] powers ... who would never take a
short cut if there was a longer, twistier road available." After
a boyhood that seems to have been spent largely fantasizing
over "having occult powers over women"—"in the woods
most days climbing trees and masturbating for mandrakes and
telling each other insane stories"—both Argalia and Vespucci
leave Florence and become high-concept adventurers (Argalia
becomes Pasha Avcalia the Turk, a warrior for the Ottoman empire; Vespucci becomes a world traveler) while the more intellectual and politically ambitious Niccolò "il Machia" remains
behind, a brooding (if bawdy) center of skeptical consciousness
meant to mirror the philosopher-king Akbar. Though the two
men never meet they are kindred spirits—Niccolò Machiavelli
would have been another of Akbar's "sons," had Akbar known
him—questioning religious tradition and the culture in which
each has been born as well as the nature of human identity.
These words of the young Machiavelli would be appropriate
for Akbar as well:

> He believed in the hidden truth the way other men believed
> in God or love, believed that the truth was in fact always
> hidden, that the apparent, the overt, was invariably a kind
> of lie. Because he was a man fond of precision he wanted to
> capture the hidden truth precisely, to see it clearly and set
> it down, the truth beyond ideas of right and wrong, ideas
> of good and evil, ideas of ugliness and beauty, all of which
> were aspects of the surface deceptions of the world, hav-
> ing little to do with how things really worked, disconnected

from the whatness, the secret codes, the hidden forms, the mystery.

Similarly Akbar, when he is not required by the author to play the buffoon-despot or the credulous fool taken in by a yellow-haired Westerner's tall tale:

> It is man at the center of things, not god. It is man at the heart and the bottom and the top, man at the front and the back and the side, man the angel and the devil, the miracle and the sin, man and always man, and let us henceforth have no other temples but those dedicated to mankind. This was his unspeakable ambition: to found the religion of man.

It may be doubtful that the historic Akbar the Great ever thought such post-Enlightenment thoughts but Rushdie eloquently provides him with the most chilling possibility of all, by which the tragic timeliness of *The Enchantress of Florence*—and the author's intention in writing it—is underscored:

> (If man had created god then man could uncreate him too. Or was it possible for a creation to escape the power of the creator? Could a god, once created, become impossible to destroy? Did such fictions acquire an autonomy of the will that made them immortal? . . .)

Both men are fascinated by the contents of their own minds, the emperor in his "omnipotence" led to brood over the nature of his own massive identity:

He, Akbar, had never referred to himself as "I," not even in private . . . He was—what else could he be?—"we." He was the definition, the Incarnation of the We. He had been born into plurality. When he said "we" he naturally and truly meant himself as an incarnation of all his subjects, of all his cities and lands and rivers and mountains and lakes . . . he meant himself as the apogee of his people's past and present, and the engine of their future . . . [But] could he, too, be an "I?" Could there be an "I" that was simply oneself? Were there such naked, solitary "I's" buried beneath the overcrowded "we's" of the earth?

(Ironically, when Akbar tries to establish himself as an "I" separate from the "we" of his role as emperor, he is rebuffed by his fantasy-queen Jodha, his mirror-self.)[2]

Though his role in the novel is a minor and muted one, Machiavelli emerges as the novel's most intriguing character, for Rushdie has given him a distinctly contemporary personality and keeps him, for the most part, free of the distracting romance-plot with its typically inflated and jocose prose; Machiavelli is the quintessential Renaissance Florentine, a mixture of the high-minded and the lasvicious ("Il Machia . . . seemed to be the reincarnation of the god Priapus, always ready for action"[3]) involved in political scheming even in his youth, and highly ambitious; when the Medicis ascend to power in Florence with the election of a Medici Pope, Machiavelli falls into disfavor, and, in scenes Rushdie chooses not to dramatize, terribly tortured. His spirit is broken:

[The people of Florence] did not deserve him . . . The pain
that had coursed through his body was not pain but knowledge. It was an educational pain followed by confession followed by death. The people had wanted his death, or at least
had not cared if he lived or died. In the city that gave the
world the idea of the value and freedom of the individual
soul they had not valued him . . .

An old man at forty-four yet Machiavelli too falls under
the predictably hypnotic spell of Qara Koz and experiences a
temporary respite from his gloom; when the Mughal princess
departs Florence, his depression returns. In the wan hope of
regaining favor at court Machiavelli immerses himself into "his
little mirror-of-princes piece, such a dark mirror that even he
feared it might not be liked"; this is *The Prince*, though Rushdie doesn't name it, and the year must be about 1518; Machiavelli would die in 1527.

Though *The Enchantress of Florence* includes a densely
printed six-page bibliography of historical books and articles
and is being described as an "historical" novel, readers in expectation of a conventional "historical novel" should be fore-
warned: this is "history" jubilantly mixed with post-modernist
magic realism. The veteran performer-author is too playful and
too much the exuberant stylist to incorporate much of deadpan "reality" into his ever-shifting, ever-teasing narrative of
the power of enchantment of cultural opposites: "We are their
dream . . . and they are ours."

The landscape of Philip Roth's America is a familiar one—mostly urban New Jersey and New York City, more recently suburban or semi-rural Connecticut. Yet, as in some of those eerie paintings of Eric Fischl in which the real is permeated by the surreal, especially where adolescent males are involved, the landscape is honeycombed with land mines and to traverse it is to enter a realm of peril. In this world outside the close-knit family unit "the tiniest misstep can have tragic consequences"—as the increasingly deranged father of Roth's *Indignation* (2008) warns his nineteen-year-old son Marcus. As in a 1950s American recrudescence of Old-Testament biblical foreboding, it's the male issue that is most at risk for Jews, for hasn't Mr. Messner the kosher butcher been warned by his friend Pearlgreen the plumber: "Mark my words, Messner: the world is waiting, it's licking its chops, to take your boy away." At its high-pitched mock-hysterical climax *Indignation* expands its focus to take in the riveting political oratory of an Ohio politician in his guise as the president of a small liberal arts college wonderfully named Winesburg College, in whose fury at the transgressions of undergraduate boys caught up in the frenzy of a panty raid there is struck the note of 1950s Cold War America, the very font of comic-patriotic paranoia:

> We as a nation are facing the distinct possibility of an atomic war with the Soviet Union, all the while the men of Winesburg College are conducting their derring-do raids on the dresser drawers of [their female classmates] . . . How's it going to serve you when a thousand screaming Chinese soldiers come swarming down on you in your foxhole, should these negotiations in Korea break down?

In Roth's earlier novel of counter-factual America *The Plot Against America* (2004) this alarming prophetic note is struck in its opening passage:

> Fear presides over these memories, a perpetual fear. Of course no childhood is without its terrors, yet I wonder if I would have been a less frightened boy if Lindbergh hadn't been president or if I hadn't been the offspring of Jews.

(Here is a bold opening worthy of Franz Kafka whose "The Metamorphosis" famously declared its young male protagonist changed overnight into a gigantic beetle—another inspired variant upon a joke.) If the proposition at the heart of *The Plot Against America* is something like a joke—that aviation hero/ Nazi sympathizer Charles Lindbergh is elected in a "landslide victory" over Franklin Delano Roosevelt in the 1940 presidential election—it quickly becomes a menacing joke as young

Jews begin to be recruited, so to speak, under the auspices of a federal program called "Just Folks"—a creation of Lindbergh's newly created Office of American Absorption as a "volunteer work program introducing city youth to the traditional ways of heartland life"—and at last a tragic joke, a nightmare-joke as "resisting" Jews are killed by patriotic "just folks" and the rightward-leaning United States prepares to enter into what will be World War II not on the side of England and England's allies but on the side of Hitler and Hitler's allies, Italy and Japan. Indeed, there may be war with Canada. FDR is "detained" along with so-called Roosevelt Jews and rabbis are arrested in the frenzied months before, as Roth's narrator Philip informs us in a hurried aside in the last chapter, Lindbergh's politics are discredited and Roosevelt is back in the White House.

At the heart of *The Human Stain* (2001) is the joke as exemplum: a joke of the most absurd "political correctness" in the context of the media hysteria of 1998 when President Bill Clinton was vilified for months as an adulterer and as a liar in contempt of court in his disclaimer of having had no "sexual relations" with the twenty-one-year-old White House aide Monica Lewinsky; this "time of nausea" as Roth's narrator Nathan Zuckerman describes it. As in *The Plot Against America*, "some sort of demon had been unleashed in the nation and, on both sides, people wondered, 'Why are we so crazy?'" but here, in the late 1990s, the craziness isn't right-wing Nazi fanaticism but a leftist tyranny of manners in which the most casual, innocent, and utterly trivial of remarks can bring down an academician as distinguished as Coleman Silk—lovely name for a very suave man!!—who'd been "one of the first of the

Jews permitted to teach in a classics department anywhere in America" and, more notably, "the first and only Jew to ever serve as a dean of the faculty at Athena College"—a small prestigious New England college not unlike Amherst. Allegedly, the incident is based upon an actual "political correctness" case investigated at Princeton University in the 1990s, though this fact, if it is a fact, has not been verified by the author, nor should it be; the incident is exemplary, illustrative of the shibboleths of the era:

> It was about midway into [the] second semester that Coleman spoke the self-incriminating word that would cause him voluntarily to sever all ties to the college—the single self-incriminating word of the many millions spoken aloud in his years of teaching and administering at Athena . . .
>
> The class consisted of fourteen students. Coleman had taken attendance at the beginning of the first several lectures so as to learn their names. As there were still two names that failed to elicit a response by the fifth week . . . Coleman opened the session by asking, "Does anyone know these people? Do they exist or are they spooks?"

As Coleman utters the word "spooks"—in a mangled interpretation a racist insult directed at the two students who happened to be not only absent but black—his fate is determined: he is vilified as a racist at the college by a majority of students and his enemies among the faculty, so excessively that his sixty-four-year-old wife Iris dies of a cerebral hemorrhage— the joke as curse. In Zuckerman's eyes "political correctness" is risible—ridiculous—even as, like the "Just Folks" patriots of *The Plot Against America*, it is deadly serious, and dangerous. Even *Portnoy's Complaint* (1969), for many readers the most famous of Roth's novels and very likely recalled as a protracted adolescent joke of obsessive-compulsive sexual behavior, is, in essence, a desperate plea for help; a frantic confession to a (faceless) psychoanalyst; a candid acknowledgment of, not sexual potency, but sexual impotence; though an adult, eager to lead an adult life, Alex Portnoy is never other than Mrs. Portnoy's son.

More clearly the "Tricky Dick" narrator of *Our Gang* (1971)—the weasely master of hypocrisy President Richard Nixon—is an extended, boldly orchestrated joke, as *The Great American Novel* (1973), a chronicle of the misadventures of a 1940s professional baseball team that has been expunged from baseball history, is a joke of another, less portentous kind, in the playful 1970s mode of Robert Coover's *The Universal Baseball Association, J. Henry Waugh, Prop.* In an abashed echo of Kafka the hapless narrator of *The Breast* (1972) can describe himself—his altered self—in pseudo-scientific terms that strike a note of pure wacky jokiness, absurdity:

I am a breast. A phenomenon that has been variously described to me as "a massive hormonal influx," "an endocrinopathic catastrophe," and/or "a hermaphroditic explosion of chromosomes" took place within my body between midnight and 4 A.M. on February 1971 and converted me into a mammary gland disconnected from any human form . . .

They tell me that I am now an organism with the general shape of a football, or a dirigible; I am said to be of spongy consistency, weighing one hundred fifty pounds . . . and measuring, still, six feet in length. [I am a] breast of the mammalian female.

My Life as a Man (1974) and *The Professor of Desire* (1977) are memoirist fictions of the utmost seeming sincerity, narrated by young male writers resembling Roth in salient ways; here, if there are jokes, they are not so much nightmare-jokes as riddles. In *My Life as a Man* the novelist Peter Tarnopol is confounded by his ill-advised marriage to a "rough" young woman named Maureen and his musings upon the nature of male-female relations are as funny as anything in Roth, though underscored by gravity verging upon despair:

Unattached and on her own (in the 1950s), a woman was supposedly not even able to go to the movies or out to a restaurant by herself, let alone perform an appendectomy or drive a truck. It was up to us then to give them the value and the purpose that society at large withheld—by marrying them. If we didn't marry women, who would? Ours, alas, was the only sex available for the job: the draft was on.

Peter Tarnopol, a reader of serious literature—Henry James, Joseph Conrad, Gustave Flaubert—dismisses mere happiness with a woman in favor of something more demanding and problematic, thus more "literary"—

What I liked . . . was something taxing in my love affairs, something problematical and puzzling to keep the imagination going . . . ; I liked most being with young women who gave me something to think about . . .

So Maureen was a rough customer—I thought about that. I wondered if I was "up"—nice word—to someone with her history and determination.

Tarnopol is devastated by both the wreck of his marriage and his stupidity in entering into it; his inability to cope with married life, and his failure to comprehend how he'd come to such a pass at the age of twenty-six. A year previously

I would have laughed had anyone suggested that struggling with a woman over a marriage would come to occupy me in the way that exploring the South Pole had occupied Admiral Byrd—or writing *Madame Bovary* had occupied Flaubert.

Maureen is a seasoned liar, outrageous, funny, disarming; the reader perceives her helplessness and desperation even as her slightly younger husband Tarnopol, fuming like a TV situation-comedy husband, is deceived by the ways in which she inventively casts herself as a "victim"—Maureen is a would-be actress, after all. She's provocative, and Tarnopol is a foil to be provoked. Roth gives Maureen the most dramatic crises:

"Do it! Kill me! Some man's going to—why not a 'civilized' one like you! Why not a follower of Flaubert!" Here she collapsed against me, and with her arms around my neck,

began to sob. "Oh, Peter, I don't have anything. Nothing at
all. I'm really lost, baby . . ."

Shrewd Maureen takes advantage of Tarnopol's naiveté by pretending to be pregnant; she knows how to play upon his sympathies as a "civilized" person even as she funnily berates him:

> "I've taken enough from men like you in my life! You're
> going to marry me or I'm going to kill myself! And I will do
> it . . . This is no idle threat, Peter—I cannot take you people
> any more! You selfish, spoiled, immature, irresponsible Ivy
> League bastards, born with those spoons in your mouths . . .
> With your big fat advance and your high Art—oh, you make
> me sick the way you hide from life behind that *Art* of yours!
> I hate you and I hate that fucking Flaubert, and you are go-
> ing to marry me, Peter, because I have had enough!"

In true literary fashion, Tarnopol berates himself: "I could not
be the cause of another's death. Such a suicide was murder. So I
would marry her instead"—though in fact he hates her, having
been "blackmailed, threatened, and terrorized" by her.

> Yes, it was indeed one of those grim and unyielding predica-
> ments such as I had read about in fiction, such as Thomas
> Mann . . . "All actuality is deadly earnest, and it is mortality
> itself that, one with life, forbids us to be true to the guileless
> unrealism of our youth."
>   It seemed then that I was making one of those moral
> decisions that I had heard so much about in college literary

courses. But how different it all had been up there in the Ivy
League, when it was happening to Lord Jim and Kate Croy
and Ivan Karamazov instead of to me. Oh, what an authority on dilemmas I had been in the senior honors seminar! . . .
I expected to find in everyday experience that same sense of
the difficult and the deadly earnest that informed the novels
I admired most. My model of reality, deduced from reading
the masters, had at its heart *intractability*.

In Maureen, who is pure *intractability*, the aspiring young
literary man is overmatched: reduced to a "twenty-six-year-old
baby boy."

But it's in *Indignation* that the tragic joke is most evident, and most devastating. Roth has so constructed this short,
deftly narrated novel that the background of the Korean War
is always evident yet in a way invisible, like scenery—it's the
petty, vexing concerns of Marcus Messner that preoccupy him
as a transfer student to Winesburg College where, like an undergraduate Everyman, inappropriately serious, devoted to his
studies, unwilling to compromise his beliefs, a young man of
unusual integrity, he's exploited by his roommates and abused
as a waiter—"More than a few times during the first weeks, I
thought I heard myself being summoned to one of the rowdier
tables with the words, 'Hey, Jew! Over here!' But, preferring
to believe the words spoken had been simply, 'Hey, you! Over
here!' I persisted with my duties." Despite his high intelligence
and his wish to graduate as valedictorian of his class and enter
law school—his wish to please his father, for whom he has
such ambivalent feelings—Marcus makes one comical blunder

after another at folksy Winesburg; he is literally if obliquely done in by failing to satisfy the college's compulsory chapel attendance. Expelled from college, Marcus is vulnerable to the draft and within a few breathless paragraphs he has been killed in Korea, along with one hundred eighty-eight young men, out of two hundred, in his company. After our intimacy with Marcus, the cruel abruptness with which his life ends is jarring, distressing. The entire text of *Indignation* has been a lament, or a rant; in a featureless nether world resembling the Hades of antiquity, though without the comfort of fellow ghosts of that Hades, Marcus Messner cries out forlornly for his father, his mother, his girlfriend; he berates himself—"If only he had gone to chapel!"

A PHOTOGRAPHER'S LIVES:
ANNIE LEIBOVITZ

Annie Leibovitz
A Photographer's Life
1990–2005

> All photographs are *memento mori*.
> —SUSAN SONTAG, *ON PHOTOGRAPHY*

Ours is an age of memoir—inevitably, faux-memoir: the highly selective and enhanced employment of "historic" individuals, events, and settings in the creation of a text; or, in the case of Annie Leibovitz's massive *A Photographer's Life 1990–2005*, a text with photographs arranged to suggest an elegiac narrative of loss, rebirth, and spiritual transcendence. After the death in December 2004—as depicted here in harrowing, painfully graphic images some observers may find offensive, not an easy death—of her longtime companion Susan Sontag, Leibovitz set herself the task of compiling photographs for a memorial book which gradually evolved into a larger memoir of the previous fifteen years of the photographer's life: "Going through my pictures to put this book together was like being on an archaelogical dig," Leibovitz says in her introduction. Initially, the memoir was going to include only personal photographs, encompassing the lingering illnesses and deaths of Sontag and of Samuel Leibovitz, the photographer's father who died in January 2005, but the project grew in size, scope, and ambition, to include highly stylized commercial work originally commissioned by such glossy publications as *Condé Nast Traveler*, *Vogue*, and *Vanity Fair*. As if to defend herself against the charge of exploiting her commercial work, with its notable emphasis upon such media celebrities as Brad Pitt, Nicole Kidman, Demi Moore, Johnny Depp and Kate Moss, to draw attention to the more modest personal material, Leibovitz has said: "I don't have two lives. This is one life, and the personal pictures and the assignment work are all part of it."

In the Brooklyn Museum exhibit of 197 photographs, most but not all included in the book, the glitzy, theatrically staged celebrity portraits are showcased while the smaller, black-and-white personal photographs, many of Leibovitz's extended family, are marginalized; the Brooklyn Museum poster for the exhibit is a reproduction of Leibovitz's *Vanity Fair* photograph of Nicole Kidman as a Hollywood fantasy concoction, while the cover of the book consists of shadowy, somber, resolutely unglamorous photographs of Annie Leibovitz in repose, taken by Susan Sontag, and a sequence of mist-shrouded, unidentified landscapes. Where the Brooklyn Museum exhibit is high-decibel, self-aggrandizing, and frequently meretricious, the book is subdued, meditative, and intimate; where the museum exhibit is aggressively glamorous, the book yields small, subtle moments of humanity, particularly in close-ups of the photographer's parents who emerge as distinct and admirable personalities. Though none of Leibovitz's intensely personal photographs of individuals from her private life, including her three very young daughters Sarah, Susan, and Samuelle, rises to the level of the intimate memoirist art of Leibovitz's contemporaries Emmet Gowin, Sally Mann, and Nan Goldin (whose *Ballad of Sexual Dependency* would seem to have been a strong influence), nor to the level of Leibovitz's friend and mentor Richard Avedon (whose photographs of his dying father have become classics of twentieth-century photography), yet these are poignant and touching, as they are resolutely unpretentious, "pictures" of ordinary life.

The photographic image would seem to be the most chameleon-like of all images, deriving meaning almost entirely from the context in which it appears, from its size vis-à-vis the viewer, and from its position in space: on the museum or gallery wall, or in a book. The glamorous celebrity photographs for which Annie Leibovitz is best known, that appeared originally in or on the cover of *Vanity Fair*, appear, on the museum wall, in a vast white space usually designated for "art," ludicrously overblown and synthetic, glossy and flat as movie posters; yet, in the book, surrounded by Leibovitz's low-keyed, candid, "artless" personal material, the identical images, greatly reduced in size, function as the memoirist intends them: as specimens of her professional work, bulletins from a distant country. The much-hyped celebrity photographs of Demi Moore, Nicole Kidman, Brad Pitt, Sylvester Stallone (in the nude, muscled and headless) are most successful as magazine photography, scaled to the page, or on the cover, where amid mundane or trashy newsstand rivals, Leibovitz's meticulously staged portraits glow like gems; in the museum exhibit, exposed on the museum wall, the famous cover of the very pregnant Demi Moore seems but a parody of Hollywood self-exhibitionism on the part of an actress of unexceptional talent in collusion with the buzz-oriented magazine (at that time edited by Tina Brown) and a high-tech photographer who routinely employs a crew of assistants and much equipment for one of her colossally expensive "shoots."

Enormous brooding photographs of such celebrities as Mick Jagger (posed topless, on an unmade bed, with cinched-in waist and darkened lips), Brad Pitt (posed sprawled atop a rumpled bed in a Vegas hotel, in a gaudy striped shirt and what appear to be faux-ocelot-skin pants and cowboy boots), and baby-faced dreamboat Leonardo DiCaprio (posed with a swan cradled in his arms and the swan's neck looped about his own neck: live swan? stuffed swan?) exude an air of comical inflation on the museum wall, while in the book, reduced to something like human scale, they might be read as individuals who have succumbed to garish fantasies about themselves. Some of the celebrity photographs verge upon kitsch-caricature, like the portrait of a fatuous-looking Jack Nicholson gripping a golf club, in a wind-ruffled bathrobe and dark glasses, reacting as if he's surprised by the camera; and the reclining B-movie pose of the young actress Scarlett Johansson in a garish Hollywood glamor costume and abbreviated satin panties. The celebrity photographs are usually portraits in isolation, as if the condition of celebrity-hood is self-enclosed, autistic; where two celebrities are photographed together, a dark-garbed Johnny

Depp slung upon the naked body of the "super-model" Kate Moss on an unmade bed in the Royalton Hotel, the effect is of two exhibitionists who have found each other, in a display of sexual intimacy for the benefit of the photographer looming over them. The effect of a sequence of such photographs is numbing, if not exasperating: for all her skill, the photographer has made no attempt to "reveal" character but merely to expose or exploit fantasies. In an interview in 7 Days, Leibovitz acknowledges being barely able to look at her commercial work, which was on display in her studio in preparation for A Photographer's Life: while insisting that she is still proud of the work, Leibovitz expresses the wish that "it had more meaning, more substance."

It is a curious fact: the more you ponder Annie Leibovitz's high-tech commercial work, the less you see in it; viewer, celebrity, and photographer come to seem crushed together, suffocated in non-meaning.

On the museum wall, these photographs predominate; in the book, they are bracketed by far more interesting personal material like pictures—to use Leibovitz's modest term—from the photographer's trip to Sarajevo in 1993 with Susan Sontag, where the women met with editors of the newspaper Oslobodjenje, and of the photographer's country place in rural Rhinebeck, New York. (In the book, as distinct from the museum exhibit, upstate New York with its densely wooded hills, mist-shrouded ponds and vistas romantically empty of human figures, functions as a much-needed contrast to the claustrophobia of the studio.) Leibovitz includes several panoramic photographs of the ruins of 9/11 followed immediately, and unabashedly, by a photograph of an enormously pregnant fifty-one-year-old Leibovitz (taken by Susan Sontag) and delivery room photographs of the birth of Leibovitz's daughter Sarah in October 2001. The symbolic meaning is blunt and yet appropriate: thousands of people have died in the World Trade Center terrorist attack, there is death in the world, but Annie Leibovitz's first daughter has been born, and the lineage that includes Leibovitz's admirable parents Marilyn and Samuel will continue. Harshly criticized by the *New York Times* art critic Roberta Smith for both the "pedestrian" nature of her personal photographs and for her exhibitionism, Leibovitz would seem to have little choice about including in her memoir such intimate material in which the "public" and the "private" intersect. How dark, how suffocating in its images of debilitating disease and death *A Photographer's Life* would have been, without the irresistible "baby pictures" of Leibovitz's three daughters! Recall Henry David Thoreau, a Transcendentalist predecessor: "I should not talk so much about myself if there were anybody else whom I knew as well."

Unguarded, unposed and painfully intimate photographs of a desperately ill Susan Sontag in hospital beds in New York City and in Seattle, in the last days of her life unrecognizable, face ravaged and stomach grotesquely bloated, appear, on the museum wall, too close by the glamour celebrity photographs of "perfect" bodies not to be cruelly diminished by them. In the public space that is the museum wall, viewed by a neutral observer who knew nothing of the photographer's longtime relationship to Sontag, such raw work reads like an exploitation of the subject's helplessness that would constitute an outrageous violation of Sontag's privacy if snapped by paparazzi who'd breached hospital security to get to her room: the viewer recoils in dismay, revulsion. Yet, in the book, where many pages of memoirist material involving Sontag and Leibovitz and their years of traveling together have prepared the viewer for such intimacy, these photographs of an aging woman in physical distress, like those of the deceased Sontag on a bier in a Fortuny-like dress, take on another, far more nuanced and poignant significance:

> I forced myself to take pictures of Susan's last days. Perhaps the pictures completed the work she and I had begun together when she was sick in 1998. I didn't analyze it then. I just knew that I had to do it . . . I cried for a month [while editing the pictures]. I didn't realize until later how far the work on the book had taken me through the grieving process. It's the closest thing to who I am that I've ever done.[1]

The photographs of Leibovitz's that work most successfully in the museum exhibit are those of bodies in motion: an astonishing leap by the (unclothed) dancer Bill T. Jones, another leap by the silhouetted Michael Jordan, close-ups of the beautifully sculpted bodies of members of the U.S. Olympics athletic teams including swimmers, gymnasts, runners and pole-vaulters, whose heroic exploits seem to transcend merely personal identity, as in the sculpted human forms of antiquity. While a close-up of the elderly Eudora Welty showing the writer vacant-eyed and seemingly without affect is a cruel exposure of Welty in an unguarded moment, close-ups of the elderly, seemingly moribund William Burroughs exude an air of something like primal terror, and human resignation in the face of such terror, as if the prankster Burroughs were peering at the viewer through the eye holes of his own death mask. There is a witty juxtaposition of President George W. Bush and his advisers followed immediately by a feisty-looking Michael Moore and his assistants, who would mercilessly lampoon Bush and his crew in the satirical film *Fahrenheit 9/11*; and there are close-up portraits of Nelson Mandela, Merce Cunningham, Joseph Brodsky, Richard Avedon, Colin Powell, Daniel Day-Lewis, and a craggy, bewhiskered Willie Nelson that gain from the exalted-heroic treatment. The museum exhibit ostentatiously concludes with a separate room containing eight gigantic landscapes that loom above the viewer with the portentousness of greeting card pictures monstrously inflated; yet, in the book, accompanying the starkly intimate photographs of the last days of Susan Sontag and of the elderly Sam Leibovitz, these identical images, in particular an Ansel Adams–inspired photograph of birch trees taken in Ellenville, New York, are beautifully understated and "Transcendental."

As a book, *A Photographer's Life 1990–2005* has the heft and intransigence of a grave marker. As befits a dream sequence, its pages are unnumbered; maddeningly, there is no table of contents, no index. Should you wish to locate certain of Leibovitz's photographs, you must page through the book, turn these enormous pages repeatedly. Still, where the museum exhibit offers, as its glitzy poster proclaims, a sensational experience, or, more precisely, to employ Samuel Johnson's remark about the Metaphysical poets, an experience of violently yoked-together images, few of them very deep or abiding, the book offers a protracted and unmistakable emotional experience. The moral of the exhibit is implicit in its staging: celebrity trumps family, public trumps private, glamour trumps the quotidian. But the book tells a very different story by rearranging images and bringing them into the same approximate scale, of the eclipsing of the public/professional life by the artist's private life: the arduous but spiritually restorative act of memorialization. In this version, the "offensive" photographs of loved ones *in extremis* are necessary components of one's own suffering; the dying individual is a part of oneself, reluctantly surrendered to death. Where an unsympathetic observer might recoil from what appears to be the ghoulish avidity with which the photographer takes "pictures" of her dying, and dead, loved ones, now corpses from which life has vanished, the sympathetic observer might interpret the act as homage, akin to a descent into death: the primitive, instinctual, visceral initial refusal to acknowledge the finality of death. The unsympathetic observer resents being forced into the position of voyeur; the sympathetic observer is willing to be forced into the position of a fellow voyager.

Granted that the memoirist impulse is fundamentally narcissistic and that the memoirist is obliged to make much of human experiences—losses of loved ones, births of babies, happy family reunions, sorrowful graveyard scenes—that are common to us all, yet the effect, in the hands of some practitioners, is an art that can speak to others. Though a project's range may be narrow, yet its roots can go deep. In *On Photography*, Susan Sontag remarks: "As the fascination that photographs exercise is a reminder of death, it is also an invitation to sentimentality." But "sentimentality" may be the risk that the more reckless and more aggrieved among us must take in the pursuit of the elusive memoirist vision.

"THE GREAT HEAP OF DAYS":
JAMES SALTER'S FICTION

[I]t was in me like a pathogen—the idea of being
a writer and from the great heap of days making
something lasting.

—JAMES SALTER, FROM *BURNING*
THE DAYS: RECOLLECTION

Born in 1925 in Passaic, New Jersey, a graduate of West Point and a fighter pilot in the Korean War, James Salter is the author of a relatively small body of prose of uncommon subtlety, intelligence, and beauty. Especially in his deftly rendered shorter fiction, gathered in *Dusk and Other Stories* (1988) and now *Last Night*, as in the remarkable *Light Years* (1975), Salter suggests not the heavy hitters of his era—James Jones, Irwin Shaw, Robert Penn Warren, John O'Hara, Norman Mailer, William Styron, and Saul Bellow, for whom prose fiction is an arena for sinewy self-display and argumentation—but such European sensibilities as Proust, Colette, Woolf, Nabokov, Marguerite Duras. Salter remarks with a kind of offhanded regret in his memoir *Burning the Days* (1997) that no work of his is filmable, but in fact Salter's elliptical, impressionistic prose suggests the films of Antonioni and Bertolucci, who may well have had some influence on his fiction. Rare in a male writer of his generation, Salter has virtually no interest in politics and social issues and very little interest in reigning ideas, popular obsessions, psychology. In his shimmeringly sensuous meditation upon mortality, *Light Years* (1975), which reads like an eroticized *To the Lighthouse*, the concerns of Salter's Caucasian-bourgeois protagonists are exclusively familial, aesthetic, sexual; though the novel moves through the violent upheaval in American society that was the 1960s, Salter's characters are untouched by assassinations, civil rights demonstrations, the Vietnam War and its protestors, the disintegration of drug-ravaged communities. *A Sport and a Pastime* (1967) is a lyric account of youthful erotic love in "[g]reen, bourgeoise France," imagined by a voyeuristic American observer, and *Solo Faces* (1979) is an impassioned account of the mystique of mountain climbing, seen primarily through the consciousness of a fanatic devotee for whom "what mattered was to be a part of existence, not to possess it." Salter's characters inhabit, not history, but time; not a snarled world of politics and events but a pastoral world forever beckoning, and forever elusive, like the highest and most treacherous peaks of the Alps.

As an Air Force pilot, James Salter flew F-86 fighter planes in more than one hundred missions during the Korean War, an interim of his life described with oneiric precision in *Burning the Days* and in his first two novels *The Hunters* (1956) and *The Arm of Flesh* (1961, revised and republished as *Cassada* in 2000). When he resigned his commission at the age of thirty-two, he'd been in uniform since the age of seventeen; he had just published, under a pseudonym, *The Hunters*: "Salter was as distant as possible from my own name. It was essential not to be identified and jeopardize a career . . . I wanted to be admired but not known." Though Salter seems to have renounced these early realistic novels in favor of his later, more experimental work, both *The Hunters* and *Cassada* are riveting works of fiction, deserving of the general praise they received at the time of publication, when Salter was favorably compared to Saint-Exupéry, one of his models. Passages from both *The Hunters* and *Cassada*, as well as previously unpublished excerpts from Salter's Korean War journal, are included in the miscellany *Gods of Tin: The Flying Years* (2004), an excellent introduction to Salter's variegated yet uniformly eloquent work. Like Salter's compelling memoir *Burning the Days, Gods of Tin* is so rich in its observations, so poetically precise in its language, one can open it virtually anywhere and be drawn into its haunting prose:

12 Feb 1952. Korea. . . . Watched a mission take off at K-14—two at a time booming down the runway, then two more, and two more. Col. Thyng was leading, north to the Yalu. A second squadron followed. They streamed out, turning, disappearing into the overcast.

Come now, and let us go and risk our lives unnecessarily. For if they have got any value at all it is this that they have got none. We arrived in Korea, as it happened, on a gloomy day. It was February, the dead of winter, planes parked along sandbag revetments and bitter cold lying over the field adding to the pall. Davis, the ranking American ace—mythic word, ineffaceable—a squadron commander, had just been shot down. With the terrible mark of newness on us, we stood in the officers' club and listened to what was or was not fact. We were too fresh to make distinctions . . .

We had come, it turned out, to join a sort of crude colonial life lived in stucco buildings in plain, square rooms, unadorned, with common showers and a latrine even the wing commander shared.

We were there together for six months, cold winter mornings with the weak sunlight on the hills, the silvery airplanes gliding forth like mechanical serpents not quite perfected in their movement and then forming on the runway amid rising sound. In the spring the ice melted in the rivers and the willow became green. The blood from a bloody nose poured down over your mouth and chin inside the rubber oxygen mask. In summer the locust trees were green and all the fields. It comes hauntingly back: silent, unknown lands, distant brown river, the Yalu, the line between two worlds.

And again,

You lived and died alone, especially in fighters. Fighters. Somehow, despite everything, that word had not become sterile. You slipped into the hollow cockpit and strapped and plugged yourself into the machine. The canopy ground shut and sealed you off. Your oxygen, your very breath, you carried with you into the chilled vacuum, in a steel bottle.

A Sport and a Pastime, published when Salter was forty-two, is a radical departure from Salter's early novels both in subject matter and in language. A perennial on those lists of "most neglected" masterpieces, this tenderly/obsessively erotic romance might be seen as a kind of homage to the Parisian publisher of scandalous novels by Sade, Henry Miller, William Burroughs, Jean Genet, Vladimir Nabokov (*Lolita*) and Pauline Réage (*Story of O*), Maurice Girodias of the fabled Olympia Press, "a sort of lanky Falstaff" as Salter recalls the man, whose books "one leafed through . . . in a kind of narcotic dream." *A Sport and a Pastime* has as an epigraph a quotation from the Koran: "Remember that the life of this world is but a sport and a pastime." It's an ironic and yet literal commentary on the novel's preoccupation with sensuous experience in a sequence of set pieces evoking, with the same lyric intensity, the countryside of France and a highly charged love affair of a twenty-four-year-old American, a Yale dropout, and a younger French shopgirl. The novel suggests Nabokov's *Lolita*, though lacking Nabokov's brilliant nastiness and allusiveness; its narrator is intrusive in the way of narrators in experimental fiction of the 1960s, a self-described "somnambulist" whose relationship to the avid young lovers is enigmatic:

> These are notes to photographs . . . It would be better to say that they began as notes but became something else, a description of what I conceive to be events. They were meant for me alone, but I no longer hide them. Those times are past.
>
> I am only putting down details which entered me, fragments that were able to part my flesh. It's a story of things that never existed although even the faintest doubt of that, the smallest possibility, plunges everything into darkness.

More mysteriously,

> Certain things I remember exactly as they were. They are
> merely discolored a bit by time ... Most of the details,
> though, have been long since transformed or rearranged to
> bring others of them forward ... One alters the past to form
> the future.

As *Lolita* is a kind of valentine to Nabokov's adopted, gor-
geously vulgar America, so *A Sport and a Pastime* is a valentine
to Salter's France, "not the great squares of Europe ... but the
myriad small towns closed tight against the traveler, towns as
still as the countryside itself." Obsessed with the young lovers
whom he has befriended, the voyeur-narrator begins to imagine their lovemaking in the most exalted terms:

> Mythology has accepted [Dean, the young man], images he
> cannot really believe in, images brief as dreams. The sweat
> rolls down his arms. He tumbles into the damp leaves of
> love, he rises clean as air. There is nothing about her he does
> not adore. When they are finished, she lies quiet and limp,
> exhausted by it all. She has become entirely his, and they lie
> like drunkards, their bare limbs crossed. In the cold distance
> the bells begin, filling the darkness, clear as psalms.

A Sport and a Pastime ends with the abrupt, accidental death
of one of the lovers and the elegiac survival of the narrator as
a kind of drifting ghost attached still to the small provincial
French towns now closed to him.

The experience of *Light Years*, like that of Virginia Woolf's most characteristic novels, is tonal, musical; the novel's plot, so to speak, seems to happen in the interstices of its characters' lives, in a sequence of wave-like motions that appear unconnected to human volition, like the play of light, obsessively described, in the Hudson Valley household that is the novel's primary setting:

> In the morning the light came in silence. The house slept. The air overhead, glittering, infinite, the moist earth beneath— one could taste this earth, its richness, its density, bathe in the air like a stream. Not a sound. The rind of the cheese had dried like bread. The glasses held the stale aroma of vanished wine.

In embryo, this is *Light Years*: an upper-middle-class suburban household touching upon infinity, irradiated with light, yet, if one looks closely, beginning to go stale as if with an excess of happiness.

> [Viri's and Nedra's] life was two things: it was a life, more or less—at least it was the preparation for one—and it was an illustration of life for their children . . . They wanted their children, in those years, to have the impossible, not in the sense of the unachieveable but in the sense of the pure . . .
>
> There is no happiness like this happiness: quiet mornings, light from the river, the weekend ahead. They lived a Russian life, a rich life, interwoven, in which the misfortune

of one, a failure, illness, would stagger them all. It was like a garment, this life. Its beauty was outside, its warmth within.

Light Years moves airily, relentlessly, from an autumn in 1958 when Viri and Nedra are a young married couple in their late twenties, attractive, enviable, "beautiful" and "handsome" as characters in an American romance by F. Scott Fitzgerald, to a spring day decades later when Viri, divorced, returns to his former house, "an old man in the woods" who has outlived his wife and has seen his daughters drift from him: "It happens in an instant. It is all one long day, one endless afternoon, friends leave, we stand on the shore."

Where novels of suburban-marital unrest at mid-century by such contemporaries of Salter's as Richard Yates, John Cheever, and John Updike are apt to be laced with a corrosive irony, *Light Years* is a more subtly modulated, Chekhovian testament to the passing of a way of life, or to the cultural elevation of that way of life: the sacred insularity of the American "nuclear family" in which adults live for, and through, their children. Viri's love for Nedra is perceived as a kind of weakness: Viri is "a good father—that is to say, an ineffective man"; eventually, he's repudiated by Nedra for being a man who "had not wanted enough." Nedra, the novel's most enigmatic character, is at once an earth mother ("Her love for [her children] was the love to which she had devoted her life, the only one which would not be consumed or vanish") entranced by the routines and rituals of her family, and a sexually restless, even predatory Mrs. Ramsey, who persists in adulterous love affairs even after her husband has found her out. Nedra insists upon a divorce, moves out of the idyllic Hudson Valley house to travel in Europe; no longer young, she embarks upon sexual adventures in anticipation of "entering the underground river" where "not even courage will help." It isn't banal happiness Nedra wants, but something more elusive and undefinable: "She meant to be free."

Like a riddle not readily solved, *Light Years* lingers in the memory. There is a melancholy enchantment in its pages redolent of Colette: prolonged happiness is a prison from which the self yearns to escape at any cost.

Fittingly, Salter's next novel, *Solo Faces* (1979), explores the search for the most extreme ecstatic freedom: solo mountain climbing in the French Alps. Where *Light Years* is a poetic meditation in prose interlarded with dramatic scenes, *Solo Faces* is an action film in prose interlarded with poetic passages. Its solitary protagonist, Rand, is a mountain climber of instinctive skill who becomes, over the course of the novel, a fanatic; a man for whom ordinary life, especially fatherhood, is terrifying. He's a type not unlike certain of the ace pilots revered in Salter's flying novels, for whom the compulsion to risk their lives is visceral; there's the yearning, too, to make oneself "heroic" in the most literal, unironic sense of the word. The pure man of action is a suicide, William Carlos Williams once noted, and so it seems, in *Solo Faces*, the purest mountain climbers are men like Rand, driven to ever more dangerous exploits as he tests his courage repeatedly, one successful climb provoking the need for another, and yet another:

He was happy, held there by the merest point of steel, above all difficulties, somehow above all fears. This is how it must feel at the end, he thought uneasily, a surge of joy before the final moment. He looked past his feet. The steepness was dazzling. Far above him was a great bulge of ice . . .

In the morning he woke among peaks incredibly white against the muted sky. There is something greater than the life of the cities, greater than money and possessions; there is a manhood that can never be taken away. For this, one gives everything.

Inevitably, Rand reaches the limit of his endurance, broken in spirit when he fails to complete a suicidal solo climb. Yet, even as he retreats in shame from the brotherhood of mountain climbers to an anonymous and posthumous life in Pensacola, Florida, he passes into legend:

They talked of him, however, which was what he had always wanted. The acts themselves are surpassed but the singular figure lives on. The day finally came when they realized they would never know for certain. Rand had somehow succeeded. He had found the great river. He had gone.

Dusk and *Last Night* are appropriate titles for Salter's slender collections of stories, that unfold with dreamlike fluidity in an atmosphere of shadows and indistinct forms, like watercolors in a dark palette. As Salter's novels are comprised of exquisite set pieces, often self-contained, so his short stories suggest novellas or novels compressed into a few pages. Both *Dusk* and *Last Night* contain memorable stories in a classic vein, yet a number of others ("Am Strande von Tanger," "The Cinema," "Lost Sons," "Via Negativa," "The Destruction of the Goetheanum," from *Dusk*; "Comet," "Eyes of the Stars," "Platinum," "Arlington," from *Last Night*) move so swiftly and disjointedly as to arouse expectation in the way of trailers for intriguing films that turn out to be the films themselves, abruptly truncated. It's as if the writer's imagination has leapt ahead of his capacity for, or interest in, the work of expression; an impatience with formal storytelling and chronological development:

> This film that he had written, this important work of the newest of the arts, already existed complete in his mind. Its power came from its chasteness, the discipline of its images. It was a film of indirection, the surface was calm with the calm of daily life. That was not to say still. Beneath the visible were emotions more potent for their concealment. Only occasionally, like the head of an iceberg ominously rising from nowhere and then dropping from sight did the terror come into view. ("The Cinema," *Dusk*)

Where narration is indirect and images are employed as a kind of emotional synecdoche, perspective tends to be coolly detached and retrospective, as in the great experimental European films of the mid-twentieth century, or the short fiction of Colette. This accounts for the protracted openings of a number of Salter's stories, their abrupt and sometimes disconcerting leaps in time, sudden endings that bring the reader up short, like sudden steps in dreams, unforeseen:

> She has small breasts and large nipples. Also, as she herself says, a rather large behind. Her father has three secretaries. Hamburg is close to the sea.

And, in a swift and somewhat desultory summing-up of a poignant story of marital betrayal:

> That was how she and Walter came to part, upon being discovered by his wife. They met two or three times afterward, at his insistence, but to no avail. Whatever holds people together was gone. She told him she could not help it. That was just the way it was.

In *Dusk* there's a perplexing story titled "Akhnilo" that tracks in microscopic detail what seems to be the mental disintegration of a man about whom we know little ("Eddie Fenn was a carpenter though he'd gone to Dartmouth and majored in history . . . He had thinning hair and a shy smile. Not much to say."), a feat of writerly obscurity that repeated readings can't decode. (In *Burning the Days*, Salter acknowledges having written a story about a man whose imagined life consumes his identity, about which Salter's wife says she couldn't "make head or tail of it.") Enough material for a substantial novel is crammed into the seven small pages of "Arlington": complicated marital relations, exotic locales, thumbnail sketches of characters, abrupt death:

In his long, admired career, Westerveldt had been like a figure in a novel. In the elephant grass near Pleiku he'd gotten a wide scar through one eyebrow where a mortar fragment, half an inch lower and a little closer, would have blinded or killed him. If anything, it enhanced his appearance. He'd had a long love affair with a woman in Naples when he'd been stationed there, a marquesa, in fact . . . Women always liked him. In the end he married a woman from San Antonio, a divorcée with a child, and they had two more together. He was fifty-eight when he died from some kind of leukemia that began as a strange rash on his neck.

Like the self-absorbed suburbanites of *Light Years*, the men and women of Salter's short fiction tend to be individuals of privilege, worldly and yet vulnerable to hurt; individuals who perceive of themselves as passionate, or deserving of passion, though, in fact, like the rare book dealer of "Bangkok," who has moved on to a domestic life of routine contentment ("You can't have ecstasy daily") they may have settled for "pretend" lives. Salter's most powerful stories tend to be about women *in extremis*, for whom all pretense has vanished, sometimes in a moment's revelation, sometimes in a protracted and horrific contemplation of mortality, as in "Twenty Minutes," in *Dusk*, when a woman living alone, a divorcée, is thrown from her horse in a desolate area, lies broken and paralyzed waiting for someone to discover her as flashes of her life scroll past her:

It was growing dark. Help me, someone, help me, she kept repeating. Someone would come, they had to. She tried not to be afraid. She thought of her father who could explain life in one sentence. "They knock you down and you get up. That's what it's all about." He recognized only one virtue. He would hear what had happened, that she merely lay there. She had to try to get home, even if she went only a little way, even a few yards.

The two most poignant stories in *Last Night* are about women who have been diagnosed with inoperable cancer: "Some Fun" reads like a dark episode of *Sex and the City* in which a woman can't share news of her impending death with her closest women friends, who are bent upon having a good time getting drunk as they exchange revelations about former husbands, but only with a stranger driving a taxi; in the harrowing "Last Night," a terminally ill woman named Marit hopes to appropriate her death by making it into a ritual involving her husband, who will inject her with a lethal amount of morphine:

> She no longer resembled herself. What she had been was gone: it had been taken from her. The change was fearful, especially in her face. She had a face now that was for the afterlife and those she would meet there. It was hard for Walter to remember how she had once been. She was almost a different woman from the one to whom he had made a solemn promise to help when the time came.

Marit, anticipating death, longs for "certain memories" to take with her, but only memories from childhood: "The rest was a long novel so like your life; you were going through it without thinking and then one morning it ended: there were bloodstains." But Marit's plan for an easeful death brings unexpected results for her, her husband, and her husband's appalled mistress.

It's a measure of James Salter's writerly gifts that one wishes each of his stories longer, as, at the somewhat premature conclusion of *Burning the Days*, one of the most engaging and beautifully composed memoirs of our time, one wishes the life, thus the art, extended:

> It is only in books that one finds perfection, only in books that it cannot be spoiled. Art, in a sense, is life brought to a standstill, rescued from time.

MARGARET ATWOOD'S TALES

Moral Disorder
by Margaret Atwood

The Handmaid's Tale
by Margaret Atwood
Introduction by Valerie Martin

> The true story is vicious
> and multiple and untrue
>
> after all. Why do you
> need it? Don't ever
>
> ask for the true story.
> —MARGARET ATWOOD, *TRUE STORIES*

But what precisely is a "true story"?—one that reveals "truth," or one that confirms the storyteller's identity? Can "truth" be an objective matter, when human subjectivities are involved? Or is truth merely—or supremely—a "story"? Through her long, energetic, and productive career Margaret Atwood has been as much an anatomist of "telling" as of "truth": the daughter of an entomologist at the University of Toronto, with a master's degree in Victorian literature from

Harvard (1962), Atwood would seem to have an instinct for taxonomy; for the casting of a cold yet not unsympathetic eye upon the stratagems by which individuals present themselves to others in narratives devised to confirm their identities or, simply, like the desperate captive "handmaid" (i.e., sexual/ breeder-slave) Offred of Atwood's most widely read novel, the dystopian *The Handmaid's Tale*, to survive. As Nell, the protagonist of the novel-in-linked-stories *Moral Disorder* thinks following the unexpected death of her husband's eccentric, troublesome ex-wife:

> All that anxiety and anger, those dubious good intentions, those tangled lives, that blood. I can tell about it or I can bury it. In the end, we'll all become stories.

In a postmodernist sleight of hand in Atwood's elaborately constructed *Alias Grace* (1996), the reader is beguiled by numerous competing variants of a central story (based upon the sensational Kinnear-Montgomery murders in Richmond Hill, Ontario, in 1843) that can never be fully resolved, as in an intricately plotted puzzle. Near the end of the lengthy novel the former defense attorney for the alleged murderess Grace Marks, whose innocence has come to seem highly likely to the reader, casually undercuts our expectations by remarking:

> Lying . . . A severe term, surely. Has [Grace] been lying to you, you ask? Let me put it this way—did Scheherazade lie? Not in her own eyes; indeed, the stories she told ought never to be subjected to the harsh categories of Truth and

Falsehood. They belong in another realm altogether. Perhaps Grace Marks has merely been telling you what she needs to tell, in order to accomplish the desired end . . . To keep the Sultan amused. To keep the blow from falling.

Still later, after Grace Marks has been pardoned and released from the penitentiary, and has married a man out of her scandalous past, she finds that she must "tell him some story or other about being in the Penitentiary, or else the Lunatic asylum in Toronto . . . He listens to all of that like a child listening to a fairy tale, as if it is something wonderful, and then he begs me to tell him yet more."

How like the author of such artful fictions, speaking of her role as storyteller! As Atwood acknowledged in a recent interview: "I'm one of the few literary writers who get lucky in their lifetimes."[1]

Author of twenty volumes of prose fiction including most notably the novels *Surfacing*, *The Handmaid's Tale*, *Alias Grace*, *The Blind Assassin*, and *Oryx and Crake*, as well as thirteen volumes of poetry, six works of non-fiction, and six children's books, Margaret Atwood has an international reputation that differs considerably from her reputation in her native Canada, where she became, virtually overnight in 1972, at the age of thirty-one, the most celebrated/controversial Canadian writer of the era. Atwood's first novel, a feminist "anti-comedy" (Atwood's description) titled *The Edible Woman*, had appeared in 1969, to enthusiastic but limited press coverage, but Atwood was most known for her distinctive poetic voice in such early, acclaimed volumes as *The Circle Game* (1966), *The Animals in That Country* (1967), *The Journals of Susanna Moodie* (1970), *Procedures for Underground* (1970), and *Power Politics* (1971) with its wonderfully terse, mordant prefatory lines:

> you fit into me
> like a hook into an eye
>
> a fish hook
> an open eye

Though Atwood's poetry has been overshadowed, perhaps inevitably, by her prose fiction, Atwood brings to her poetry the identical sharp, acerbic eye and ear, and the identical commingling of the tragic and the farcical, that have characterized her most ambitious fiction; her prevailing concerns (sexual politics, the endangered environment), foregrounded in the cautionary dystopias *The Handmaid's Tale* and *Oryx and Crake* (2003) are sounded decades before in such mordant, bleakly funny poems as "Backdrop Addresses Cowboy" (excerpted):

> Starspangled cowboy
> sauntering out of the almost-
> silly West, on your face
> a porcelain grin,
> tugging a papier-mâché cactus
> on wheels behind you with a string,

you are innocent as a bathtub
full of bullets.

Your righteous eyes, your laconic
trigger-fingers
people the streets with villains:
as you move, the air in front of you
blossoms with targets

and you leave behind you a heroic
trail of desolation:
beer bottles
slaughtered by the side
of the road, bird-
skulls bleaching in the sunset.
            The Animals in That Country (1968)

Curiously, and ironically, the book that in 1972 catapulted the young author to such unexpected celebrity has never been published in any country outside Canada: this is *Survival: A Thematic Guide to Canadian Literature*. (Now published in a revised edition by McClelland & Stewart, *Survival* was originally published by the small Toronto-based press House of Anansi as one in a series of "self-help guides" to help defray the costs of literary publishing.) Conceived as an "easy-access" book for the use of high school and college instructors of Canadian literature (a category that, in 1972, scarcely existed and was more likely to arouse derision than admiration), *Survival* is, as its subtitle indicates, not a survey of Canadian literature, not an evaluation of distinctive Canadian texts, nor a compendium of histories and biographies, but a taxonomy outlining "a number of key patterns [intended to] function like the field markings in bird-books: they will help you distinguish this species from all others." Atwood's methodology follows that of such influential critical theorists of the time as Leslie Fiedler, Perry Miller, and Northrop Frye whose student Atwood had been at the University of Toronto; her intention in *Survival* is to identify "a series of characteristics and leitmotifs, and a comparison of the varying treatments of them in different national and cultural environments."

Immensely readable, entertaining, and insightful, a treasure trove for non-Canadian readers to whom such gifted Canadian poets and writers as Susanna Moodie, Margaret Avison, Margaret Laurence, Sheila Watson, Graeme Gibson, Jay Macpherson, E. J. Pratt, Tom Wayman, A. M. Klein, Anne Hébert, Gabrielle Roy, Marie-Claire Blais, Earle Birney, Sinclair Ross, Austin Clarke, W. O. Mitchell, and numerous others are likely not to be well known, *Survival* exudes a schoolgirl zest and playfulness rarely found in works of literary criticism, as unique in its way as D. H. Lawrence's brilliantly cranky *Studies in Classic American Literature*. In her opening chapter Atwood ventures the "sweeping generalization" that each country or culture has a single dominant symbol at its core, notably The Frontier (America), The Island (England), and Survival, or *la Survivance* (Canada):

Our central [Canadian] idea is one which generates, not the excitement and sense of adventure or danger which The

Frontier holds out, not the smugness and/or sense of security, or everything in its place, which The Island can offer, but an almost intolerable anxiety. Our stories are likely to be tales not of those who made it but of those who made it back from the awful experience—the North, the snowstorm, the sinking ship—that killed everyone else. The survivor has no triumph or victory but the fact of his survival.

Atwood divides her material into thematic categories that suggest an ambitious course syllabus: "Nature the Monster," "Animal Victims," "First People: Indians and Eskimos as Symbols," "Ancestral Totems: Explorers, Settlers," "The Casual Incident of Death: Futile Heroes, Unconvincing Martyrs and Other Bad Ends," "Ice Women vs. Earth Mothers," and, particularly appropriate in 1972 when sales of most Canadian literary novels and volumes of poetry were minuscule, "The Paralyzed Artist." (Born in 1939, Margaret Atwood began her career like most Canadian writers of the era: traveling the vast country giving readings and toting cardboard boxes of her own books to sell afterward since there wasn't likely to be a bookstore to supply them.) That Canadian writers such as Michael Ondaatje, Alice Munro, Robertson Davies, Carol Shields, and Atwood herself would one day acquire critical and commercial success outside Canada could not have been predicated in a culture in which the expression "World-famous in Canada" was always good for a laugh; and in which, in academic and literary circles, it was taken for granted that the work of Canadian writers did not constitute a "literature" since it was merely colonial, derivative, and third-rate. One can see how traditional academics were roused to indignation by a "mere chit of a girl" not only venturing into their territory but approaching their subject with such panache and vernacular directness:

> Let us suppose, for the sake of argument, that Canada as a whole is a victim, or an "oppressed minority," or "exploited." Let us suppose that Canada is a colony . . .
>
> If Canada is a collective victim, it should pay some attention to the Basic Victim Positions . . .
>
> Position One: To deny the fact that you are a victim . . .
>
> Position Two: To acknowledge the fact that you are a victim, but to explain this as an act of Fate, the Will of God, the dictates of Biology (in the case of women, for instance), the necessity decreed by History, or Economics, or the Unconscious, or any other large general powerful idea.
>
> Position Three: To acknowledge the fact that you are a victim but to refuse to accept the assumption that the role is inevitable.
>
> Position Four: To be a creative non-victim.

Much in *Survival* remains provocative and illuminating, as in Atwood's discussion of the paralysis of the artist lacking an audience ("He is blocked, he is like a man shouting to no one") and in the chapter "Animal Victims" in which animal figures in the literatures of Britain, America, and Canada are compared:

> It is true that stories ostensibly about animals appear in British literature; but . . . the animals in them are really, like the

white rabbit in *Alice in Wonderland*, Englishmen in furry
zippered suits, often with a layer of human clothing added
on top . . .

Animals appear in American literature minus clothes and
the ability to speak English, but seldom are they the center of
the action. Rather they are its goal, as these "animal stories"
are in fact hunting stories . . . American animal stories are
quest stories—with the Holy Grail being a death—usually
successful from the hunter's point of view, though not from
the animal's; as such they are a comment on the general imperialism of the American cast of mind.

[Canadian] animal stories are far from being success
stories. They are invariably failure stories, ending with the
death of the animal; but this death, far from being the ac-
complishment of a quest, to be greeted with rejoicing, is seen
as tragic or pathetic, *because the stories are told from the
point of view of the animal.*

Published in the same year as *Survival*, and seemingly
written with the predominant themes of the "guide" to Canadian literature in mind, Atwood's lyric, quasi-mystical second novel *Surfacing* drew a good deal of attention, not all
of it sympathetic. By the standards of Atwood's carefully researched, multi-layered and often multi-narrated later novels,
Surfacing is a slighter work, at times almost parable-like, or
diagrammatic, in its structure: the pilgrimage of an unnamed,
wounded and self-deluded young woman narrator to enlightenment in a remote wilderness setting. In this paradigm of a
feminist "quest" novel, Atwood's emotionally repressed narra-

tor travels with her laconic lover and a singularly disagreeable married couple to a lakeside cabin in northern Quebec, where she'd come with her family as a child; the narrator's friends are filmmakers, but her purpose in journeying to the cabin is to search for her missing father, who seems to have vanished into the wilderness. In the course of this minutely introspective novel, in which the protagonist examines herself as one might examine a biological specimen, she comes to terms with her distorted and self-lacerating memories: the humiliation of a failed love affair, the trauma of an abortion. Journeying into northern Quebec would seem to mimic a journey into the heart of darkness if by "darkness" is meant the demons of the self, imagined as ghosts, as in a vision of her aborted fetus glimpsed in a dive into the lake:

> It was below me, drifting towards me from the furthest level where there was no life, a dark oval trailing limbs. It was blurred but it had eyes, they were open, it was something I knew about, a dead thing, it was dead.

The release of this blocked memory empowers the narrator to resist her lover's crude demands for quick sex:

> I didn't want him in me, sacrilege, he was one of the killers, the clay victims damaged and strewn behind him, and he hadn't seen, he didn't know about himself, his own capacity for death.

What is most compelling about *Surfacing* isn't the self-absorbed, rather generic young-woman narrator but the wilderness setting Atwood so vividly evokes, clearly a memorialization of the wilderness site to which her entomologist father took her and his family while Atwood was growing up: the small, simply constructed cabin where "there were always books,"[2] the nearby lake, the endless, intriguing and unfathomable forest in which one could become hopelessly lost. It's a setting that reverberates in Atwood's fiction, with the power of recalled emotion, in stories like "Hurricane Hazel" and "In Search of the Rattlesnake Plantain" (*Bluebeard's Egg*, 1983), and the spooky "Death by Landscape" (*Wilderness Tips*, 1991) in which the wilderness setting is a girls' camp that provides the background for an unnerving episode in a young girl's life, from which she never fully recovers.

Where nature is sacred, the violation and exploitation of nature are sacrilege. *Surfacing* casts a cold, furious eye upon star-spangled intruders from south of the Canadian border: "Bloody fascist pig Yanks." The pristine wilderness is vulnerable to invasion by American appropriation—"Rotten capitalist bastards"—and by direct assault, as in this encounter with American fishermen:

American flag at the front and another at the back, two irritated-looking businessmen with pug-dog faces and nifty outfits and a thin shabby man from the village, guiding...

"Getting any?" one of the Americans yells, teeth bared, friendly as a shark...

The other American throws his cigar over the side. "This don't look like much of a place," he says.

As Atwood's narrator ruefully recalls: "We used to think that [Americans] were harmless and funny and inept and faintly lovable, like President Eisenhower." Now, American crassness conjoined with American ingenuity inspires paranoia in the Canadian male:

> "They're running out of water, clean water, they're dirtying up all of theirs, right? Which is what we have a lot of, this country is almost all water if you look at a map. So in a while, I give it ten years, they'll be up against the wall. They'll try to swing a deal with the government, get us to give them the water cheap or for nothing . . . and the government will give in, they'll be a bunch of puppets as usual. But by then the Nationalist Movement will be strong enough so they'll force the government to back down; riots or kidnappings or something. Then the Yank pigs will send in the Marines."

Atwood's narrator would seem to speak for Atwood herself in such melancholy observations:

> In the bay the felled trees and numbered posts showed where the surveyors had been, power company. My country, sold or drowned, a reservoir; the people were sold along with the land and the animals, a bargain, sale, *solde*. Les soldes they called them, sellouts . . .

So virulent is Canadian outrage against imperialist America, even those rapacious individuals who are in fact Canadians, not Americans, are Americans:

But they'd killed the heron . . . It doesn't matter what country they're from, my head said, they're still Americans, they're what's in store for us, what we are turning into. They spread themselves like a virus, they get into the brain and take over the cells and the cells change from inside and the ones that have the disease can't tell the difference . . . If you look like them and talk like them and think like them then you are them, I was saying, you speak their language, a language is everything you do.

It's significant that Atwood's two most bleakly pessimistic novels, the dystopias *The Handmaid's Tale* and *Oryx and Crake*, are set on American soil, if not precisely in the "United States"; by the time of *Oryx and Crake*, set sometime in the near future, the rapacious Americans of *Surfacing* have morphed into an entire race:

> Human society . . . was a sort of monster, its main byproducts being corpses and rubble. It never learned, it made the same cretinous mistakes over and over, trading short-term gain for long-term pain. It was like a giant slug eating its way relentlessly through all the other bioforms on the planet, grinding up life on earth and shitting it out the back-side in the form of manufactured and soon-to-be-obsolete plastic junk.

Surfacing, published more than thirty years before *Oryx and Crake*, ends with a mystical immersion of its heroine in nature, and an ecstatic revelation of the primacy of her female, daughterly identity. Having hidden from her friends to remain alone at the lake, the narrator experiences a derangement of the senses of a benign, Jungian sort: she "sees" the ghost of her dead mother, as her mother would have been "thirty years ago, before I was born," and imagines her mother as one of several blue jays; yet more dramatically, she "sees" her mysteriously missing father, and understands what has become of him:

> His job was wrong, he was really a surveyor, he learned the trees, naming and counting them so the others could level and excavate . . . He is standing near the fence with his back to me, looking in at the garden . . . He has realized that he was an intruder; the cabin, the fences, the fires and paths were violations; now his own fence excludes him, as logic excludes love . . . I see now that although it isn't my father it is what my father has become. I knew he wasn't dead.

Set in the near future, in a fundamentalist-Christian totalitarian state called the Republic of Gilead, *The Handmaid's Tale* retains the ease and intimacy of the first-person narration of *Surfacing* but is far more ambitious and provocative in scope. Originally published in 1986, *The Handmaid's Tale* is now, appropriately for our times, reissued, with a thoughtful introduction by Valerie Martin that notes that the novel was conceived out of Atwood's alarm at the frequency with which she heard, from her American friends, the facile expression "It can't happen here" in response to Atwood's accounts of "excursions into the darker side of religious fanaticism in Iran and Afghanistan." Atwood's ongoing views of the cultural contrasts between her native Canada and its "starspangled" neighbor underlie the grim, punitive puritanism of the Republic of Gilead:

> The founding Puritans had wanted their society to be a theocratic utopia, a city upon a hill, to be a model and a shining example to all nations. The split between the dream and the reality is an old one and it has not gone away.
>
> Canada suffers from no such split, since it was founded not by idealists but by people who'd been kicked out of other places. Canada was not a city upon a hill, it was what you had to put up with.

The historical time of *The Handmaid's Tale* would seem to be 2005, no longer our uneasily shared "future." The novel in no way resembles science fiction but rather "speculative fiction": a psychologically "realistic" and persuasive exploration of a counterworld bearing a significant if surreal relationship to reality. In essence a Gothic tale of a young woman's cruel imprisonment, her shifting relationship with her captors and her eventual escape, *The Handmaid's Tale* differs from its classic dystopian predecessors in the intimacy of the protagonist's voice and in the convincing domestic background Atwood has established for her. The ominously named "Offred" (so named by her captors, who seem to have appropriated an entire caste of fertile, breeding-age females to become impregnated by the Gilead commanders whose wives are infertile) is rendered with the admirable attentiveness to detail and psychological nuance that is the province of the realistic novel, not the fable. Where the mostly male characters of H. G. Wells's prophetic novels, Aldous Huxley's *Brave New World*, and George Orwell's *1984* are primarily functions of plot, Atwood's character is distinct and individual, with sharp, painful memories of what she has lost (husband, daughter, radical-feminist mother, college roommate). Narrated in the breathless present-tense, like *Surfacing*, much of *Alias Grace* (another captive-female novel) and *The Blind Assassin* as well as numerous short stories by Atwood, *The Handmaid's Tale* achieves the feat of rendering the bizarre, the ludicrous, and the improbable a new sort of quotidian as Offred moves through the prescribed routine of her essentially dull, housewifely day of shopping for household items ("Our first stop is at a store with another wooden sign: three eggs, a bee, a cow. Milk and Honey. There's a line, and we wait our turn, two by two."), a stroll to the Wall, formerly the Harvard Wall, now appropriated by the Republic of Gilead for the displaying of executed enemies of the state ("Beside the main gateway there are six more bodies hanging, by the necks, their hands tied in front of them, their heads in white bags tipped sideways onto their shoulders. There must have been a Men's Salvaging early this morning"), and a sly, catty peek at her sexual rival in the Commander's household, the Commander's middle-aged wife Serena Joy who'd been a Christian-family-values stump-speaker before the Gilead overthrow of the federal government:

> She doesn't make speeches any more. She's become speech-
> less. She stays in her home, but it doesn't seem to agree with

her. How furious she must be, now that she's been taken at her word.

She's looking at the tulips. Her cane is beside her, on the grass. Her profile is towards me . . . It's no longer a flawless, cut-paper profile, her face is sinking in upon itself.

Atwood's greatest challenge in *The Handmaid's Tale* is to make the ritual-copulation Ceremony something other than comical, if not slapstick, as the Handmaid lies, mostly clothed, between the spread legs of the Wife, fully clothed, to be sub-jected to sexual intercourse as performed by the Commander, also mostly clothed. Granted the absurdity of the physical situ-ation, and the improbability of a middle-aged man's sexual potency in such a situation, very likely this is how it might be:

> Serena Joy grips my hands as if it is she, not I, who's be-ing fucked, as if she finds it pleasurable or painful, and the Commander fucks, with a regular two-four marching stroke, on and on and on like a tap dripping . . . It's as if he's some-where else, waiting for himself to come, drumming his fin-gers on the table while he waits . . .
>
> Why does he have to wear that stupid uniform? But would I like his white, tufted raw body any better?

Given that Gilead is run by men, one would suppose that Al-pha males like the Commander could rationalize more com-fortable ways of reproducing their precious DNA, as Mormon men seem to have done in their early, polygamous Protestant-

Christian church. And given the fact of plummeting birth rates attributed to disease, nuclear-plant accidents, leakages from chemical- and biological-warfare stockpiles and toxic-waste disposal sites, it would seem likely that the Handmaids as a class would have been forcibly subjected to artificial insemination.

Yet how eerily prescient, that the Republic of Gilead was established by a coup when Christian fundamentalists, revulsed by an overly liberal, godless and promiscuous society, assassinated the President, machine-gunned Congress, declared a national state of emergency, and laid blame to "Islamic fanatics"; as in Orwell's *1984*, the Republic consolidates its strength by maintaining continual wars against demonized "enemies."

Among its other features, *The Handmaid's Tale* is a treasure trove of feminist/gender studies issues. Here, as elsewhere, Atwood examines sexual politics from numerous angles. Is there a basic, essential difference between the sexes, and is this difference biological, or culturally determined? Women can't add, says the Commander, for women "one and one and one and one don't make four" only just "one and one and one and one," and this Offred concedes:

> What the Commander said is true. One and one and one and one don't equal four. Each one remains unique, there is no way of joining them together. They cannot be exchanged, one for the other. They cannot replace each other.

Yet women beware women!—for the patriarchy has shrewdly conscripted categories of women to control and exploit other women: in the Gilead social hierarchy there are Wives, Aunts, Marthas with grim, obligatory duties to perform. If they fail to bear children, or when they're beyond the age of childbearing, Handmaids are likely to be shipped off to the dread Colonies with other rebellious, useless or elderly women, where their fate is to clear away corpses after battles, to prevent the outbreak of plague, and to clean up toxic dumps and radiation spills: "They figure you've got three years maximum, before your nose falls off and your skin peels away like rubber gloves." As in pre-Gilead America, or Victorian England, men of the privileged class have access to brothels, in which, in secret, the hypocritical "family values" of their society are cheerfully flouted; the Commander takes Offred, in ludicrous sex-pot costume, to Jezebel's, a *Playboy*-fantasy bordello exclusively for the use of officers and "trade delegations, of course." And, as in Shirley Jackson's "The Lottery," ordinary, repressed individuals in Gilead, in this case women, are regularly forced to, or allowed to, participate in bloody Dionysian murders called Participutations, in which a man, said to be a "rapist," is literally torn into pieces: "The air is bright with adrenaline, we are permitted anything and this is freedom." Offred, who has no wish to participate in such bloodshed, finds herself ravenously hungry after the ceremony: "This is monstrous, but nonetheless it's true. Death makes me hungry."

Like other Atwood fictions, *The Handmaid's Tale* is not a simple narrative. As she tells her story Offred frequently remarks that it's a "reconstruction" and that, at crucial times, she is not telling the truth, or offering variants of the truth, in her description of her furtive love affair with the Commander's chauffeur Nick, for instance:

> It didn't happen that way either. I'm not sure how it happened; not exactly. All I can hope for is a reconstruction: the way love feels is always only approximate.

In the startling appendix to the novel titled "Historical Notes on *The Handmaid's Tale*," we learn that Offred has not been writing her story but recording it in a sequence of secret tapes, to be discovered long after her death in the ruins of what was once the city of Bangor, Maine. Abruptly the reader is catapulted into a more conventionally science-fiction future, provided with a "partial transcript of the proceedings of the Twelfth Symposium on Gileadean Studies held at the University of Denay, Nunavit, on June 25, 2195"; our narrator Offred has long since vanished, like the nightmare Republic of Gilead, preserved two hundred years later in historical archives under the supervision of pompous (male) academics like Professor Pieixoto, Director, Twentieth and Twenty-first Century Archives, Cambridge University, England. (Reassuring to know that, though the United States is no more, there yet remains not only England, but a university protective of "liberal arts.") As the Handmaid's Tale is an urgent, personal, "female" document, so the academics' "male" commentary on it is glib, condescending, fatuous, and self-serving. Atwood has said in interviews that she wanted to end *The Handmaid's Tale* on an optimistic note[3] to indicate that the Republic of Gilead did not last forever, and to provide the reader with "historical" information unavailable to Offred, yet how deflating is this heavily ironic coda, how much more appropriate to that most perishable of literary genres, the academic satire, than to a work of such raw, urgent power as the Handmaid's Tale within *The Handmaid's Tale*. The appendix makes of the novel an astute, provocative social commentary, where its absence would have made the novel an abiding work of art ending with Offred's hopeful voice ("And so I step up, into the darkness within; or else the light").

The strikingly titled *Oryx and Crake*, Atwood's other notable work of speculative fiction, is a yet more ambitious and darkly prophetic work than *The Handmaid's Tale*, set in a near-future, post-apocalyptic terrain that is reverting to wilderness after a plague deliberately induced by the deranged scientist-genius Crake has wiped out most of mankind. (The madman/idealist Crake, self-named for the red-necked crake, a rare Australian bird extinct by the era of *Oryx and Crake*, is a credible descendent of Mary Shelley's Dr. Frankenstein and a younger variant of the genocidal-minded idealist of "The Last Flight of Dr. Ain" by James Tiptree, Jr.) Narrated from the perspective of Jimmy, or Snowman as he calls himself, but not in Jimmy's first-person voice, *Oryx and Crake* is a highly conceptual, skillfully executed performance by a writer clearly impassioned by her subject: our endangered environment, and our endangered species. By turns tragic, serio-comic, farcical and blackly satiric, the novel suggests such classic films as Stanley Kubrick's *Dr. Strangelove*, Ridley Scott's *Blade Runner*, and the Australian-set Mad Max films of George Miller; its literary predecessors include Jonathan Swift's *Gulliver's Travels* ("The Voyage to Laputa"), Mary Shelley's *The Last Man*, H. G. Wells's *The Time Machine* and *The Island of Dr. Moreau*, and Huxley's *Brave New World*. Atwood's epigraph from Swift, a typically Swiftian double entendre, is instructive:

> I could perhaps like others have astonished you with strange improbable tales; but I rather chose to relate plain matter of fact in the simplest manner and style; because my principal design was to inform you, and not to amuse you.

In the nightmare world recalled by Jimmy, before Crake's plague-apocalypse, as in a parody of Marxist expectation the repressive nation-states of such dystopias as *1984* and *The Handmaid's Tale* seem to have withered away, replaced by gigantic global corporations ("HelthWyzer," "CorpSetCorps") whose control over individuals is invisible and near absolute; and whose financing of science is chillingly utilitarian and unprincipled. In this all-too-credible variant of Huxley's narcotized utopia, "demi-autistic" young scientists like Jimmy's school friend Crake of the Watson-Crick Institute are developing drugs like BlyssPluss, a super-Viagra with, as Crake says enthusiastically, the power to "protect the user against all known sexually transmitted diseases" as well as simultaneously "provide an unlimited supply of libido and sexual prowess, coupled with a generalized sense of energy and well-being"—all this, and it prolongs youth. A fourth capability, Crake says, would not be advertised:

The BlyssPluss Pill would also act as a sure-fire one-time-does-it-all-birth-control pill, for male and female alike, thus automatically lowering the population level ...

"So basically you're going to sterilize people without them knowing it under the guise of giving them the ultra in orgies," [Jimmy said].

"That's a crude way of putting it," said Crake.

Yet more diabolically, pharmaceutical companies are researching new diseases for which new, expensive medical technologies and drugs will be required: "The best diseases," said Crake, "would be those that cause lingering illnesses."

Both Jimmy and Crake are the offspring of scientists in the hire of giant corporations; both Jimmy's (fugitive) mother and Crake's (murdered) father were rebels. Jimmy is a feckless arts major who must attend the under-funded, falling-down Martha Graham Academy surrounded by slummy "pleeblands" while the science-prodigy Crake attends the prestigious, lavishly funded Watson-Crick Institute fondly known as "Asperger's U." Like one of Swift's enthusiastic Laputians, Crake takes Jimmy on a guided tour through the research center whose grotesque mascot is a "spoat-gider" ("one of the first successful splices ... goat crossed with spider") and where highly specialized young scientists are working in such fields as "NeoAgriculture" (their project is a rapidly growing, seemingly headless chicken to be marketed as "Chickie Nobs") and "BioDefences" ("wolvogs"—wolf-dogs). Inevitably, some of these exotic new transgenic species have slipped out of Watson-Crick laboratories to reproduce their kind in nature—or what remains of nature: "snats," "cane toads," "rakunks." In his trek in the jungle-terrain (somewhere in what was once the United States, in approximately 2025), Jimmy encounters such cinematic creatures as a rabbit that glows in the dusk, "a greenish glow filched from the iridicytes of a deep-sea jellyfish in some long-ago experiment." (Lest one think that the fiction-writer is inventing such transgenic wonders, see Suzanne Anker and Dorothy Nelkin's appallingly fascinating *The Molecular Gaze: Art in the Genetic Age* where on page 94 an identical rabbit by the bio-artist Eduardo Kac, "GFP Bunny," appears as "art.")[4]

Crake is the deranged idealist who would rid the world of human cruelty and destructiveness, though he doesn't himself believe in either God or Nature and would appear to be wholly amoral. In place of *Homo sapiens* Crake has created a new species of humanity: simple, placid, dull-normal creatures lacking any sense of ego, or humor, for whom sex is a routine physiological function and who are programmed by their creator to die suddenly at the age of thirty, in the prime of life. The Children of Crake, as Jimmy calls them, are physically beautiful, perfectly proportioned, of no more human interest than "animated statues." For these child-like creatures, the world's civilizations have been wiped out. New birth myths must be created for them by Snowman, who ironically finds himself revered by the Children of Crake as their savior, after Crake's death.

The constraining mantle of post-apocalyptic genre is borne lightly by Atwood in *Oryx and Crake*, but such cautionary fantasies have become so popular in recent decades that revitalizing the form is a considerable challenge. Where there is an apocalypse, there must be an apocalypse-catalyst, or causer: the monomaniac Mad Scientist. Where there is such a villain, there must be a foil: the sensitive witness, the survivor who, like Ishmael, lives to tell the tale. There may even be a third person, a love object, for whom the two contend, in this case the former prostitute Oryx, whom Crake hires to educate the new breed of humans. She becomes for the Children of Crake the truly female figure. How to humanly register, still more feel any emotional involvement with characters like Jimmy/Snowman and the elusive Oryx when, as the novel hopes to persuade us, the earth's entire population, billions of men, women, children, are dying? Such vast cataclysms leave us unmoved no matter how skillfully rendered by so trenchant and committed a writer as Atwood, though visual dramatizations, as in Steven Spielberg's recent remake of *The War of the Worlds*, can rouse the viewer to a visceral horror that might seem to substitute for an emotional engagement. With its plethora of freaky forms, *Oryx and Crake* suggests one of those unnerving Saul Steinberg drawings in which recognizable human figures are surrounded by bizarre cartoon characters, human and animal and geometrical, some of them here stick figures.

Like *The Handmaid's Tale* and *Surfacing*, *Oryx and Crake* is tantalizingly open-ended. Jimmy/Snowman discovers that he isn't the last specimen of *Homo sapiens* left on earth after all—but will he, can he, dare he approach the other survivors? In a moment that replicates that of Atwood's unnamed protagonist in *Surfacing*, who contemplates her lover at a distance, undecided whether to answer his calls to her, Jimmy/Snowman contemplates his fellow human beings at a similar distance and withdraws: "Zero hour, Snowman thinks. Time to go."

Where Atwood's recent novels *Alias Grace* and *The Blind Assassin*, like *Oryx and Crake*, have been ambitiously high-concept fiction buttressed by a considerable amount of research, *Moral Disorder*, Atwood's newest gathering of short stories, is domestic realism at its most compelling: eleven sharply focused, intensely personal stories that function like chapters in an elliptical memoirist novel. In the seemingly artless, anecdotal prose of such previous stories of Atwood's as "Rape Fantasies," "Hair Jewellery," and "Giving Birth" (*Dancing Girls*, 1982) and the beautifully rendered "Significant Moments in the Life of My Mother" (*Bluebeard's Egg*, 1986), Atwood takes us through the life of her protagonist Nell from the age of eleven, when her sister is born, to late middle age when Nell's children are grown and gone and she and her husband Tig are living in an age of "bad news": "We don't like bad news, but we need it. We need to know about it in case it's coming our way." As Nell's life is inextricably entwined with the lives of others—family, friends, lovers, her husband and his family, even an assortment of wonderfully individualized farm animals—we come to know her small, narrowly focused world as if it were our own. *Moral Disorder* is likely to be read, perhaps misread, as Margaret Atwood's most explicitly autobiographical fiction though Nell is not a writer, nor even a creative artist, but, simply, a decent, morally responsible and astute individual upon whom nothing is lost. As Nell thinks at the end of the funny, heartrending title story:

Maybe she would grow cunning, up here on the farm. Maybe she would absorb some of the darkness, which might not be darkness at all but knowledge. She would turn into a woman others came to for advice. She would be called in emergencies. She would roll up her sleeves and dispense with sentimentality, and do whatever blood-soaked, bad-smelling thing had to be done. She would become adept with axes.

Early in *Moral Disorder*, in the ironically titled "The Art of Cooking and Serving," we return another time to the wilderness setting of *Surfacing*, except that the focus isn't now on an adult daughter who has lost both her parents but on an eleven-year-old girl anxiously caught up in the mystery and dread of her middle-aged mother's pregnancy: "I couldn't understand why [my mother] had chosen to do what she'd done—why she'd turned herself into this listless, bloated version of herself, thus changing the future—my future—into something shadow-filled and uncertain. I thought she'd done it on purpose. It didn't occur to me that she might have been ambushed." Warned by her father that her mother could become "very ill" unless the daughter takes over the most strenuous household tasks, the girl thinks: "He always thought I knew more than I knew, and that I was bigger than I was, and older, and hardier. What he mistook for calmness and competence was actually fright." Only after the baby's birth, when the family has returned to the city, and the girl is older, does she become empowered, impulsively, to rebel against her mother and the household duties that have shadowed her; at the cusp of adolescence, Atwood's yet-unnamed narrator is alert to "seductive and tawdry and frightening pleasures" of her own.

Subsequent linked stories—"The Headless Horseman," "My Last Duchess"—take the girl through a relatively conventional middle-class adolescence, distinguished by an uncommon interior life:

> I hadn't yet discovered that I lived in a sort of transparent balloon, drifting over the world without making much contact with it, and that the people I knew appeared to me at a different angle from the one at which they appeared to themselves; and that the reverse was also true. I was a lot smaller to others, up there in my balloon, than I was to myself. I was also blurrier.

In flash-forwards we learn that the younger sister, imagined as a "menace" before her birth, has turned out to be in fact a menace of a kind: she is an emotionally unstable, chronically depressed individual for whom Atwood's narrator feels a helpless sort of sisterly responsibility. The depressed sister speaks obsessively of "leaving": "I should just check out. I'm useless here. It's too much effort," which the narrator interprets as:

> She doesn't mean my house. She means her body. She means the planet Earth. I can see the same thing she's seeing: it's a cliff edge, it's a bridge with a steep drop, it's the end. That's what she wants: *The End*. Like the end of a story.

Because *Moral Disorder* is rooted in domestic realism, and not in tragedy, or Gothic melodrama, the depressed younger sister never kills herself but survives, unremarkably, into adulthood: "She takes a pill every day, for a chemical imbalance she was born with. That was it, all along."

As *Moral Disorder* moves forward in time, out of the relatively staid 1950s and into the "moral disorder" of the 1960s. Atwood's unnamed narrator acquires the no-nonsense name of Nell as she acquires, apparently through the maneuvering of her lover's wife Oona, a very nice man named Tig, and Tig's two sons for whom she must care, as a responsible (if unmarried) stepmother. Belatedly Nell realizes:

> She was being interviewed, in a way: Oona had her fingered for the position of second wife, or if not a second wife exactly, something second. Something secondary. Something controllable. A sort of concubine. She was to serve as Tig's *other company*, so that Oona could get on with the life of her own she was so determined to lead.

Poor Nell, who doesn't even cheat at solitaire! In the heady 1960s where "all games had changed at once and earlier structures had fallen apart and everyone had begun pretending that the very notion of rules was obsolete" Nell finds herself in approximately the position she'd been boxed into, at eleven: caretaker.

In the linked stories "Moral Disorder" and "White Horse" Atwood ventures into the rural Ontario that has been Alice

Munro's literary province, as into a canny, often very funny dissection of the sexual politics of the era. These are poignant stories crammed with richly nostalgic detail, rueful, wise, elegiac; years later, Nell drives past the farm where she'd lived so crowded and tumultuous a life, seeing how "[t]he farmhouse itself had lost its ramshackle appearance. It looked serene and welcoming, and somewhat suburban."

The two linked stories that end the collection, "The Labrador Fiasco" and "The Boys at the Lab," return us to Atwood's unnamed narrator, now a middle-aged woman caring for her elderly parents. In the first of these, the father, weakened from a stroke, takes comfort in being read to by his daughter from an account of the ill-fated expedition into the wilds of Labrador undertaken by the doomed American explorers Hubbard and Wallace in 1903; in this somber story the narrator's father suddenly peers at her with the remark: "You seem to have become very old all of a sudden." "The Boys at the Lab" is essentially a portrait of the narrator's mother that will evoke, to readers familiar with Atwood's fiction, similar portraits of strong yet elusive maternal figures, including the ghostly mother of *Surfacing*. Now the mother is bedridden, near-blind and near-deaf:

> Talking into her ear is like talking into the end of a long narrow tunnel that leads through the darkness to a place I can't really imagine. What does she do in there all day? All day, and all night. What does she think about? Is she bored, is she sad, what's really going on?

Like Atwood's captive "murderess" Grace Marks who saves herself by emulating that prototype of all female storytellers Scheherazade, Atwood's narrator understands that her function at her mother's bedside is to tell stories; to make "legendary" what was once, decades ago at the summer wilderness camp, the stuff of ordinary life: "The stories she most wants to hear are about herself, herself when younger; herself when much younger." When the mother's memory at last fades, the narrator must evoke, out of her own imagination, an ending to the final story she has told her mother. What more eloquent and heartrending ending to this work of fiction published nearly thirty-five years after *Surfacing*, a final evocation of the wilderness site in northern Quebec to which Atwood's father brought his family each summer: "Then they all climb up the hill, toward the Lab, and vanish among the trees."

IN THE EMPEROR'S DREAM HOUSE:
CLAIRE MESSUD

The Emperor's Children
by Claire Messud

> Great geniuses have the shortest biographies. Their
> cousins can tell you nothing about them. They
> lived in their writings, and so their house and
> street life was trivial and commonplace.
>
> —RALPH WALDO EMERSON, QUOTED IN
> *THE EMPEROR'S CHILDREN*

1.

Nietzsche tells us: "Poets behave shamelessly toward their
experiences: they exploit them." But is this so, invariably? In
prose fiction, as in poetry? It has become a commonplace as-
sumption that even writers of ambition are inspired primarily
by their own lives and by the experiences of their generations,
fed by the influence of the great, self-absorbed and -obsessed
Modernists (Joyce, Proust, Lawrence) and by mid-twentieth-
century American "confessional" poets (Lowell, Berryman,
Sexton, Plath); as if the autobiographical pulse is ubiquitous,
beating visibly, or invisibly, fueling the very act of creation.

Who needs a muse, where there is a mirror? What need for any effort of the imagination, in the creation of poetry or prose in the mode of Robert Lowell: "Yet why not say what happened?"

Yet there is an equally powerful instinct to resist autobiography/confession, to forge purely imagined, or assimilated, literary subjects; for some writers, even those for whom the stylistic experimentations of Modernism are extremely attractive, the very act of "identification" must involve distance, difference. "If Art does not enlarge men's sympathies, it does nothing morally," as George Eliot once remarked. That art should be guided by, or even suggest, a moral compass seems, in the post-Modernist era, quaintly remote, quixotic; yet there are numerous, notable writers for whom the nineteenth-century ideal of "enlarging sympathy" is predominant. Among contemporary writers whose inspiration seems, at times magically, to be the very antithesis of self, Claire Messud has demonstrated a remarkable imaginative capacity.

Born in 1966 in the United States, educated at Yale and Cambridge, Messud has set her several novels in such widely disparate places as the remote, punishing islands of Bali and Skye (*When the World Was Steady*, 1994); in a meticulously realized south of France and in Algeria under French colonization (*The Last Life*, 1999); in Ukraine, wartime (World War II) Europe, and Toronto ("A Simple Tale," in *The Hunters*, 2001). Messud's debut novel *When the World Was Steady* is a tenderly ironic double portrait of two hapless middle-aged English sisters who travel to very different islands: Emmy, abruptly di-

vorced by her Australian husband, leaves her affluent residence
in Sydney to make a pilgrimage of sorts to the exotic island
of Bali, for no reason other than a wish to escape the place
of her humiliation; Virginia, the younger and more naive sister, a spinster caretaker of an aging, difficult mother, agrees
to accompany her mother on a misguided sentimental journey
to the mother's birthplace in a remote area of the Scottish island of Skye. Each of the Simpson sisters has adventures on
her island, of a kind that might be called romantic, or mystical; each leaves her island a changed woman, but not very
changed. Emmy leaves Bali and almost immediately reverts to
her former, superficial self, in a flurry of planning her daughter's wedding: "This was her way of being, she recognized, and
her way of not suffering too much, which was why she had
come home to the mantles—however tattered—that she knew
how to wear." Virginia, the more thoughtful of the sisters, as
she is the lonelier and more poignant, seems to have lost even
her wan, anemic Christian faith when she returns from her island adventure:

> Virginia had concurred, falsely, that God might Him-
> self be in the wrong, or at least, might be cruel. But for
> herself, she attributed fault to human inadequacy and
> she continued to try to believe that He Himself could not
> disappoint . . . But out in the world, in the London that
> looked ruthlessly and exactly the same since her return from
> Skye . . . she could discern only emptiness and terror, a mo-
> rass of humanity's failure masked only by its transparent il-
> lusions of meaning.

As if the "good women" so attentively observed by Barbara Pym and Anita Brookner were taken out of their routine, domestic lives, given a shake and made to experience a metaphysical chill, before being brought back safely home again.

Messud's most ambitious novel is the very long, very detailed and coolly impassioned *The Last Life*, a sustained feat of ventriloquism narrated by an expatriated young Frenchwoman named Sagasse La Basse, living now in New York City ("with my burden of Original Sin" and studying at Columbia University, who looks back upon her turbulent early adolescence in a resort town on the Mediterranean, amid a family of French Algerian emigrants. Sagasse's mother is an American in exile who is never allowed to imagine that she really belongs in France, or in the stultifyingly close-knit and self-regarding bourgeois La Basse family; Sagasse's paternal grandfather is a well-to-do hotelier with French Nationalist leanings, whose single, impulsive act of violence, discharging a firearm at teenaged trespassers on his property, precipitates the disintegration of the family, including the suicide of Sagasse's father. The novel is recounted in a tone of obsessive memoir, in which each recalled detail is equivalent to all others as in an inviolable incantation, an expression of a doomed yet prideful lineage:

> we knew ourselves to be bound to our faith, cement-bound, blood-bound, in a proximity shared by only a few hundred thousand, those who were, like us, exiles of French Algeria . . . The logic of my upbringing was indisputable: we were Catholics, we were French, we were Algerian. Ours,

as a personal heritage, a gift indeed, most particularly for us, the Europeans of North Africa, was the doctrine of Original Sin.

There is a curious, largely unexamined rift between the highly sophisticated inner language of Sagasse and Sagasse's outer life, in which she behaves like a spoiled, somewhat dyspeptic fifteen-year-old, a moody child of privilege with (somehow) the power of an artist to re-create La Basse family histories in France and in Algeria, at second hand; as if the precocious young narrator of Françoise Sagan's *Bonjour Tristesse* were gifted with the political/cultural insight of a Camus, or the young Thomas Mann of *Buddenbrooks*. So deeply immersed is Sagasse in her subject, so persuasive in her interior voice, the La Basse clan, somewhat petty, self-destructive and exasperating individuals, emerges as figures of significance, and sympathy. Sagasse's lengthy homage to her past is an homage to the mystique of French Algeria, where Sagasse herself never lived; and to the imperial France that colonized Algeria, only to fall fatally in love with its creation. Both Augustine and Camus are quoted liberally in *The Last Life*, but it is Augustine whose melancholy fatalism, disguised as religious piety, speaks to the La Basse sensibility: "From the evidence of this life itself, a life so full of so many and such various evils that it can hardly be called living, we must conclude that the whole human race is being punished."

How necessary, then, that the exiled Sagasse reinvent herself as an American, which is to say as anonymous:

And in time, America becomes a kind of home, without the crippling, warming embrace of history . . . In a gesture of perversity, I studied history, as an undergraduate, the wild idealism of the Founding Fathers, the piling, stone upon recent stone, of a culture notable for its interest not in the past but in the future: a different, an American, way of thinking.

At the novel's end, in an eloquent coda, the solitary Sagasse hints at a future involving a fellow graduate student at the university, whom, so far, she has only observed from a distance:

Not long in America, he has washed up here like Phlebas the Phoenician, but alive, from the wars of his homeland—and of mine—a home that exists only in the imaginary. His name is Hamed. How to tell him, who might have been my cousin, the stories I know? How to avoid it?

The oddly paired novellas of Messud's *The Hunters* would seem to proffer variants on themes of alienation and urban dislocation: "A Simple Tale" is the radically compressed life-story of an aging Ukrainian woman, a kind of European immigrant Everywoman, who has worked for an eccentric Canadian woman named Mrs. Ellington for nearly fifty years, in the vein of Flaubert's self-effacing homage to "ordinary" life, "A Simple Heart"; "The Hunters," set in a grubby district of London, is narrated by an eccentric individual of no evident sex, age, or ethnic background ("This was . . . a time in which I had no life. Or rather, in which I had no life that could be seen"), given to arch Nabokovian observations and fantastical speculations about his, or her, neighbors, in the vein of that most riddlesome of Henry James's late voyeuristic novels *The Sacred Fount*.

What links these seemingly antithetical works of fiction is the singular author who would seem to exhibit, perhaps more convincingly than James Joyce himself did, those ideal attributes of the artist set forth in Stephen Dedalus's credo in *A Portrait of the Artist as a Young Man*:

> The personality of the artist, at first a cry or a cadence or a mood and then a fluid and lambent narrative, finally refines itself out of existence, impersonalizes itself, so to speak . . . The artist, like the God of creation, remains within or behind or beyond or above his handiwork, invisible, refined out of existence, indifferent, paring his fingernails.

2.

Curiously titled, *The Emperor's Children* suggests a gloss on the cliché of the emperor's "new clothes": shared delusion, communal madness, nullity. One of the characters in the novel has a work-in-progress titled *The Emperor's Children Have No Clothes*, described in the hyperventilated terms of contemporary publishing jargon:

> Marina Thwaite's groundbreaking debut book demystifies [parental neuroses], unraveling them through the threads of

our clothing, and more particularly of our children's clothes. In this brilliant analysis of who we are and the way it determines how our kids dress, Marina Thwaite reveals the forms and patterns that both are and lie beneath the fabric of our society. In so doing, she bares children, their parents, and our culture at large to an unprecedented and frank scrutiny, and in her truth-telling shows us incontrovertibly that the emperor's children have no clothes.

(How skillful, and how funny, Claire Messud is in her new role as satirist! An entire chapter of *The Emperor's Children*, titled "Vows by Lisa Solomon, Special to *The New York Times*," is virtually indistinguishable from the "real thing.") The speaker here is a self-styled "revolutionary" named Ludovic Seeley with a "pale, oval, Nabokovian [and] predatory face" and the young woman to whom he is speaking is Marina Thwaite, daughter of the prominent public intellectual Murray Thwaite, who has been working halfheartedly for years on a pseudo-cultural exposé of children's fashions. All that the oddly named Ludovic Seeley does, or says, is seductive, or manipulative, for Seeley is both a stock figure of women's romance ("His face, so distinctive, struck her as that of a nineteenth-century portrait, a Sargent perhaps, an embodiment of sardonic wisdom and society, of aristocratic refinement") and a figure of sinister foreboding, exuding the fascination of a "reptile, a beautiful but dangerous one"; Seeley speaks openly of his admiration for Napoleon, and his wish to "unmask" and "debunk" individuals of prominence, like Marina's father Murray Thwaite, the novel's "emperor": "the country's liberal conscience."

The classic European novel which *The Emperor's Children* most resembles is Flaubert's *L'Éducation sentimentale* (1869), the author's third novel and by some, including Flaubert himself, considered his masterpiece. In the guise of naturalism, *L'Éducation sentimentale* is a lengthy, relentless satire fueled by Flaubertian contempt for the hypocrisy, venality, and vanity of Parisian men and women during the general period 1840 to 1851, an era, in Flaubert's vision, of money-grubbing madness. The "sentimental education" of Flaubert's zestfully misanthropic novel is that of an idealistic young man from the provinces who has come to Paris to study law: the romantic-minded Frédéric Moreau, naive, credulous in the way of a male Emma Bovary, doomed to perpetual disappointment by life and revealed, in time, in a typical Flaubertian flourish, to be as empty-headed as everyone else. The "young man from the provinces" of *The Emperor's Children* is an awkward American cousin of Flaubert's Frédéric, one Frederick "Bootie" Tubbs, overweight, slovenly, with intellectual/writerly pretensions, who has dropped out of college at Oswego and has plummeted, as his anxious mother notes, from being a brainy "phenomenon" (valedictorian of his Watertown High School class) to being a "freak"; a resident of dreary Watertown, New York, who somehow has the conviction that he is, or is meant to be, a genius. Unemployed, unemployable, supported by his doting mother, "Bootie" feeds upon the fantasy of living "like a philosopher, the way Emerson said that Plato had, alone and invisible, known to the world only through his work . . . He had to get to New York, for this: to his as yet unalerted teacher and mentor. To Murray Thwaite."

As these excerpts suggest, *The Emperor's Children* is a work of satiric comedy, a considerable departure for Claire Messud whose prose style has exuded a certain *gravitas* in the past. Ambitious, multi-layered, set predominantly in Manhattan in the months leading up to, and following, 9/11, *The Emperor's Children* is Messud's first American-set novel, as it is her first work of fiction to rapidly shift perspective from chapter to chapter, leaping about, with authorial freedom, among a number of interlocked characters. Such omnipotence suggests the airy glibness of a comedy of manners, or satire; Messud eschews here the dramatic intensity of a single perspective, like that of Sagasse La Basse, in the service of an "unmasking" and "debunking" project of her own. Yet *The Emperor's Children* is never so bleakly misanthropic as *L'Éducation sentimentale*, nor even so corrosive as the urban satires of Messud's contemporaries Martin Amis and Zadie Smith; its prevailing tone of crisp bemused irony suggests the less savage comedies of manners of Alison Lurie, Diane Johnson, and Iris Murdoch. Even as she unmasks them, Messud can't resist evoking sympathy for her mostly foolish, self-deluded characters; and can't deny even the fatuous Bootie the possibility of regeneration and redemption in the chaotic aftermath of 9/11.

At the center of *The Emperor's Children*, in the ambiguous, and precarious, role of the "emperor," is the aging, yet still charismatic writer Murray Thwaite, an adjunct professor at Columbia University whose prominence within his circle of admirers seems to cast more a blinding glare than an illumination. Messud's subtly nuanced portrait of a public intellectual as both a revered role model and a "disintegrating giant" is

specific enough to suggest that *The Emperor's Children* is, at
least in part, a *roman à clef*, and yet generic enough to suggest
that Thwaite is an idealized, or inflated, American type:

> Murray Thwaite has built his reputation on being a straight
> shooter. On telling it like it is. From the civil rights move-
> ment and Vietnam right down through Iran Contra and
> Operation Desert Storm, from education policy to work-
> ers' rights and welfare to abortion rights to capital punish-
> ment—Murray Thwaite has voiced significant opinions. We
> have believed him, and believed in him.

(This double-edged encomium has been written by Thwaite's
nephew Bootie who, working as Thwaite's assistant, and living in Thwaite's impressively sprawling Central Park West
apartment, is secretly preparing an exposé titled "Murray
Thwaite: A Disappointed Portrait.") Apart from publishing
so frequently that he has begun to plagiarize his own material, Murray Thwaite has been secretly composing his life's
work, titled *How to Live*, part aphorisms, part essay, in the
grandiloquent manner of Emerson; a project that, if it is ever
completed, "would at last and indisputably elevate his name
from the ranks of competent, even courageous journalists and
thoughtful columnists to the rare air of the immortals." And
Thwaite has not resisted beginning an affair with a woman not
only young enough to be his daughter, but a woman who is his
daughter's best friend.

Yet more vulnerable is Murray Thwaite as the father of
the badly spoiled thirty-year-old ingenue Marina, a "celebrated

native beauty (surely this wasn't of no account?)" who frets about winding up "ordinary, like everyone else." Marina has done virtually nothing since graduating from Brown ten years before except to work as a *Vogue* intern and to have accepted a publisher's advance for her book "about children's fashions and—for this was the spin—about how complex and profound cultural truths—our *mores* entire—could be derived from a society's decision to put little Lulu in a smocked frock or tiny Stacey in sequined hotpants." Having long ago spent the advance for this project, Marina has drifted about in Manhattan literary circles in a "pretense of work," trading on her looks and on being Murray Thwaite's daughter; her vaporous life is given a sudden, if misguided, focus when Marina is seduced by the opportunistic Ludovic Seeley who has been brought to New York to start a high-profile, well-financed "revolutionary" magazine with the goal of exposing hypocrisy, called *The Monitor*. A flashy amalgam of such publications as *New York*, the *New York Observer, Vanity Fair* and the late, buzz-oriented *Talk, The Monitor* is funded by a billionaire publisher ("August Merton, the Australian mogul. Busy buying up Europe, Asia, North America. Everything in English and all to the right") and would seem to be a prime example of what an observer calls "the blurring of left and right politics in pure contrarianism. People who aren't *for* anything, just against everything." Unfortunately for the reptilian Ludovic Seeley and his billionaire backer, the lavish "launch" for *The Monitor* is scheduled for September 12, 2001—by which time its mixture of malice and frivolity has become instantly passé.

The most sympathetic, as she is the most industrious and least self-deluded of the emperor's children, is Marina's college friend Danielle Minkoff, a TV producer for a PBS-like channel who retains the idealism of youth even as she is confronted by the cynicism of the TV marketplace: Danielle's suggestions for programs about the mistreatment of Australian aborigines or an update on AIDS are rejected by her supervisor who urges her toward trendier subjects like cosmetic surgery. Danielle naively rationalizes her affair with Murray Thwaite in the vocabulary of popular romance: "She considered that their connection was almost eerie, a meeting of minds, a Platonic reunion of divided souls." Though Danielle feels a "moral repugnance" for sleeping with a man whose wife has befriended her, she can't resist the primitive charms of the "country's liberal conscience":

> [Thwaite] had loomed shaggy and grand like a crumbling castle, a half-ruin, in the semidarkness of her pristine apartment, his belt unbuckled and his bare torso monumental, and had held her to him so that she could hear his heart beating beneath the grayed fur against her cheek. When he spoke, his voice resounded in his chest, and entered her ear like an echo ... Pressed to his chest she'd felt safe and exhilarated at once, as if swept by an internal breeze; and there seemed little point telling herself that this was immoral.

Messud tries valiantly to pump credibility and feeling into Danielle's love affair with Murray Thwaite ("Like an addict— no, she *was* an addict. She thought about him all the time, or else thought about thinking about him, and the fact that she shouldn't," but the coolly bemused, sardonic tone of much of *The Emperor's Children*, like the swiftly moving chapters, works against the myopia of romance. One feels that Danielle has been pressed into service in a role not suited for her, like a miscast actress, who, apart from the romantic scenes expected of her, is more convincing elsewhere. When Thwaite breaks off his affair with Danielle immediately, on the morning of 9/11, Danielle reacts by succumbing to a protracted depression that conflates the blow to her ego and the terrorist catastrophe:

> there was no call to feel anything, there was nothing to feel because you weren't worth anything to anyone, you'd had your heart, or was it your guts, or both, taken out, you'd been eviscerated ... she had known, she had known all along, and now there was nothing but sorrow and this was how it was going to be, now, always.

The most vividly imagined of Thwaite's erstwhile children is "Bootie" Tubbs the overweight, egomaniacal, parasitic nephew from upstate New York who imagines that he is of the elect company of Plato, Emerson, Tolstoy though he has difficulty reading a book to its conclusion; from the vantage point of youth, he soon discovers flaws in his uncle/benefactor:

> He couldn't have known beforehand how he would feel about it, that the manuscript [*How to Live*] would seem to him both pretentious and trite ... He believed now that

the Great Man had been an illusion all along, mere window dressing. Reluctantly, he slid into alignment with Ludovic Seeley: Murray Thwaite was one great con trick, a lazy, self-absorbed, star-fucking con trick.

Naturally, with the pitiless rectitude of youth, Bootie feels the need to "expose" Murray Thwaite in an article for *The Monitor*. Exasperating, irrepressible, Bootie is an ideal comic creation; real enough to make any of us shudder at the prospect of a youthful relative coming to visit, especially one who professes to "admire" us. So obtuse is Bootie that, after he gives "Murray Thwaite: A Disappointed Portrait" to his uncle to read, he's genuinely surprised that Thwaite responds angrily: "Where the fuck do you get off, you little nullity, you common little piece of shit, snooping around in my papers and crapping all over them?" Expelled from the emperor's lofty residence on Central Park West, the forlorn but unrepentant Bootie rents a room in Brooklyn and, on the morning of 9/11, somewhere in the vicinity of ground zero, disappears. (Or so it seems to Bootie's relatives.)

The terrorist attack leveling the World Trade Center towers is placed strategically late in *The Emperor's Children*, in chapter fifty-eight of sixty-seven chapters, and, viewed primarily through Danielle's stricken eyes, it is elliptically and convincingly rendered. Such profound "historic" events, introduced into works of fiction, in which nothing can be accidental, have the force of cosmic rebukes against the pettiness of human beings and the vanity of human wishes; at once, the threat of Ludovic Seeley and *The Monitor* evaporates, and the sinister Seeley fades from the narrative like a banished demon. Murray Thwaite not only returns to his devoted wife Annabel (who'd been entirely unaware that he was having an affair with their daughter's closest friend) and, true to his reputation as the country's liberal conscience, responds to the demands of "his public":

> He had much writing, and speaking, to do. He formulated a reasoned middle ground that, while not stretching so far as those who claimed America deserved it, nevertheless reminded his suffering companions of the disenfranchised agonies of the West Bank, or of the ever-growing population of disenfranchised Muslim youth around the globe . . . Murray couldn't help but be aware of the irony that Bootie's [supposed] death had granted him greater nobility, an importance—he knew it to be false—as a man of justice, unswayed by the arrows of misfortune. But perhaps, had he been there to see it, Bootie would at last have been proud of his uncle.

As for the invincible Bootie: hurriedly fleeing the chaos of 9/11, on foot, Bootie thrills to feel himself utterly alone in an "unknown country," granted a vision he interprets as Emersonian: "He had been given—his fate—the precious opportunity to *be* again, not to be as he had been. Because as far as anyone knew, he *wasn't*." In the spirit of Musil's *The Man Without Qualities*, another weighty book he'd been trying to read, indifferent to his mother's and relatives' probable concern for him, Bootie simply relocates to Miami and re-invents himself, in a fitting conclusion to Messud's mirror of our foundering times:

> This time, he was ready. This person in motion was who he was becoming: it was something, too: a man, someday, with qualities . . . Great geniuses have the shortest biographies, he told himself; and take them by surprise. Yes. He would.

AFTER THE APOCALYPSE: JIM CRACE

The Pesthouse
by Jim Crace
Nan A. Talese/Doubleday

> Sometimes she wondered if America had once been
> populated by a race of fools. So many old things
> from that time had lost their grip on the world and
> dropped away.
> —*THE PESTHOUSE*

Long the province of genre entertainments—science fiction, dystopian fantasy, pre- and post-Apocalyptic films like *On the Beach, Blade Runner*, and the *Mad Max* trilogy—the future has been boldly explored in recent years by such writers as P. D. James (*The Children of Men*, 1993), John Updike (*Toward the End of Time*, 1997), Margaret Atwood (*The Handmaid's Tale*, 1986; *Oryx and Crake*, 2003), Doris Lessing (*Mara and Dann*, 1999), Michael Cunningham ("Like Beauty," in *Specimen Days*, 2005), Cormac McCarthy (*The Road*, 2006). Now comes a grim prophetic fable by the much-admired British writer Jim Crace who has so imaginatively evoked long-ago, even prehistoric worlds (*The Gift of Stones*, 1988, is set in the Bronze Age; *Quarantine*, 1997, in the time of Christ) and whose brilliantly executed *Being Dead* (1999) manages the considerable feat of being both the most pitilessly unromantic love story you are likely to encounter—a minute observation, as through a microscope, of the processes of organic decay in the lifeless bodies of a middle-aged married couple—and the most unexpectedly romantic: "This was the world as it had always been, plus something less which once was doctors of zoology."

Kingsley Amis once remarked that there isn't much point to writing if you can't offend someone; it might be said that there isn't much point to writing about the future unless you frighten someone. Certainly the great majority of future-set fictions, from H. G. Wells's *The Time Machine* (1895) to Aldous Huxley's *Brave New World* (1932), George Orwell's *1984* (1949), and Margaret Atwood's two, very different dystopian novels *The Handmaid's Tale* and *Oryx and Crake*, are designed to unsettle and to make the reader think. The genre to which such fiction belongs is fundamentally didactic, instructive; beyond the visceral unsettling, there are crucial lessons to be imparted. In contemporary fiction, such literary excursions into the unknown belong to the sub-genre "speculative fiction": not old, free-style science fiction, involving extraterrestials, but fictions set upon our earth, confronting the consequences of current conditions. The aptly titled *The Pesthouse* is set in "America" in an indeterminate future scarcely distinguishable from a frontier, if not a Neanderthal, past. What remains of the old America has largely reverted to wilderness, much of its soil contaminated by toxins, in the wake of a sequence of catastrophes only vaguely recalled by survivors: the "Grand

Contagion"; "mocking" storms, floods, mud-slides, droughts, famines; "anarchy and spite." Survivors of these catastrophes and their offspring are uneducated, illiterate, in some cases mentally impaired, lacking not only a history of their own predicament, but any sense of its loss. What remains are ill-understood but unquestioned folk sayings: "Metal has brought death into the world. Rust and fire are God's reply." In mounds of old debris, illiterate searchers find what they call "word-ings": "a looping example of the forgotten text that had sur-vived on so many relics of the old country and that for some reason always begged to be touched." Adult men and women are childlike, credulous "like children in a fairy tale" beyond their comprehension. Contemplating an old pair of binoculars, strapping young Franklin Lopez, whose episodic adventures and misadventures *The Pesthouse* tracks, wonders at this mys-terious object "of some material too unnatural and perfect for anybody to make or find anymore." Pre-catastrophe America has only a mythic, not an historic past:

> the country their grandpas and grandmas had talked about,
> a land of profusion, safe from human predators, snake-free,
> and welcoming beyond the hog and hominy of raw place; [a
> country of] good climate, fertile soil, wholesome air and wa-
> ter; plenty of provisions, good pay for labor, kind neighbors,
> good laws, a free government, and a hearty welcome.

In present-day America, Franklin and his young woman com-panion Margaret, embarked upon a pilgrimage of sorts, are continually confronted by ruins:

a debris field of tumbled stone and rock, stained with rust and ancient metal melt. Colossal devastated wheels and iron machines, too large for human hands, stood at the perimeter of the semicircle, as if they had been dumped by long-retreated glaciers and had no purpose now other than to age. Hardly anything grew amid the waste. The earth was poisoned, probably . . . The smell was oily, acidic, and medicinal, the sort of smell even a skunk would avoid.

Mysteriously in *The Pesthouse*, and not very plausibly, the "United States of America" has vanished utterly, without a trace: not a vestige of government remains, nor even a memory of government officials or politicians. Not a vestige of law, the military, science, education, industry, technology, culture, religion. (No churches? No religious leaders, priests? Only a writer unfamiliar with the ever-volatile presence of religion in America from the reign of seventeenth-century Puritans to the political clout of twenty-first-century Born-Again Christians could imagine a post-Apocalyptic America in which fundamentalist Christian sects would not be flourishing.)

The novelty of Crace's somewhat under-imagined blighted Eden is that the population is migrating eastward, ironically reversing the westward migrations of earlier centuries, in a desperate attempt to "emigrate" to Europe, though no one seems to know anything about this promised land, or what experiences might befall them on the gigantic sail ships that have materialized at the water's edge, like apparitions out of Crace's 1994 historical novel *Signals of Distress*, to carry them there:

[Franklin] could not imagine exactly what awaited them when they set foot aboard, what type of people they might be, what language they might speak. But he was sure that life would be more prosperous. How could it not be better there?

Crace's irony is indistinguishable from mockery:

Here was where disease was in command. But there'd be no fever where they were going, would there? They wanted to believe it. There'd be no ague or calenture, no tick disease or cholera, no canker or malaria. Why, they had persuaded themselves, illness would be so rare on that side of the ocean that people would travel for a day just to watch a man sniff.

Franklin Lopez is so naive as to react to his first sighting of what we assume to be the Atlantic Ocean in this way: "But heaven's glory, see the size of it. Who's to say how long you'd need on board a ship before you reached the other bank? All day, I'd say." In the novel's most chilling scene, at the water's edge, mobs of would-be emigrants are examined by men in un-identified black uniforms who mark their foreheads with blue dye if they approve them for passage to Europe and red dye if they reject them; only the few wealthy families, able-bodied young men and boys, and attractive women of child-bearing age are chosen. So desperate are the Americans to escape the "taints and perils" of their country, they seem to be oblivious of the risk of surrendering their freedom and signing on for a wholly unknown fate. Are the sinister great-masted sailing ships slave ships? Are the naive "emigrants" but human cargo to be delivered to European masters? (And why are the European ships nineteenth-century sail ships? Has Europe suffered a crash of civilization like America's?) We never learn, since the principals of *The Pesthouse* decide against emigrating and decide to journey westward, in an abrupt and not very convincing reversal of intention:

> [Franklin and Margaret] knew they had only to find their strength. And then—imagine it—they could begin the journey west again. They could. They could imagine striking out to claim a piece of long-abandoned land and making home in some old place, some territory begging to be used. Going westward, they go free.

The Pesthouse is Jim Crace's eighth novel, and the most self-consciously "mythic." Unlike *Being Dead*, a virtuoso fusion of high-concept fabulism and psychological realism, or such magically evoked imagined worlds as those of *Continent* (1986), *Signals of Distress*, *The Gift of Stones*, and *Quarantine*, *The Pesthouse* is almost purely conceptual, an idea-driven work of prose fiction that might have been more effectively executed in graphic novel form, or in film. Though repeatedly described, the "post-Apocalyptic" landscape is never more than generic, like a film backdrop, and is never made specifically American, which is to say regional—for rural America is regional, and not simply "wilderness." Where in Crace's first, Calvino-inspired novel *Continent*, Crace evoked an imaginary seventh continent through the sheer poetry of language, *The Pesthouse* is blandly and perfunctorily narrated, as if in the debased speech of Dogpatch residents:

> Here were men who'd come from places with flat and functional names like Half-Day Bridge, Boundary Wood, Center Island, and, yes, Ferrytown, but within a day or two they expected to travel on the Dreaming Highway, which led, so they believed, through Give-Your-Word Valley to Achievement Hill and a prospect of the Last Farewell . . . The journey to the boats . . . would be an easy and speedy one. "A hog could roll there in a sack."

We are told that the land was once so fertile "it used to be boasted that you had only to flick a booger on the ground for a mushroom to grow overnight." With deadpan earnestness it is explained how tying a living pigeon against the sole of one of Franklin's feet—"pinioning its wings and backs against his insteps"—once saved Franklin from a deathly illness, since it's known that "diseases depart from the body through the soles of the feet." Franklin is described repeatedly as "tall"— "immensely tall"—while his future mate Margaret is "tiny"— figures of romantic clichés. There is a droll, mock-fairy-tale tone to *The Pesthouse* that grates on the nerves, for it isn't clear, given the faux-naif folksiness of Crace's approximation of American "rural" speech, whether he wants us to feel sympathy for his mentally challenged characters, or laugh at them as fools who have brought their collective doom upon themselves. Here is the affable simpleton Franklin:

he proved to be a useful beast of burden, willing and easily tamed. But making him menacing and dangerous would be beyond the ingenuity of the Devil himself. The man might be big, but he was hardly daunting. He laughed inexplicably and too loudly every once in a while. He blushed like a girl. He did what he was told too readily.

Held captive by a crew of rustlers, as in a Western film, Franklin is menaced by their chief, the worst kind of villain, one who threatens in rhyme: "The man who quits is cut to bits. His toes are separated from his nose." Meanwhile, in a protracted scene of pursuit and escape, Margaret eludes would-be rapists and murderers on foot and on horseback, clutching a baby in her arms; though she has seen the corpse of a recent rape victim, yet she thinks that "probably her danger would prove to be brief and somewhat comical." Comical? Margaret is thirty-six years old and has seen numerous corpses yet she remains inexplicably, absurdly childlike: "*Rape* and *death* were only words to her. Pain she understood a little more." But how is this possible, given what Margaret has experienced? The reader has the uneasy suspicion that the author has forgotten who Margaret is, or is supposed to be, like Franklin an unconvincing character symbolizing Simplicity, Innocence. Yet more forced is an interlude meant to be broadly satiric, when Margaret takes up residence in the Blessed Ark, a commune of sorts presided over by a twenty-member monastic order mysteriously called the Finger Baptists/Helpless Gentlemen whose "flaccid arms and lifeless hands" have become atrophied for want of use. Gaining entrance to the Blessed Ark seems to (comically?) replicate the experience of airline passengers making their way through security checkpoints:

> "Nothing metal, nothing metal," [one of the Finger Baptist devotees] was commanding, walking up and down the line, repeating his instructions and devotions to every group, "Remove all metal from your hair—no antique combs—no knives at all, no silverware, no ear or finger rings, no pans. Metal is the Devil's work. Metal is the cause of greed and war. In here we are . . . the enemies of metal. Check your pockets. Shake out all your rust. Remove your shoes. Unlace your bags."

Inside the Ark, Margaret discovers peculiar rites of homage: devotees spoon food into the mouths of the Finger Baptists/Helpless Gentlemen, who "did not want to feed themselves." Since it is believed that "Hands do Devil's work" these holy men must be serviced by devotees, preferably attractive young women like Margaret who finds herself, as in a campy rerun of Atwood's *Handmaid's Tale*, pressed into duties that include bathing the holy men, cleaning their teeth, dressing and undressing them, massaging and masturbating them: "She found the whole procedure unpleasant and disturbing." No plausible reason is suggested how, or why, in a hardscrabble near-anarchic post-Apocalyptic world, such fatuous individuals as the Helpless Gentlemen have come to exist, still less why anyone would service them; if this is Crace's idea of satire, one is obliged to ask satire of what? (Surely not the Baptist Church? Yet why "Finger *Baptists*"?) The holy men are deluded idealists, perhaps, and/or plain crazy: "The Helpless Gentlemen had set their minds and bodies against the country's ferrous history. Wingless and with withered arms, they'd earned their places at the side of God." None of this is made remotely credible, convincing, or even interesting, calling to mind Aristotle's exasperation in the *Poetics* with episodic plots: "Of imperfect plots and actions the episodic are the worst. By an episodic plot I mean one in which the episodes do not have to each other the relation of either probability or necessity."

What is most baffling about *The Pesthouse* is that, unlike Crace's more characteristic fiction, it seems to lack an inner, intellectual core and to be, in essence, more an action-adventure romance akin to Hollywood Westerns of the 1950s than an original work of speculative fiction. The great strength of Crace's work—nowhere more in evidence than in *Being Dead*, with its fascinating narrative perspective, and *Quarantine*, which so compellingly imagines the fabled "forty days" of Christ's fast in the desert—is its inwardness; yet *The Pesthouse* is all surface, suffused with an air of *déjà vu*. It's as if, setting out for a "happy ending," Crace could only employ puppet-figures as characters. The conclusion of the novel reunites Margaret and Franklin ("joy was fizzing in [Franklin's] lungs"), imagined as mythic Adam and Eve figures destined to re-settle and re-populate America. Abruptly, the novel's tone changes, as in a parody of a sentimental romance:

> It was as if the country that had once been hostile to them
> was regretful for it and was now providing recompense—
> fewer dangers, warmer nights, softer going in a season that

was opening up rather than shutting down. It even decorated the way with early flowers.

No more toxic soil? No more "mocking" storms? Where have "anarchy and spite" disappeared to? In this mawkish upbeat ending in which "Good fortune showed its face" after so much hardship and peril, we are meant to rejoice at the prospect of a new, American-born Adam and Eve lighting out for the territory. If the future is anything like the past, good luck to them.

THE STORY OF X:
SUSANNA MOORE'S *IN THE CUT*

Susanna Moore is the author of three previous novels, set for the most part in her native Hawaii: *My Old Sweetheart* (1982), *The Whiteness of Bones* (1989), and *Sleeping Beauties* (1993). Each is a novel of substance and achievement in the fullest Hawthornian sense—rich with "minute fidelity" to the socially ambiguous, physically seductive world, narrated with sensitivity and intelligence by young women who have broken with their mesmerizing pasts. Of the three, *My Old Sweetheart* is perhaps the most delicately realized, an elegiac reminiscence of an island childhood passed under the spell of the narrator's charismatic but mentally unstable mother, who eventually kills herself. *My Old Sweetheart* is one of those elusive, shimmering works of fiction, bold, impressionistic, subtle, and mysterious, that resist paraphrase and summary, like Marilynne Robinson's equally haunting first novel, *Housekeeping*; like the prose of Katherine Mansfield, Virginia Woolf, the early stories of Eudora Welty. One is reminded too of Jean Rhys's masterpiece *Wide Sargasso Sea*, with its obsessive lyricism and mounting dread. The poisoned paradise of subtropical islands, for those of white skin! *My Old Sweetheart* evolves into something of a mystery as the narrator searches for her eccentric physician-father who seems to have disappeared into Cambodia as a medical relief worker, but the mystery is never resolved.

Perhaps because more structurally ambitious, with many more characters and settings, and many more discursive prose passages, Moore's other two novels are less certain achievements; as if, in exorcising the spell of an island childhood, the author were casting off its power to spellbind as well. Yet, for the writer, there is no direction other than forward, outward. The historical/mythological/archetypal heritage of the past, however richer than the contemporary civilization beyond the island, is simply too much of a burden to be borne. Moore's young women protagonists initiate themselves sexually as a way of self-definition, but the initiations are not always edifying. Mamie of *The Whiteness of Bones* thinks uneasily, in the minutes before, in fact, she is clumsily assaulted in a Chicago hotel room:

> She had always suspected that the mistake of feminism was its refusal to admit the superior, undeniably superior, strength of men—not economic or political strength, that was another thing altogether—but the simple fact that at any moment, [a man] could reach over and snap her narrow wrist in two.

Leaving aside for the moment the fact that feminism has not exactly been unaware of male "superiority" in physical terms, and that the very foundation of feminism may be a reaction in defiance of this "superiority," Moore's passage is notable for its air of passivity, fatalism; it is consistent with Moore's depiction generally in her fiction of unchallenged male aggression. The young woman narrator of Moore's new novel *In the Cut*, inexorably drawn to "big, handsome" men who will abuse her, ponders the difference between male and female perversion: "The action of the man is directed toward a symbol, not himself. The woman acts against herself." "In the cut" means, quite bluntly, "in the cunt." Yet "cut" with its implications of slashing, maiming, is very much to the point.

Where Moore's Hawaii-generated novels are lush, sensuous, capacious in their sympathies, *In the Cut*, set in a New York City imagined as an anteroom to Hell, is minimalist in both concept and execution. For Moore, as for many novelists, physical settings have the potency of characters, and *In the Cut* is very much dominated by its gritty urban background. Some of the strongest passages in this generally rather underdeveloped novel have to do with place; or, more accurately, with the tremulous intersection between person and place, as if "place" had the power to infiltrate soul.

I stood on the street, smelling the diesel from the trucks on the West Side Highway and the odor of brine from the Hudson River, too faint to be really pleasing, and that particular New York smell, at least in summer, of urine . . .

As I walked north, cars shooting past now and then like noisy comets, I decided I would not mind excessively the seeing of a rat (Pauline once saw hundreds of them pour out of a Con Edison hole at the corner of Desbrosses and Hudson and undulate in ripples across the cobbled street and then undulate back again, diving into the hole as if the Pied Piper himself had summoned them back), but I would not be very happy to hear a rat. The sound fills me with particular dread. It is a high, beseeching call, like that of newly hatched birds, and it causes my hair to stand on end.

In this city stray men urinate publicly, sometimes on the very doorstep of the (unnamed) protagonist's Washington Square apartment building. Other men, including one of her writing students at NYU (where she teaches a single course, presumably as an adjunct), are overly attentive to her and may even be following—stalking?—her. Moore's New York is a city in which it is distressing but not inordinately surprising to learn that the mutilated body of a young woman has been found virtually across the street from one's apartment, in Washington Square Park. Yet X, the protagonist, never draws the blinds to windows that are open to the street and even sleeps, as she informs an investigating NYPD homicide detective, with her windows open. Though a psychotic serial killer appears to be operating in the city, she continues to walk alone at night in deserted neighborhoods.

She meets her cynical, shopworn friend Pauline ("Her sexual swagger is only the convention of a woman who suspects that there is little hope for happiness with a man, and who hedges her bet by pretending that she is grateful to be alone") in a singularly disagreeable place called the Pussy Cat which is patronized mainly by truckers and "downtown artists who think it's cool to be in a bar filled with truckers" and staffed by topless waitresses, of whom one has mastered the knack of "lifting paper money, preferably twenties, from the bar-top with her vagina." ("[Tabu] offered to teach me the vagina trick but I explained I had trouble enough with situps.") X has journeyed a long distance from her sketchily recalled Philippine childhood.

X presumably represents the elusiveness of self, the emptiness, the "cut" at the core of the female in an overwhelmingly male, and violent, world. She declares that she is not a masochist even as she acknowledges that her passivity rejects an "expectation of causality" that might result in the drift into "a certain collusive masochism." Moore's implication is that the drift is cultural, collective, and not individual. Physiognomy, too, is presented as destiny: X identifies with her body (as perceived and acted upon by men), and for a woman, in the claustrophobic genre of erotic horror at least, the body is solely the sexual being, the female genitalia. Or is X unusually unlucky? Her former husband, a photographer, seems to have been even more sinister than her homicide detective lover, having nagged her for years to allow him to "realize his life's ambition of photographing a scorpion in my vagina." ("I'm sick of beauty," this absent male has said, though there is no evidence that he has tried it.) X's meager memories of her absent father involve his having literally abandoned her in a hotel room in Geneva when she was thirteen years old, and his pornography collection in which she'd discovered a print of a geisha "with the heel of her bare foot in her vagina."

In *The Whiteness of Bones*, following a violent sexual assault which for some reason the young heroine Mamie does not report to the police, she seems to blame not the drug-addled assailant but herself, in fact not herself but her genitalia: "It is what started everything, you know, all my trouble, a vagina . . . The bad thing is, I don't know what I can do about it." In a delirium of self-loathing she muses, "Vagina as fate. Vagina as fight. Vagina as fête."

Intermittently, through X, Susanna Moore demonstrates a flair for witty, understated irony in the manner of Joan Didion, but overall X's lack of self-definition weakens the novel. It is difficult to believe in X as a coherent character and not rather a floating cluster of impressions, ideas, memories, and a physical body to which things are done by others, namely men; a sequence of artful notebook entries, perhaps, by a mordantly gifted writer living in New York City in debased times. Often, despite her alleged intelligence, X behaves not only stupidly, but inexplicably; unless her desire to fall prey to a marauding male is meant to explain everything. It is as if Muriel Spark had imagined the frenzied, doomed anti-heroine of *The Driver's Seat* as passive, endearingly "feminine"—the perfect victim, in other words. X lacks even the self-destructive energies of Judith Rossner's lonely schoolteacher in *Looking for Mr. Goodbar*, which *In the Cut* recalls.

Closet admirers of LAPD Detective Mark Fuhrman will be intrigued by NYPD Detective Jimmy Malloy, a Vietnam veteran in his late forties with a flair for macho speech and even more macho sexual behavior. Like the notorious Fuhrman, Malloy serves as a swaggering initiator into a sinister world of police ethics and comportment for a young woman university instructor and writer who becomes enthralled by him and the slang with which he and his fellow NYPD officers define the world. Where Laura Hart McKinny seems to have maintained a skeptical distance between herself and the boastful racist Fuhrman, however, over the course of their sixteen-hour taped interview, X is infatuated with Malloy at their first meeting. (He has come to interview her regarding the brutal murder/"disarticulation" of the young woman whose body has been found in Washington Square Park.) X's attraction to Malloy is immediately sexual, to his macho self, and romantic, the yearning of the weakly passive for the strong, unpredictable male. Attaching herself to Malloy, X begins to assemble a dictionary of police slang: "The words themselves—in their wit, exuberance, mistakenness, and violence—are thrilling to me." The dictionary entries, interspersed through the narrative, are a measure of X's increasingly obsessive involvement with Malloy. They constitute a jarring poetry of assault:

> virginia, n., vagina (as in "he penetrated her virginia with a
>   hammer")
> snapper, n., vagina
> gash-hound, n., someone who loves gash
> brasole, n., vagina (from the Sicilian? bresaola? cured meat?)
> to knock boots, phr., to have sexual intercourse
> to do, v., to fuck
> to do, v., to kill
> smudge, n., black person
> Ape Avenue, n., Eighth Avenue (police slang)

cocola, n., black person (Puerto Rican word)

spliv, n., black person

to pull a train, v., to have group sex, gang-bang

dixie cup, n., a person who is considered disposable

hamster, n., black person (Bronx word)

to get some pink, phr., to have sexual intercourse

bloodclot, n., worst possible insult in Jamaican slang

The suspense of *In the Cut* has much to do with the reader's suspicion that Detective Malloy may be the serial killer he and his handsome partner "Richie" Rodriguez are looking for. Is it a clue, or meant to mislead, when Malloy describes "disarticulation" to X: "It is when an arm or a leg is pulled out of the joint, not cut, not sawed, but pulled out . . . It makes a funny sound." Certainly Malloy is not a model of integrity: "[He] lies to bosses. Lies on the stand. He boasts about it. Lies under oath. It's called testilying, he'd told me." In a less cynical time, Jimmy Malloy would be a "rogue cop"—a subspecies of "rogue male"—but the term has become anachronistic. "Rogue" suggests isolation, a romantic estrangement or expulsion from the herd; the police officers of *In the Cut*, like those Los Angeles officers for whom Fuhrman would seem to have been a spokesman, are herd animals themselves, bonded by deeply entrenched attitudes and acts of racism, sexism, casual and continuous violations of police ethics. Though necessary for the development of the plot, X's awe for these macho swaggerers is not treated ironically and rather quickly begins to grate.

In the Cut is advertised by its publisher as an "erotic

thriller," which seems harshly reductive for a work of serious literary ambition. ("Erotic horror" seems to me the more accurate, more inclusive category, if categorizing is required.) On the whole, however, it's a fair assessment, given the exigencies of plot and the sketchiness of X's character. In genre works of this kind, essentially cinematic in outline, plot is the engine that relentlessly drives character, as in literary fiction character is usually the engine that drives plot. Everything must move swiftly forward along action/suspense lines to a dramatic denouement that should both surprise the reader and explain, if not resolve, the mystery. Probability in the Hawthornian sense—"the probable and ordinary course of man's experience"—is sacrificed in servitude to plot. Would a seasoned veteran like Jimmy Malloy really allow himself to be handcuffed to a chair by his skittish lover? (This curious scene replicates an equally curious scene in *The Whiteness of Bones*, when Mamie handcuffs herself to a chair out of what seems to be masochistic whimsy. She can only be freed from her self-imposed bondage by a man.) Equally improbable is the total lack of awareness of AIDS among X's well-educated, sexually promiscuous New York friends. And would even a closet-psychotic homicide detective leave his victims' bodies in his own jurisdiction? Nor is the clichéd cinematic scene avoided in which the (male) stalker accosts the (female) victim as she walks alone, at night, on West Broadway:

> Clothed not in the black suit of an undertaker, not even black-skinned, but in some black and shiny material like plastic, or, more terrifying, rubber, an arm wrapped casually,

easily around my neck. My head was yanked back, my neck pulled taut, a hand over my gaping mouth.

He wore a black stocking mask, black holes for eyes. There was a strange odor on his gloves, like glue or acetone. Formaldehyde.

For all that *In the Cut* is clearly a lesser literary achievement by a fine writer, it is also powerful, shameless (or fearless) in its depiction of female passivity in the face of ubiquitous male aggression. Here is a repudiation in a sense not merely of mature womanhood but of personhood itself, with its obligations of personal responsibility and integrity. To allow others, of the category "male," to identify one in terms of one's genitalia, is to invite death. X, no surprise to the reader, is X'd out. It seems to have been her deepest, not quite secret wish, like that of the enthralled heroine of *Story of O*, whose final request is for extinction and whose final happiness is her lover's fulfillment of that request.

"IT DOESN'T FEEL PERSONAL": THE POETRY OF SHARON OLDS

> If I read a book and it makes my whole body so cold no fire can warm it I know that is poetry. If I feel physically that the top of my head were taken off, I know *that* is poetry. Is there any other way.

These ardent words of Emily Dickinson, written in a letter to an editor and "romantic friend" Thomas Higginson, might have been coined to describe Sharon Olds's poetry. There are many poems in our literature that inspire admiration, even awe for their technical virtuosity; but there are not so many poems that make us feel anything so immediate, visceral and overwhelming. In her astonishing books—the aptly titled *Satan Says* (1990), *The Dead and the Living* (1983), *The Gold Cell* (1987), *The Father* (1992), *The Wellspring* (1996), *Blood, Tin, Straw* (1999), *The Unswept Room* (2002), *Strike Sparks: Selected Poems* (2004)—Sharon Olds has cultivated an inimitable voice that is both fearless and heartrending, wise—and wounded—with experience yet childlike with yearning. Her original and startling images of domestic life—the "erotics of family love and pain" as Alicia Ostriker has noted—her willingness to speak from the heart, at times of subjects so extreme (the excruciating details of her alcoholic father's death from cancer, for instance, as well as the trauma of having been abused by her mother, as a child "tied to a chair," the vicissitudes of sexual love)—have made her a lightning rod of a kind, a beacon of admirable audacity in the eyes of some—Billy Collins has called her a "poet of sex and psyche . . . infamous for her subject matter alone"—Michael Ondaatje has called her poetry "pure fire in the hands"—and a threatening and disturbing breaker of taboos in the eyes of others—like Helen Vendler who has called her poetry "pornographic"—(probably the best endorsement the prissy Harvard critic has ever given).

Like William Blake, as well as Dickinson, Sharon Olds has consciously cultivated a perspective of radical innocence. Her characteristic tone is seemingly simply, artless—the voice so ostensibly neutral, we are pulled into it, as in a recollection of childhood nightmare mis-recalled as something very different that might be called "family fun"—

> In the evenings, during the cocktail hour,
> My mother's new husband would sometimes inspect
> the troops. Your mother has the best damn fanny
> in the house, he would say to my sister and me—in our
> teens, then twenties, thirties, forties. Turn around! He'd
>   cry out, Turn
> around! We wouldn't
> turn around . . . And when I'd pass him next,
> he'd bear-hug me, as if to say

> no hard feelings, and hit me hard
> on the rear and laugh very loud, and his eyes seemed to
> shine as I otherwise never saw them shine,
> like eyes of devils and fascists in horror
> comic books. ["Paterfamilias"]

There is something subversive, even mutinous in the poet's unflinching child-eye; we sense a kinship with the unflinchingness of Emily Dickinson as with Sharon Olds's older contemporaries Anne Sexton and Sylvia Plath—the quintessential Confessional poets of mid-century American poetry. Like these numinous sister-poets, Sharon Olds is a natural mythographer—all that falls within her scrutiny, all that she sees with her finely wrought poet-eye is myth, fairy tale, legend even as, for Olds, it is utterly domestic, ordinary. Unlike her tormented predecessors, particularly Sylvia Plath who cultivated an air of grievance and discontent with the very fabric of the universe, Sharon Olds is fundamentally a celebrant of what *is*.

> "I want to be able to write about any subject . . .
> I'm just interested in human stuff like hate, love,
> sexual love and sex. I don't see why not."
> —SHARON OLDS

"It became the deep spring of my life, this love for men,/ I don't know if it is a sickness or a gift"—these are the opening lines of "The Wellspring," a poem of intense openness and intimacy that begins as a lyric rhapsody to erotic love—"it is all I want, to meet men/ fully, as a twin, unborn, half-gelled,/ frontal in the dark, nothing between us but our/ bodies, naked, and when those melt/ nothing between us—as if I want to die with them." Suddenly the poem shifts and takes on another tone, acquires another subject, the poignancy of raw unspeakable need. The conclusion:

> For a moment,
> after we wake, sometimes we are without desire—
> five, ten, twenty seconds of pure calm, as if each one of
>   us is whole

One Secret Thing completes the cycle of scrupulously wrought family poems she has been writing through much of her career. The book focuses upon conflict—the outward, political conflict of war endured from numerous—anonymous—perspectives and the inward, scarring conflict of strife within a family. The book begins with an elegy—"Most of us are never conceived./ Many of us are never born ... And some who are born live only for minutes,/ others for two, or for three, summers,/ or four, and when they go, everything/ goes—the earth, the firmament ..." ["Everything"] By degrees a double portrait emerges of the poet—the entranced child's eye—and the poet's mysteriously driven, essentially unfathomable mother: "When I think of people who kill and eat people/ I think of how lonely my mother was./ She would come to me for comfort, in the night,/ she'd lie down on me and pray. And I could say/ she fattened me, until it was time/ to cook me, but she did not know,/

she'd been robbed of a moral sense that way." ["Freezer"] In "The Dead" a calm thought intrudes—"For a moment I see that it might not be entirely bad if my mother died."

With the candor and delicately nuanced emotional ambivalence with which Sharon Olds wrote about her dying father, in earlier poems, now in the concluding poems of *One Secret Thing* she speaks of the terrible blood-kinship of mother-daughter—"I do not want her/ to die. This feels like a new not-want,/ a shalt-not-want not-want . . . Now if she goes/ when she goes/ to me it is like the departure of a/ whole small species of singing bird from the earth." ["Little End Ode"]

It has been charged against Sharon Olds—as it was, in an earlier era, charged against poets as diverse as W. D. Snodgrass, Robert Lowell, and John Berryman as well as Sexton and Plath—that she has exploited her personal life in her poetry; that she writes of "sensational" subjects. But poetry has always been fueled upon the obsessions of poets, and what subject of lasting significance isn't, in some way, "sensational"? Though Sharon Olds writes with intensity and passion of the personal life it should be clarified that she perceives her work as *written*—undergoing many revisions and transformations until it emerges as a text. For the poet, as for most artists, personal life is but the raw material that requires shaping into an artwork, in this case a highly stylized text. In an interview the poet says:

> It doesn't feel personal. It feels like art—a made thing—the "I" in it is not myself anymore but, I hope, some pronoun that a reader or hearer could slip into.

Born in San Francisco and raised as a "hellfire Calvinist"—as the evidence of her poems suggests—Sharon Olds has a B.A. from Stanford and a Ph.D. from Columbia in American literature. For many years she has been an immensely popular and influential presence in the contemporary poetry scene: she has taught in the Graduate Creative Writing Program at NYU since 1983; in 1984 she founded and continues to run a poetry workshop at Goldwater Hospital for the severely disabled. Though she didn't publish her first book until the age of thirty-seven—"That sure seemed old then, and it sure seems young to me now"—*Satan Says* attracted much admiring attention and was awarded the San Francisco Poetry Prize. Her second book *The Dead and the Living* won the 1983 National Book Critics Circle Award. She has received numerous awards including the Lamont Poetry Prize, the T. S. Eliot Prize and her books are poetry best sellers. In 2005, one of very few poets invited by Laura Bush to participate in the National Book Festival in Washington, D.C., Sharon Olds wrote a letter to the President's wife that was subsequently published in *The Nation*. The letter is a model of tact and integrity:

So the prospect of a festival of books seemed wonderful to me. I thought of the opportunity to talk about how to start up an outreach program. I thought of the chance to sell some books, sign some books and meet some of the citizens of Washington, D.C. I thought that I could try to find a way, even as your guest, with respect, to speak about my deep feeling that we should not have invaded Iraq, and to declare my belief that the wish to invade another culture and another country—with the resultant loss of life and limb for our brave soldiers, and for the noncombatants in their home terrain—did not come out of our democracy but was instead a decision made "at the top" and forced on the people by distorted language, and by untruths. I hoped to express the fear that we have begun to live in the shadows of tyranny and religious chauvinism—the opposites of the liberty, tolerance and diversity our nation aspires to . . .

But I could not face the idea of breaking bread with you. I knew that if I sat down to eat with you, it would feel to me as if I were condoning what I see to be the wild, highhanded actions of the Bush administration . . . So many Americans who felt pride in their country now feel anguish and shame, for the current regime of blood, wounds, and fire. I thought of the clean linens at your table, the shining knives and the flames of the candles, and I could not stomach it.

In her early twenties when she was a graduate student at Columbia, Sharon Olds "made a vow to Satan to write her own poetry"—on the steps of Low Library : "Give me my own poems and I'll give up everything that I've learned. It doesn't have to be any good, just as long as it's mine."

TOO MUCH HAPPINESS:
THE STORIES OF ALICE MUNRO

O f writers who have made the short story their *métier*, and whose accumulated work constitutes entire fictional worlds—William Trevor, Edna O'Brien, Peter Taylor, Eudora Welty, and Flannery O'Connor come most notably to mind— Alice Munro is the most consistent in style, manner, content, vision. From the first, in such aptly titled collections as *Dance of the Happy Shades* (1968) and *Lives of Girls and Women* (1971), Munro exhibited a remarkable gift for transforming the seemingly artless—"anecdotal"—into art; like the short-story writers named above, Munro concentrated upon provincial, even back-country lives, in tales of domestic tragicomedy that seemed to open up, as if by magic, into wider, deeper, vaster dimensions—

So my father drives and my brother watches the road for rabbits and I feel my father's life flowing back from our car in the last of the afternoon, darkening and turning strange, like a landscape that has an enchantment on it, making it kindly, ordinary and familiar while you are looking at it, but changing it, once your back is turned, into something you will never know, with all sorts of weathers, and distances you cannot imagine. ["Walker Brothers Cowboy," from *Dance of the Happy Shades*]

Though Munro has set stories elsewhere—Toronto, Vancouver, Edinburgh and the Ettrick Valley of Scotland, even, in this new volume, Russia and Scandinavia—her favored setting is rural/small-town southwestern Ontario. This region of Canada, settled by Scotch Presbyterians, Congregationalists, and Methodists from the north of England, is characterized by frugality, rigidly "moral" principles, and Christian piety of the most severe, judgmental sort; a dour sort of Protestantism that has inspired what has been called Southern Ontario Gothic— a heterogeneous category of writers that includes Robertson Davies, Marian Engel, Jane Urquhart, Margaret Atwood, and Barbara Gowdy, in addition to Alice Munro. Like the American rural south; where Protestantism has flourished out of very different roots, the strait-laced xenophobic Anglo-Canadian culture nonetheless throws up all sorts of "queer streaks" and "fits"—lesions in the carapace of uniformity that provide the writer with the most extraordinary material: Munro's "A Queer Streak" charts the consequences of a fourteen-year-old's bizarre threatening letters written to her own family; "Fits" charts the consequences of a murder-suicide within the family of the wife and mother who discovered the corpses. How to explain such a domestic tragedy, in the house next door?

"What this is like . . . it's like an earthquake or a volcano. It's that kind of happening. It's a kind of fit. People can take a fit like the earth takes a fit. But it only happens once in a long while. It's a freak occurrence." ["Fits," *The Progress of Love*, 1986]

Possibly not, Munro suggests. Possibly not a "freak" occurrence at all.

In her new, thirteenth collection of short fiction, *Too Much Happiness*—a title both cuttingly ironic and passionately sincere, as the reader will discover—Munro explores themes, settings, and situations that have come to seem familiar in her work, seen now from a startling perspective of time. Her use of language has scarcely changed over the decades, as her concept of the short story remains unchanged; Munro is a descendent of the lyric realism of Chekhov and Joyce for whom the taut stark dialogue driven fiction of Hemingway holds little interest and the ostentatious writerly hauteur of Nabokov is altogether foreign, like "experimentation" of any sort. (One is inclined to suspect that Munro would agree with Flannery O'Connor's dismissal of experimental literature—"If it looks funny on the page, I don't read it.") Munro's voice can seem deceptively direct, even unadorned, but it is in fact an elliptical and poetic sort of vernacular realism in which the ceaselessly ruminative, analytic, and assessing voice comes to seem utterly natural, as if it were the reader's own voice:

The thing she was ashamed of . . . was that she might have been paying attention to the wrong things, reporting antics, when there was something further, a tone, a depth, a light, that she couldn't get and wouldn't get. . . . Everything she had done could sometimes be seen as a mistake. . . . She was enough of a child of her time to wonder if what she felt . . . was simply sexual warmth, sexual curiosity; she did not think it was. There seemed to be feelings which could only be spoken of in translation; perhaps they could only be acted on in translation; not speaking of them and not acting on them is the right course to take because translation is dubious. Dangerous as well. ["Who Do You Think You Are?," *The Beggar Maid*, 1978]

The Beggar Maid has the intimate, confiding tone of memoirist fiction, leading the reader to assume that Rose's voice is not distinct from Alice Munro's voice; in "Child's Play," from *Too Much Happiness*, this voice recurs scarcely altered though the narrator is much older than Rose, and her recollection of the past isn't tempered by the sort of ironic-wistful yearning for what she has lost that has brought Rose—a "career" woman now living in a large city—back to her grim little hometown of Hanratty, Ontario. In "Child's Play" the narrator Charlene undertakes an entirely different sort of self-exploration, or self-incrimination:

What I was trying to explore [in an anthropological study titled *Idols and Idiots*] was the attitude of people in various cultures—one does not dare say the word "primitive" to describe such cultures—the attitude towards people who are mentally or physically unique. The words "deficient," "handicapped," "retarded," being of course consigned to the dustbin and probably for good reason—not simply because such words may indicate a superior attitude and habitual unkindness but because they are not truly descriptive. Those words push aside a good deal that is remarkable, even awesome—or at any rate powerful, in such people. And what was interesting was to discover a certain amount of veneration as well as persecution, and the ascribing—not entirely inaccurately—of quite a range of abilities, seen as sacred, magical, dangerous, or valuable. ["Child's Play"]

The fear of—the revulsion for—what is "awesome" in a retarded neighborhood girl whom the narrator knew when they were children, is the subject of the ironically titled "Child's Play"; at the outset of the story the reader is primed to expect a nostalgic look back at the protagonist's United Church of Canada background in and near Guelph, Ontario, and her intensely close friendship with a girl named Charlene, but this expectation is revealed as naive:

Charlene and I kept our eyes on each other, rather than looking down at what our hands were doing. Her eyes were wide and gleeful, as I suppose mine were, too. I don't think we felt wicked, triumphing in our wickedness. More as if we were doing just what was—amazingly—demanded of us, as if this were the absolute high point, the culmination, in our lives, of our being ourselves. ["Child's Play"]

In this case "ourselves" is the very expression of the girls' cultural heritage—a deep suspicion of people who seem to deviate from the norm, who threaten the protocol of narrow domesticity. The "wicked" girls grow into—not "wicked" adults—but, simply, their elders. One will seek—belatedly—absolution; the other, the self-condemning yet self-sparing narrator, one of Munro's intelligent witnesses, quite decisively eludes it:

> Was I not tempted, during all this palaver? Not once? You'd think that I might break open, be wise to break open, glimpsing that vast though tricky forgiveness. But no. It's not for me. What's done is done. Flocks of angels, tears of blood, not withstanding. ["Child's Play"]

Like Flannery O'Connor, whose fiction, for all its surface dissimilarity, has been a powerful influence on Munro's, Munro tracks her characters in their search for "forgiveness"—or grace. Where O'Connor's vision is otherworldly, and "grace" is a gift of God, Munro's vision is steadfastly secular; her characters lack any impulse toward transcendence, however desperate their situations; their lives are not susceptible to sharp, defined moments of redemption but to more mundane acts of human love, magnanimity, charity. In "Wood," for instance, in this new collection, a somewhat eccentric, crankily independent furniture refinisher is drawn to the forest to cut wood, an interest, or obsession "which is private but not secret." Suffering a fall in the woods, Roy can barely drag himself back to his truck—"He can't believe the pain. He can't believe that it would continue so, could continue to defeat him"—his plight is so extreme, he's being tracked by a buzzard—when, unexpectedly, his wife, who has been near-paralyzed with chronic depression, comes to his rescue: "She came in the car, she says—she speaks as if she'd never given up driving at all— she came in the car but she left it back at the road." In a moment, Roy's terrible predicament is eased; he has not been lost in a "deserted forest," as he'd believed, but has been saved— redeemed—by his wife; as his wife, too, in being obliged to rescue her husband, has been awakened from her spell of depression: "To his knowledge, she has never driven the truck before. It's remarkable the way she manages it." "Wood" comes to a plausibly happy ending, where the reader has been primed to expect something very different, as in one of Jack London's gleefully grim little allegories of men succumbing to the wild.

So too, the first story in the volume, "Dimensions," charts the progress of a woman who has remained married, unwisely, to a mentally unstable, abusive husband: ". . . it was no use contradicting [Lloyd]. Perhaps men just have to have enemies, the way they have to have their jokes." Even after their children are murdered by Lloyd, and Lloyd has been declared criminally insane and hospitalized, Doree can't quite bring herself to separate from him; like Lloyd, she wants to think that the children are in some sort of "heaven"—"It was the idea that the children were in what [Lloyd] called their Dimension that came sneaking up on her . . . and for the first time brought a light feeling to her, not pain." In another unexpected conclusion, Doree is abruptly freed of her morbid dependence upon her ex-husband by way of a spontaneous act of her own when she saves the life of an accident victim by giving him artificial respiration:

> Then she felt it for sure. A breath out of the boy's mouth. She spread her hand on the skin of his chest and at first she could not tell if it was rising and falling because of her own trembling.
> Yes. Yes.
> It was a true breath. The airway was open. He was breathing on his own. He was breathing. ["Dimensions"]

In the similarly poignant "Deep-Holes," in the new volume, a woman must acknowledge the painful fact that her adult son is lost to her, for all her effort to reclaim him; he has vanished from her life only to resurface as a guru of sorts to homeless and disfigured individuals in a Toronto slum, for whom "normal" relations with his family are repugnant. Bluntly he tells her:

> "I'm not saying I love you...I don't use stupid language...I don't usually try to get anywhere talking to people. I usually try to avoid personal relationships. I mean I do. I do avoid them."

For Sally's son there is no spiritual dimension—"There isn't any inside stuff...There is only outside, what you do, every moment of your life. Since I realized this I've been happy." Rebuffed, dismissed, the guru's mother comes finally to feel a kinship with others like herself. Her victories will be small ones, but attainable:

> There is something, anyway, in having got through the day without its being an absolute disaster. It wasn't, was it? . . .
> And it was possible, too, that age could be her ally, turning her into somebody she didn't know yet. She has seen the look on the faces of certain old people—marooned on islands of their own choosing, clear sighted, content.

The story in *Too Much Happiness* most clearly derived from Flannery O'Connor is the oddly titled "Free Radicals" in which a boy with a "long and rubbery" face—"a jokey look"— inveigles his way into the home of an elderly widow who lives alone, under the pretense of being from the electric company; then, he claims to be a diabetic, who needs quick nourishment; at last, in a TV-psychotic monologue he reveals that he's a murderer—he has killed his family—"I take out my nice little gun and bin-bang-bam I shoot the works of them." The terri- fied woman whose house he has entered in the hope of stealing her car—herself in remission from cancer—contrives to save her life by humoring the boy, and by telling him a story of how years before she'd poisoned a girl to whom her husband was attracted; the story isn't true, and doesn't seem to make much difference to the psychotic boy, but seems to be revelatory of Nita's own guilt for having stolen another woman's husband when she was young. After the boy has fled with her car, Nita comes to the belated realization that she hasn't really grieved for her husband until now: "Rich. Rich. Now she knows what it is to really miss him. Like the air sucked out of the sky." It's a curious story, an ungainly amalgam of O'Connor and Munro, intriguing rather than satisfying, ending with Nita being informed by a police officer that the murderous boy died crashing her car: "Killed. Instantly. Serves him right." It's often said that Munro's short stories, richly detailed and dense with psychological observation, read like compact novels, but "Free Radicals," like one or two others in this collection, rather more suggest the thinness of anecdote.

The jewel of *Too Much Happiness* is the title story, an ambitiously imagined and exquisitely structured novella-length work in the mode of Munro's longer, intricately structured stories "The Love of a Good Woman," "Carried Away" and "The Albanian Virgin," as well as the linked stories of *The View from Castle Rock* (2006). In the Russian mathematician/novelist Sophia Kovalevsky (1850–1891)—the first woman to be appointed to a university teaching position in North Europe—Munro has discovered one of her most compelling and sympathetic young-woman protagonists, in temperament closely akin to such earlier Munro heroines as Rose of *The Beggar Maid* of whom it's said "[her] nature was growing like a prickly pineapple, but slowly, and secretly, hard pride and skepticism overlapping, to make something surprising even to herself." As Sophia Kovalevsky is eventually doomed by her very independence, physically exhausted and made ill by having to undertake an arduous winter train-journey alone, so Rose is made to feel miserably out of place in her provincial Ontario town of Hanratty; though Rose is never in any physical danger, the threat to her sense of her self-worth is ceaseless through childhood and adolescence, a continual questioning by her elders of the integrity of her very nature. The final story of *The Beggar Maid* is titled "Who Do You Think You Are?"—this terrible, taunting, and corrosive question put to independent-minded young women, often by older women who should be their mentors and supporters, like Rose's high school English teacher, who maddeningly persists in demanding that Rose follow every insipid rule of her classroom. With the authority of the repressive Protestant community behind her Miss Hattie persecutes Rose as if Rose were a young disobedient child instead of an intellectually gifted high school girl: "You can't go thinking you are better than other people just because you can learn poems. Who do you think you are?" Though inwardly raging Rose reacts in the way that, the reader guesses, Alice Munro herself reacted, as a bright high school girl in the small Ontario town of Wingham, in the 1940s:

This was not the first time in her life Rose had been asked who she thought she was; in fact that question had often struck her like a monotonous gong and she paid no attention to it. But she understood, afterward, that Miss Hattie was not a sadistic teacher. . . . And she was not vindictive; she was not taking revenge because she believed Rose had been proved wrong. The lesson she was trying to teach here was more important to her than any poem, and one she truly believed Rose needed. It seemed that many other people believed she needed it, too.

Of course Sophia Kovalevsky lives in a yet more provincial and restrictive world than rural southwestern Ontario, at least when she resides in her native Russia where unmarried women are not allowed to travel out of the country without permission from their families. In the cause of female emancipation Sophia marries a young radical-minded man without loving him, in order to leave the country to study abroad; after his death, by suicide, she is left with their young daughter, and the challenge of establishing a career. In 1888, Sophia wins first prize in an international mathematics competition in which entries are blind and genderless. At the swanky reception for the Bordin Prize in Paris

> [Sophia] herself was taken in by it at first, dazzled by all the chandeliers and champagne. The compliments quite dizzying, the marveling and the hand-kissing spread thick on top of certain inconvenient but immutable facts. The fact that they would never grant her a job worthy of her gift, that she would be lucky indeed to find herself teaching in a provincial girls' high school . . . ["Too Much Happiness"]

No more would the gentlemen-mathematicians who so honor Sophia give her a university position than they would employ a "learned chimpanzee." Like the smug, self-righteous women of provincial Ontario the wives of the great scientists "preferred not to meet her, or invite her into their homes." Most painful of all, Sophia loses—at least provisionally—the man who is the great love of her life, a professor of sociology and law, a Liberal forbidden to hold an academic post in Russia, named Maxsim Maxsimovich Kovalevsky. (It's a coincidence that their last names are identical—Sophia's first husband was a distant cousin of Maxsim.)

Sophia's adoration of Maxsim both illuminates her life as a woman and endangers it. The reader senses, beyond the young woman's fantasies of domestic life with this most unusual man—"He weighs 285 pounds, distributed over a large frame, and being Russian, he is often referred to as a bear, also as a Cossack"—that Maxsim isn't nearly so infatuated with Sophia as she is with him. Both are forty years old, but Sophia is the more mature of the two, as she is the more vulnerable emotionally. Maxsim can't seem to forgive Sophia for being at least as brilliant as he is, if not, with her "freaky glittery fame" more of a prodigy. Where Sophia writes of Maxsim with girlish adoration—

> He is very joyful, at the same time very gloomy
>> Disagreeable neighbor, excellent comrade
>> Extremely light-minded yet very affectionate
>> Indignantly naïve nevertheless very blasé
>> Terribly sincere and at the same time very sly—

Maxsim includes in his love letters "terrible" sentences:

> If I loved you I would have written differently.

It would seem that Sophia's fortunes take a turn for the better when she's offered a position to teach in Sweden—"the only people in Europe willing to hire a female mathematician for their new university." But to travel by herself from Berlin to Stockholm in the winter, at a time when Copenhagen is under quarantine with an outbreak of smallpox, is a dangerous, if not foolhardy undertaking: "Would Maxsim ever in his life board such a train as this?" By the time Sophia finally arrives in Stockholm she is ravaged by pneumonia and never regains consciousness. Speaking at her funeral, Maxsim refers to her "rather as if she had been a professor of his acquaintance" and not his lover. It's a melancholy end to this vibrant and accomplished "emancipated" woman who lived before her time, bravely and without the protection of men.

"Too Much Happiness" gathers considerable narrative momentum in its final pages, which chart poor Sophia's fatal train to the only country in Europe—if not the world—that will hire her as a university professor. Like those long, elaborately researched and documented stories of Andrea Barrett that chronicle the lives of nineteenth-century scientists—see *Ship Fever* (1996) and *Servants of the Map* (2002)—"Too Much Happiness" contains enough densely packed material for several novels and is burdened at times by expository material presented in undramatic and somewhat improbable passages, as if the author were eager to establish her subject as *real, historical* and not merely imagined:

> Suppose this girl had been awake and Sophia had said to her, "Forgive me, I was dreaming of 1870. I was there, in Paris, my sister was in love with a Communard. He was captured and he might have been shot or sent to New Caledonia but we were able to get him away. My husband did

it. My husband Vladimir who was not a Communard at all but only wanted to look at the fossils in the Jardin des Plantes."

In her acknowledgments Munro notes that parts of "Too Much Happiness" are derived from translated Russian texts including excerpts from Sophia's diaries, letters, and other writings, and that her primary source is Nina and Don H. Kennedy's biography *Little Sparrow: A Portrait of Sophia Kovalevsky* (1983), a work that "enthralled" her. Sophia Kovalevsky is indeed an enthralling figure, the single most interesting individual Munro has written about to date. It's appropriate that Munro prefaces "Too Much Happiness" with a remark by the historic Sophia Kovalevsky:

Many persons who have not studied mathematics confuse it with arithmetic and consider it a dry and arid science. Actually, however, this science requires great fantasy.

III.

NOSTALGIAS

NOSTALGIA 1970: CITY ON FIRE

"Almost pathetically serious"—so it was said of the thirty-two-year-old novelist whose photograph appeared in *Vogue*'s "People Are Talking About" feature for September 1970. The caption writer went on to note that the writer whose third novel *them* had received the National Book Award for 1970 was "tentative, hush-voiced, with the fixed brown eyes of a sleepwalker" and that "daydreaming" had given to her writing a "peculiarly floating quality" somewhat at odds with the violence of her subject. I was quoted, with enigmatic brevity: "What an artist has to resist and turn to his advantage is violence." This replica of my face of 1970, so strangely without expression, mask-like and dreamy and "serene" was, ironically, no indication of the maelstrom of emotions I was feeling at the time: excitement, wonderment, stress, a kind of chronic ontological anxiety. ("Ontological anxiety": the doubt that one exists as merely *one*, and the doubt that one can know the identity of this *one*, in any case. "Ontological anxiety" is an invaluable stimulus for creative endeavor since, in such endeavors, though we may have grave doubts about our own existence, we are likely to throw ourselves passionately into the construction of artworks with which to bond with others.)

Photographed for *Vogue*! The most elegant, as it was the most daunting and mysterious of the glossy magazines my grandmother, herself a somewhat mysterious woman, brought to our farmhouse in Millersport, New York, while I was growing up in the 1950s. Other magazines were the more populist, practical-minded *Redbook*, *Ladies' Home Journal* and *Good Housekeeping*; the career-girl *Mademoiselle* (where, in 1959, my first published story would appear as a co-winner of that magazine's short story competition); and *The New Yorker*, most prized in our household for its cartoons, often as perplexing as they were funny, and inhabited by fey, epicene individuals we assumed were New York sophisticates. By far, it was *Vogue* that evoked the most fascination to a girl living on a small, not-very-prosperous farm in the upstate New York region known as the Snow Belt. Here was a treasure trove of the mystical, magically empowered Feminine, distinct from the merely utilitarian Female (on a farm, female creatures have their specific uses, none of which is romantic in the slightest): *Vogue* was, among other things, a shrine honoring sheer, non-utilitarian Beauty, most of which happened to be Feminine. It would be decades before I encountered Sigmund Freud's remark in his late, melancholy *Civilization and Its Discontents*: "Beauty has no obvious use; nor is there any clear cultural necessity for it. Yet civilization could not do without it." Yet I was, in early adolescence, an astute observer of worlds so foreign to my own, images of beauty so remote from my experience, I might have been contemplating photographs of men and women from a species other than my own captured by the camera lenses of such legendary photographers as Richard Avedon and Irving Penn. No more than I might have fantasized looking like any of these celebrities, socialites and models, wearing such extraordinary clothes, jewelry, makeup, could I have imagined seeing myself one day in *Vogue*, or the image of one identified in a caption as "Joyce Carol Oates." As my childhood heroine Alice, of *Alice in Wonderland*, exclaimed: "Curiouser and curiouser!"

On the evening of March 4, I'd received the 1970 National Book Award for my novel *them* at a gala celebration; this photograph was taken by the distinguished photographer Jack Robinson on the morning of March 6, nearing 9:30 A.M. Amid a flurry of interviews and photography sessions during my brief but distressingly crowded visit to New York this image is the single one to remain dramatically imprinted in my memory. What is evoked in the portrait for me is a perverse sort of nostalgia: the recollection of an era of peril, beginning with the tragic assassination of John F. Kennedy in 1963 and continuing through a dazed, near-anarchic decade of assassinations (Robert Kennedy, Martin Luther King, Jr., 1968) and "race" riots in American cities (as in Detroit, in July 1967, when we were living in that beleaguered city) through the end of the bloody, protracted and exhausting Vietnam War in 1973. It is an era difficult to describe to those who didn't live through it when paranoia flourished, and with justification; drug use became as promiscuous and commonplace as smoking cigarettes; and isolated acts of terrorism, bombs on college campuses, for instance, or detonated at the Pentagon, were purely homegrown,

"American-revolutionary-radical" and not foreign. For that morning, after a night of fitful sleep on a very hard (horsehair?) mattress in a guest room in a distinguished old Central Park West apartment building listening to the nighttime sounds of the great city (if sirens were neon-red traceries in the sky, how like a cat's cradle the sky above New York City would look!), as I sat stiff and self-conscious, trying not to blink in the glaring lights, trying, as the photographer gently urged me, to "relax," there came suddenly, from somewhere close by, a deafening explosion. Windows rattled, the floor, walls, ceiling of the studio shook.

Abruptly, the photography session ended.

Perhaps at the instant this image was "captured" on film: the instant when the private and inward is waylaid, appropriated and redefined by an act of violence.

In that instant, you feel a sick, animal fear. As we'd felt, over a period of hours, even days, at the time of the "civil unrest" in Detroit, arson fires, looting, street violence and gunfire less than three blocks from our house in a residential neighborhood near the University of Detroit, where I taught at the time. At such moments of peril you think *This can't be happening! This can't be happening to me.* And if you are lucky, it isn't.

We staggered out of the photographer's studio, out of the brownstone in the West Village and onto the sidewalk where already the air was smoky and gritty. We were dazed, panicky. With such stunning abruptness the intimate moment of art had ended and had been replaced by this brute and utterly perplexing reality. Around us were frightened pedestrians, stalled traffic, a cacophony of horns and sirens. No one had any idea what had happened: an exploding boiler? Gas line? A *bomb*?

A block or so away, flames shot upward from what appeared to be a brownstone town house. It would turn out to be an elegant nineteenth-century house with a Greek-revival facade, the boyhood home of the poet James Merrill.

Later, it would be revealed that the terrible explosion had been inadvertently caused by an amateur bombmaker who'd triggered a timer on a homemade "antipersonnel" bomb being assembled in the basement of the house at 18 West Eleventh Street, by two zealot members of the radical antiwar group Weatherman, with the intention of setting off the bomb at a dance at the Fort Dix, New Jersey, army base. ("Antipersonnel" is a particularly nasty kind of bomb, tightly packed with screws and nails, intended to dismember human targets.) The bomb fortuitously detonated that morning killed three individuals, two men and a woman named Diana Oughton, a former debutante and Bryn Mawr graduate, whose body was grotesquely dismembered in the blast; fleeing from the burning house, naked, on foot were two female Weathermen, one of them Kathy Boudin, later to acquire notoriety of her own.

That season of peril. The sour, sick dregs of 1960s counterculture idealism. In such rocky soil the seeds of nostalgia yet grow.

We left New York the next day. We returned to Windsor, Ontario. We lived there in a white-brick house with plate glass walls overlooking the Detroit River. Living in Ontario during the ongoing crisis of the Vietnam War, in a foreign country with the advantage of hardly seeming foreign, in a city that is, by a geographical quirk, south of Detroit, I would stare out the window of my study at the fast-flowing, choppy and often leaden-colored river and would remember, with a pang of loss, how curious and fleeting is the intimacy between photographer and "subject," how abruptly it can end; and the image that remains can be both timeless and time-bound, a memory of nightmare crystallized in art.

THE MYTH OF THE
"AMERICAN IDEA": 2007

How heartily sick the world has grown, in the first seven years of the twenty-first century, of the "American idea"! Speak with any non-American, travel to any foreign country, the consensus is: the "American idea" has become a cruel joke, a blustery and bellicose bodybuilder luridly bulked up on steroids, consequently low on natural testosterone, deranged and myopic, dangerous. In 1923 D. H. Lawrence remarked that the essential American soul is "hard, isolate, stoic, and a killer" and except for "stoic" this description is as accurate in 2007 as it was more than eighty years ago when Lawrence's brilliantly unorthodox *Studies in Classic American Literature* was published. How would Lawrence react to the quasi-mystical, shamefully self-aggrandizing "American idea"? Very likely, along these lines:

> Freedom . . . ? The land of the free! This is the land of the free! Why, if I say anything that displeases them, the free mob will lynch me, and that's my freedom. Free? Why, I have never lived in any country where the individual has such an

abject fear of his fellow countrymen. Because, as I say, they are free to lynch him the moment he shows that he is not one of them. [D. H. Lawrence, "The Spirit of Place"]

(If not "lynch" precisely how about "crucify in the media"? The ravenous tabloid press, tabloid TV and ever more ominously "mainstream" media have become the lynch mob of contemporary times, pummeling those guilty of the most innocuous of blunders with the ferocity with which they pummel outright criminals.)

What is most questionable about the "American idea"— indeed, most dangerous—is its very formulation: that there is a distinctly "American idea" in contrast to Canadian, British, French, Chinese, Icelandic, Estonian, or mere human "ideas." Our unexamined belief in American exceptionalism has allowed us to imagine ourselves above anything so constrictive as international law. American exceptionalism makes our imperialism altruistic, our plundering of the world's resources a healthy exercise of capitalism and "free trade." From childhood we are indoctrinated with the propaganda that, as Americans, we are superior to other nations; our way of life, a mass-market "democracy" manipulated by lobbyists, is superior to all other forms of government; no matter how frivolous and debased, our American culture is the supreme culture, as our language is the supreme language; our most blatantly imperialistic and cynical political goals are always idealistic, while the goals of other nations are transparently opportunistic. Perhaps the most pernicious of American ideas is the revered "My country right or wrong" with its thinly veiled threat of punishment against those who hesitate to participate in a criminal patriotism. The myth of American exceptionalism begins with the revolt of the colonies against the British crown. In 1776, what a thrilling, exhilarating "American idea"! But in the first decade of the twenty-first century, in a vastly altered world, and considering the higher degree of civilization embodied by Canada, that waged no war against the British—that country's reluctance to rush into war, its disinclination to celebrate the violence of the frontier, and to display itself as exceptional—it might be a timely American idea to examine our very origins.

"WHY IS HUMANISM NOT THE PREEMINENT BELIEF OF HUMANKIND?" ADDRESS UPON RECEIVING THE 2007 HUMANIST OF THE YEAR AWARD

Humanism—like "the humanities"—indeed, all of the arts—has sometimes seemed, amid the turbulence of history, a frail vessel bearing us onward along a treacherous stream, and yet, the ideal of humanism prevails: a faith in reason, in the strategies of skepticism and doubt, a refusal to concede to "traditional" customs, religious convictions, and superstitions. Yesterday, in San Francisco, interviewed on Michael Kresnick's popular *Book Forum*, which is a call-in radio show, I inadvertently aroused the anger of a number of individuals who called in to protest my remark in passing that I did not believe in "evil"—that I thought that "evil" is a theological term, and not adequate to explain, nor even to suggest, psychological, social, and political complexities. When we label someone as "evil" we are implicitly identifying ourselves as "good." The issue was Islamic suicide bombers who are surely motivated by political passions and so to call them merely "evil" is to fail to understand the phenomenon of terrorism. Though I said repeatedly that I wasn't defending terrorism, I was questioning the terms in which it was being discussed, it seemed to make no difference: my critics remained angry, and unplacated. There would seem to be a powerful need in many—most?—people to believe in literal "evil"—"good"—"God"—"Heaven"—"Hell." Terms we might interpret as metaphorical have acquired an eerie Platonic "realism."

Why is humanism not the preeminent belief of humankind? We must imagine our distant ancestors discovering death—baffled and terrified by death—and needing to ascribe to this natural phenomenon a supernatural explanation. As T. S. Eliot observed, "Humankind cannot bear very much reality"—especially, humankind can't bear the crushing evidence of a reality that limits human delusions of immortality and omniscience. A primitive fear of the unknown—of death—a disbelief that "this can't be all there is" prevails in all of us, tempting us to believe in a deity that will guarantee not only our immortality but our worth; and will unite us with "loved ones" in the afterlife, as in the country and western classic "May the Circle Be Unbroken" ("in the sky, Lord, in the sky"). As a novelist I tend to be sympathetic with persons who are religious, though I can't share in their convictions; it has always been something of a mystery to me, that intelligent, educated men and women—as well as the uneducated—can "have faith" in an invisible and non-existent God. One hundred years ago a gathering like this would have consisted of a majority of individuals who believed in the "perfectability" of mankind. In the wake of Charles Darwin's revolutionary work, scientists and educators like the distinguished T. H. Huxley believed in both biological and social/moral evolution. The optimism of the turn of the century—the previous century—is expressed in H. G. Wells's youthful, Utopian work; though there is a check to that work in Wells's brilliantly conceived and executed "scientific romances" (*The Time Machine, The Invisible Man, The Island of Dr. Moreau, The War of the Worlds*). By 1920, a more cautious note is sounded in Wells's monumental *The Outline of History*: "Human history becomes a race between education and catastrophe." By 1945, in *The Mind at the End of Its Tether*, the former Utopianist was predicting the destruction of human civilization, in a tone comparable to that of Sigmund Freud in his late, melancholy essays *The Future of an Illusion* and *Civilization and Its Discontents*. In fifty years, in the wake of not one but two devastating world wars, the Holocaust and the revelation of the Nazis' genocidal agenda against Jews, the "perfectability of mankind" would seem to have been turned inside-out. And yet, humankind—and humanism—prevails. And in succeeding generations, I would like to predict that humanism—a secular ethical analogue to the old religions of tradition—will be the preeminent belief of humankind.

IN THE ABSENCE OF
MENTORS/MONSTERS:
NOTES ON WRITERLY INFLUENCES

How solitary I've always felt, in my writing life. Unlike nearly all my writer friends, especially my poet friends, I never really had a "mentor"—never anyone to whom I might show my work in progress in anything approaching an ongoing, still less an intimate or "profound," relationship.

Even during my marriage of many years—which ended in February 2008 with the sudden death of my husband, Raymond Smith—my writing occupied another compartment of my life, apart from my married life. I am uneasy when people close to me read my writing—my fiction—as if I were intruding on their sense of me, which I would not wish to violate; I think that the life of the artist can be detached from the life of the "art"—no one is comfortable when others perceive, or believe they can perceive, the wellsprings of their "art" amid the unremarkable detritus of life.

Since my husband was an editor and publisher, overwhelmed with reading, assessing, annotating and editing manuscripts to be published in *The Ontario Review* or by *Ontario Review Press*, I was reluctant to take up his time with yet more writerly projects of my own. I did ask him to read my nonfiction essays and reviews for such publications as the *New York Review of Books*—which, in any case, as an avid reader of that publication, he would have read when they were printed.

Rarely did he read my fiction. Not in progress or after publication.

Maybe this was a mistake. I am willing to concede that much in my life has been mistaken—and yet: what is the alternative, superior life I might have led? Is there such a Platonic fantasy?

I haven't had significant mentors in my writing life, nor have I had "monsters"—but I have had, and have now, fascinating writer friends. It's altogether likely that these writer friends have influenced me in ways too subtle and diffuse to examine except anecdotally.

The Rival. The day of Vladimir Nabokov's death—July 2, 1977—is firmly fixed in my memory, for on the following day Donald Barthelme said casually to me, with a puckish lift of his upper lip and what in non-Barthelmian prose might be described as a *twinkle of the stone-colored eye* behind wire-rimmed glasses: "Happy? Nabokov died yesterday, we all move up a notch."

(And how did I respond to this? Probably with a startled or an embarrassed smile, and a murmur of mild disapprobation. *Oh Don, you don't mean that—do you?*)

Well, no! Don was just kidding.

Well, yes. What is kidding but deadly serious?

We were in an Italian restaurant within a few blocks of Donald's apartment at 113 West Eleventh Street in New York City. We were having a late lunch after drinks at the apartment with Donald's wife, Marian—Don's second wife, young, blond, attractive and, it seemed, warily in love with this complex, difficult, elliptical man, who behaved much more naturally—graciously—with my husband than with me, with whom he spoke in a manner that was jocular and subtly needling, edged with irony, sarcasm. As if Don didn't know what to make of me—at least in person. This was the first time we'd met after a friendly/funny correspondence following a literary feud of sorts conducted in public, in the pages of the *New York Times Book Review* (me) and *Newsweek* (Donald)—a disagreement of the kind writers had in the 1970s, or perhaps have had through the centuries, regarding the "moral"/"amoral" nature of literature. (The following year, John Gardner would publish his controversial polemic *On Moral Fiction*, praised in some quarters and condemned in others.) For the purposes of writerly combat "Joyce Carol Oates" weighed in on the side of moral seriousness; "Donald Barthelme" on the side of amoral playfulness. In an interview in the *Times* the Dada-inspired Barthelme had stated that "Fragments are the only form I trust," which in retrospect sounds reasonable enough but, at the time, at the height of whatever literary issue was raging in whatever literary publications, struck me as dubious, or in any case a vulnerable position that might be questioned, if not attacked and repudiated. Subsequently, Donald "attacked" me in print, as one might have foreseen, and somehow it happened that we began writing to each other, and not long afterward we arranged to meet on one of my infrequent trips to New York, and so Donald Barthelme and I became not friends—for we saw each other too rarely for friendship, and when we did meet, Don was so clearly more at ease with my husband than with me—but "friendly acquaintances."

Perhaps Don thought of me as a "friendly rival"—it may have been that he thought of all writers, especially his contemporaries, as "rivals"—in the combative, macho way of Stanley Elkin, John Gardner, Norman Mailer, and numerous (male) others. The notion of our being "competitors" in some sort of public contest made me feel very ill at ease, and so invariably I found myself murmuring something vaguely embarrassed and/or conciliatory, usually some variant of *Oh Don, you don't mean that—do you?* with a hope of changing the subject.

With one so strong-minded as Donald Barthelme, you could not easily change the subject. You would remain on Don's subject for as long as Don wished to examine that subject, he with the air of a bemused vivisectionist. As Don's prose fiction is whimsical-shading-into-nightmare, cartoon-surreal-visionary, so Don's personality on such quasi-social occasions was likely to be that of the playful bully, perversely defining himself as an outsider, a marginal figure, a "loser" in the marketplace, in contrast to others whose books sold more, or so he believed. No sooner had my husband and I been welcomed into the Barthelmes' brownstone apartment—no sooner had I congratulated Don on what I'd believed to be the very positive reviews and best-seller status of his new book of stories, *Amateurs*—than he corrected me with a sneering smile, informing me that *Amateurs* wasn't a best seller, and that no book of his had ever been a best seller; his book sales were "nothing like" mine; if I doubted this, we could make a bet—for $100— and check the facts. Quickly I backed down, I declined the bet—no doubt in my usual embarrassed and conciliatory way, hoping to change the subject.

But Don wasn't in the mood to change the subject just yet. To everyone's embarrassment—Ray's, mine, his wife's—Don picked up a phone receiver, dialed a number, and handed the receiver to me with the request that I speak to his editor—he'd called Roger Straus at Farrar, Straus & Giroux—and ask if in fact Donald Barthelme had ever had a best seller; and so, trying to fall in with the joke, which seemed to me to have gone a little further than necessary, I asked Roger Straus—whom I didn't know, had scarcely heard of at this time in my life—if Don had ever had a best seller, and was told no, he had not.

Plaintively I asked, "He hasn't? Not ever? I thought..."

The individual at the other end of the line, whom I would meet years later, the legendary Roger Straus of one of the most distinguished publishing firms in New York, said coolly, "No. He has not. Put Don on the phone, please, I want to talk to him."

Of course, Donald Barthelme was hardly a "mentor" of mine— I had the distinct idea that he'd read very little of my writing, probably not a single book, only just short stories in collections in which we both appeared, such as *Prize Stories: The O. Henry Awards* or magazines like *Harper's* and *The Atlantic*. (It would be a long time before my fiction began to appear, not very frequently, in *The New Yorker*, in which Barthelme's wildly experimental short fiction had become a fixture rivaling the well-crafted traditional short fiction of John Updike. How upset Don would be were he living now, to see how George Saunders has usurped his *New Yorker* space with his deftly orchestrated Barthelme-inspired American-Gothic-surreal short fiction.) In my presence, at least, as on that uncomfortably hot July day in 1977 when we had lunch in the Village, it seemed important to Donald to establish himself as both a martyr of sorts—the brilliant iconoclastic/experimental writer whose books sold less than they deserved to sell—and the most strong-willed among us. Social engagements with Donald Barthelme were conducted strictly on Barthelmian terms.

If he were still alive—he died in 1989, of cancer—Don would be seventy-six years old at the time of this writing, December 2008. Very likely the Barthelmian edginess would have subsided by now. Very likely even Nabokov wouldn't have been considered a rival but something like a colleague, a brother, or a friend.

The Friend. Though I was on friendlier, more relaxed and affectionate terms with my fellow western–New Yorker John Gardner, who'd published an early short story of mine titled "The Death of Mrs. Sheer" in his literary magazine *MSS*—and who regarded me, somewhat embarrassingly, as a "major American writer"—like himself—it can't be said that John Gardner was a mentor of mine, either. John was my sole writer friend who read my writing with enormous seriousness, which was both flattering, and unsettling; it sometimes seemed that John took my books almost as seriously as he took his own. His model would seem to have been the elder, didactic, somewhat tiresome Tolstoy: *Art must be moral.* Another model might have been the zealous reformer Martin Luther. For this reason, John took it as his duty to chide, criticize, scold—in particular he scolded me about my "pessimism"—my "tragic view of life"; it was John's hope to enlist me in the quixotic enterprise of writing what he called "moral fiction"—see the preacherly *On Moral Fiction* (1978). My next novel should be, for instance, a novel that John's young daughter could read and be left with the feeling that "life was worthwhile"—so John argued, with grim persistence, pushing aside his near-untouched plate of food (thick sirloin steak leaking blood), and drinking glass after glass of Scotch.

How I replied to this, as to other admonitions of John Gardner's, I have no idea.

Though John professed to admire my novels *A Garden of Earthly Delights, Expensive People, them, Wonderland*—though he gave my postmodernist Gothic *Bellefleur* a long, thoughtfully written, and generous review on the front page of the *New York Times Book Review,* and always spoke highly of me in public in venues in which he mischievously and maliciously denounced many of our cohorts—he always seemed disappointed in me. I might have been an acolyte who'd managed to elude the gravitational pull of a powerful planetary force—an American Tolstoy-visionary in the mortal form of John Gardner.

With my longtime predilection for the playful experimentation of James Joyce, no less than for the intransigent tragic humanism of D. H. Lawrence and the absurdist surrealism of Franz Kafka, I was not likely to be influenced by my fellow western New Yorker from Batavia. I was not likely to be told what to do, still less why I must do it. Nor did I understand the passion with which John attacked his slightly older postmodernist contemporaries, of whom a number were his friends, or had been—John Barth, Robert Coover, Stanley Elkin. I never understood the bitterness of some of these rivalries, which hurt John more than they hurt others and made enemies of individuals who should have been friends and supporters at a time when John badly needed support.

But then, I don't really understand the messianic personality—the hectoring Tolstoy, the righteous Martin Luther. I never understood why so exceptional a personality as John Gardner wanted so much to influence others. During our often noisy evenings together, when John lectured in one of his lengthy, lurching, eloquently drunken monologues or argued with someone who dared to challenge him, the calm, still, sane words of Henry David Thoreau came to me: *I never found the companion that was so companionable as solitude.* Why this compulsion to enjoin others to think as you believe they should? It seemed futile to me, foolish.

Years of proselytizing, preaching and sniping at other writers provoked a considerable backlash against John in the late 1970s and early 1980s, as he might have anticipated. I have no doubt that some of the negative publicity John drew helped to account for his moods of depression, which in turn provoked drinking, and driving while drinking—recklessly, on the motorcycle that would eventually kill him, in an accident on a graveled country road near his home in Susquehanna, Pennsylvania, in 1982.

At the time of his death, John had been divorced from two wives, and was about to marry another, a much younger woman writer, a former student of his at SUNY-Binghamton.

I remember first hearing of John's death. I'd been invited to give a reading at the Princeton Public Library, and my librarian-hostess told me the shocking news: "John Gardner is dead." Not for a moment did I think that this John Gardner might be the other Gardner, a writer of popular mysteries; I'd known immediately that this Gardner was my western–New York friend. And I'd known, or seemed to know, that John's death (at the age of forty-nine) would turn out to be both accidental and—perhaps, to a degree—self-willed.

What would John Gardner's life be now, if he hadn't drunk so heavily? So compulsively, like a fated character out of Dostoyevsky or Eugene O'Neill? If he hadn't succumbed to an alcoholic's wildly inflated vision of himself—in which he saw his destiny loom large in the writing of the "great American novel" that would "alter the consciousness" of his time? My most vivid memories are of John hugging me, hard. This was John's customary greeting, as it was John's customary farewell. I remember John kissing my cheek, smelling of whiskey—his silvery hair falling disheveled to his broad, slightly rounded shoulders, his gesturing hands edged with grime, like fingerless gloves. I remember the glisten of his eyes, and the sharp smell of his smoldering pipe: "Joyce, you know that we're as good as—maybe better than—Lawrence, don't you? Lawrence, Joyce—Faulkner—we are their equals, or will be. You know that, don't you? Come on!"

Early Influences. Often it's said that the only influences that matter greatly to us come early in our lives, and I think that this must be so. Of the thousands—tens of thousands?—of books I've probably read, in part or entirely, many of which have surely exerted some very real influence on my writing life, only a few shimmer with a sort of supernatural significance, like the brightest stars in the firmament: Lewis Carroll's *Alice's Adventures in Wonderland* and *Through the Looking-Glass*, Frances Hodgson Burnett's *The Secret Garden*, and *The Gold Bug and Other Stories* by Edgar Allan Poe—the great books of my childhood.

Add to which, in early adolescence, at a time when I borrowed books from the Lockport Public Library each Saturday when my mother drove into town to shop for groceries, such thrilling titles as Henry David Thoreau's *Walden*, Emily Brontë's *Wuthering Heights*, Ernest Hemingway's *In Our Time*, William Faulkner's *The Sound and the Fury*—the great books of a more self-consciously literary era in my life.

Of course as a student I had influential teachers—a succession of wonderfully encouraging, inspiring and insightful teachers both at Williamsville High School, in Williamsville, New York, and at Syracuse University, from which I graduated in 1960. As a child, I attended a one-room schoolhouse in rural Niagara County, New York, north of Buffalo, of which I've written elsewhere—a hardscrabble "education experience" that has provided useful memories of the kind we all retrieve and hone for nostalgic purposes but not an education of which one might reasonably boast, still less present as ideal or "influential" in any significant way. (My memory of our Amazonian teacher Mrs. Dietz, confronted with the rebelliousness and general obtrusiveness of six-foot-tall farm boys with no love of book learning or even of sitting still for more than a few minutes at a time, approaches the succinctness of Faulkner's terse encomium for the black housekeeper, Dilsey: *They endured.*)

If I had a single mentor who guided me into my writing life—or at any rate encouraged me—it wasn't any of my teachers, wonderful though they were, or any of my university colleagues in the years to come, but my grandmother Blanche Woodside, my father's mother. ("Oates" was the name of my grandmother's first husband.) In our not-very-prosperous farmhouse in Millersport, New York, at the northern edge of Erie County near the Erie Barge Canal, there were no books at all—*not even a Bible*. (How curious this was wouldn't occur to me until I was much older. Though eventually my parents converted to Catholicism after the sudden, premature death of my mother's father, when I was in junior high school, the household of my early, formative years was utterly without religion of any kind—the prevailing tone of secular skepticism was set by both my mother's father, a Hungarian immigrant who worked in a steel foundry in Tonawanda and as a village blacksmith at home in Millersport, and by my father, Fred Oates, who'd had to drop out of grade school to help support his mother after his father, Carleton Oates, abandoned them in or about 1917.) Along with articles of clothing she'd sewed or knitted for me, my grandmother gave me books for Christmas and my birthday, year after year; when I was fourteen, inspired by my predilection for filling tablet after tablet with my school-girl handwriting and drawings, in the way of a budding serial novelist, my grandmother stunned my parents and me by giving me a Remington portable typewriter for my birthday!—an astonishing gift, considering that my grandmother had very little money and that typewriters were virtually unheard-of in rural households like ours.

Most of the children's storybooks and young-adult novels my grandmother gave me have faded from my memory, like the festive holiday occasions themselves. The great single—singular—book of my childhood, if not of my entire life, is *Alice's Adventures in Wonderland* and *Through the Looking-Glass*, which my grandmother gave me when I was eight years old, and which, with full-page illustrations by John Tenniel, in a slightly oversized edition with a transparent plastic cover, exerted a powerful influence on my susceptible child's imagination, a kind of hypnotic spell that lasted for years.

Here is my springboard into the imagination! Here is my model of what a storybook can be.

I was too young for such exalted thoughts, of course. Far too young even to grasp that the name stamped on the spine of the book—*Lewis Carroll*—was the author's name, still less that it was the author's pen name. (Many years would pass before I became aware that the author of the *Alice* books was an Oxford mathematician named Charles Dodgson, an eccentric bachelor with a predilection for telling fantastical stories to the young daughters of his Oxford colleagues and photographing them in suggestive and seductive poses evocative of Humbert Humbert's nymphets of a later, less innocent era.) My enchantment with this gift began with the book itself as a physical and aesthetic object, quite unlike anything else in our household: both *Alice* books were published in a single volume under the imprint Illustrated Junior Library, Grosset & Dunlap (1946). Immediately, the striking illustrations by John Tenniel entered my imagination, ranged across the field of the book's cover—back and front—in a dreamlike assemblage of phantasmagoric figures as in a somewhat less malevolent landscape by Hieronymus Bosch. (I still have this book. It is one of the precious possessions in my library. What a surprise to discover that the book that loomed so large in my childhood imagination is only slightly larger than an ordinary book.)

The appeal of *Alice* and her bizarre adventures to an eight-year-old girl in a farming community in upstate New York is obvious. Initially, the little-girl reader is likely to be struck by the fact that the story's heroine is a girl of her own approximate age who confronts extraordinary adventures with admirable equanimity, common sense, and courage. (We know that Alice isn't much more than eight years old because Humpty-Dumpty says slyly to her that she might have "left off" at seven— meaning, Alice might have died at seven.) Like most children, Alice talks to herself—but not in the silly prattling way of most children: " 'Come, there's no use in crying like that!' said Alice to herself rather sharply; 'I advise you to leave off this minute!' " (Obviously, Alice is echoing adult admonitions—she has interiorized the stoicism of her elders.) Instead of being alarmed or terrified, as a normal child would be, Alice marvels, "Curiouser and curiouser!"—as if the world so fraught with shape-changing and threats of dissolution and even, frequently, cannibalism were nothing more than a puzzle to be solved or a game to be played like croquet, cards, or chess. (Alice discovers that the Looking-Glass world is a continual game of chess in which, by pressing forward, and not backing down in her confrontations with Looking-Glass inhabitants, she will become Queen Alice—though it isn't a very comfortable state pinioned between two elderly snoring queens.) The *Alice* books are gold mines of aphoristic instruction: "Who cares for you? . . . You're nothing but a pack of cards!" Alice cries fearlessly, nullifying the authority of malevolent adults as, at the harrowing conclusion of *Looking-Glass*, she confronts the taboo-fact of "cannibalism" at the heart of civilization:

> [The Pudding] was so large that [Alice] couldn't help feeling a *little* shy with it, as she had been with the mutton; however, she conquered her shyness by a great effort, and cut a slice and handed it to the Red Queen.
>
> "What impertinence!" said the Pudding. "I wonder how you'd like it, if I were to cut a slice out of *you*, you creature!"
>
> It spoke in a thick, suety sort of voice, and Alice hadn't a word to say in reply; she could only sit and look at it and gasp.

The banquet dissolves into nightmare as the White Queen seizes Alice's hair in both hands and screams "Take care of yourself! . . . Something's going to happen!"

There was not a moment to be lost. Already several of the guests were lying down in the dishes, and the soup ladle was walking up the table toward Alice's chair . . . "I can't stand this any longer!" [Alice] cried, as she jumped up and seized the tablecloth with both hands; one good pull, and plates, dishes, guests, and candles came crashing down together in a heap on the floor.

Both *Alice's Adventures in Wonderland* and *Through the Looking-Glass* are brilliantly imagined fantasies that shade by degrees into nightmare—only to be routed by Alice's impetuousness and quick thinking. The child reader is meant to take solace in the possibility that, like Alice, she can exorcise adult vanity and cruelty; she may be very young, and very small, but she can assert herself if she knows how. Both *Alice* nightmares end with Alice simply waking up—returned to a comfortable domestic world of kittens and tea things—and no adults in sight.

In essence, I think I am, still, this child-self so like an American cousin of Lewis Carroll's Alice: my deepest, most yearning and most (naively) hopeful self. I think that I am still waiting to be "influenced"—by a loving mentor, or even a monster. By someone.

Who?

W riters, particularly novelists, are inextricably linked to *place*. It's impossible to think of Charles Dickens and not to think of Dickens's London; impossible to think of James Joyce and not to think of Joyce's Dublin; and so with Thomas Hardy, D. H. Lawrence, Willa Cather, William Faulkner, Eudora Welty, Flannery O'Connor—each is inextricably linked to a region, as to a language-dialect of particular sharpness, vividness, idiosyncrasy. We are all regionalists in our origins, however "universal" our themes and characters, and without our cherished hometowns and childhood landscapes to nourish us, we would be like plants set in shallow soil. Our souls must *take root*—almost literally.

For this reason, "home" isn't a street address, or a residence, or, in Robert Frost's cryptic words, the place where, "when you have to go there, they have to take you in"—but where you find yourself in your most haunting dreams. These may be dreams of numinous beauty, or they may be nightmares—but they are the dreams most embedded in memory, thus encoded deep in the brain: the first memories to be retained and the last memories to be surrendered.

Over the years of what seems to me both a long and a swiftly passing lifetime "home" has been, for me, several places: Millersport, New York, and nearby Lockport, where I was born and lived until the age of eighteen; Detroit, Michigan, where I lived with my young husband Raymond Smith, 1961 to 1968—when he taught English at Wayne State University and I taught English at the University of Detroit; and Princeton, New Jersey, where we lived for forty-eight years at 9 Honey Brook Drive, while Ray edited the *Ontario Review* and Ontario Review Press books and I taught at Princeton University until Ray's death in February 2008. Now I live a half-mile from that house in a new phase of my life, with my new husband Charles Gross, a neuroscientist at Princeton University who is also a writer and photographer. The "contemporary French provincial" house in which we live on three acres fronting a small lake is "home" in the most immediate sense—this is the address to which our mail is delivered, and each of us hopes that this will be the last house of our lives; but if "home" is the repository of our deepest, most abiding and most poignant dreams, the landscape that haunts us recurringly, then "home" for me would be upstate New York—the rural crossroads of Millersport, on the Tonawanda Creek, and the city of Lockport on the Erie Barge Canal.

As in a vivid and hallucinatory dream I am being taken—my hand in hers—by my grandmother Blanche Woodside to the

Lockport Public Library on East Avenue, Lockport. I am an eager child of seven or eight and this is in the mid 1940s. The library is a beautiful building like no other I've seen close up, an anomaly in this city block beside the dull red brick of the YMCA to one side and a dentist's office to the other, across the street is Lockport High School, another older, dull-brick building. The library—which, at my young age, I could not have known had been built by WPA funds in 1936—has something of the look of a Greek temple; not only is its architecture distinctive, with elegantly ascending steps, a portico and four columns, a facade with six large, rounded, latticed windows and, on top, a kind of spire, but the building is set back from the street behind a wrought iron rail fence with a gate, amid a very green jewel-like lawn.

The library for grown-ups is upstairs, beyond a dauntingly wide and high-ceilinged doorway; the library for children is more accessible, downstairs and to the right. Inside this cheery brightly lit space there is an inexpressible smell of floor polish, library paste, books—that particular *library smell* which conflates, in my memory, with the *classroom smell* of floor polish, chalk dust, books so deeply imprinted in my memory. For even as a young child I was a lover of books and of the spaces in which, as indeed in a sacred temple, books might safely reside.

What is most striking in the children's library are the shelves and shelves of books—bookcases lining the walls— books with brightly colored spines—astonishing to a little girl whose family lives in a farmhouse in the country where books are almost wholly unknown. That these books are available for children—for a child like me—all these books!—leaves me dazed, dazzled.

The special surprise of this memorable day is that my grandmother has arranged for me to be given a library card, so that I can "withdraw" books from this library—though I'm not a resident of Lockport, nor even of Niagara County. Since Blanche Woodside is a Lockport resident, and I am her grand-daughter, some magical provision has been made to include me; or maybe, as I would not suspect until later, years later, my grandmother paid for my library card.

The Lockport Public Library has been an illumination in my life. In that dimension of the soul in which time is col-lapsed, and the past is contemporaneous with the present, it still is. Growing up in a not-very-prosperous rural community lacking a common cultural or aesthetic tradition, in the after-math of the Great Depression in which people like my family and relatives worked—worked, and worked—and had little time for reading more than newspapers—I was mesmerized by books and by what might be called "the life of the mind"—the life that *was not* manual labor, or housework, but seemed in its specialness to transcend these activities.

As a farm girl, even when I was quite young I had my "farm chores"—but I had time also to be alone, to explore the fields, woods and creek side, and to read.

There was no greater happiness for me than to read—children's books at first, then "young adult"—and beyond. No greater happiness than to make my way along the seemingly infinite shelves of books in the Lockport Public Library, drawing my forefinger across the spines. My grandmother Blanche Woodside was an avid reader whom all the librarians knew well, and whom they obviously liked very much; two or even three times a week my grandmother checked books out of the library—novels, biographies—I remember the plastic covers—I remember once asking Grandma about a book she was reading, a biography of Abraham Lincoln, and how she answered me: this was the first conversation of my life that concerned a book, and "the life of the mind"—and now, such subjects have become my life.

What we dream of, that we are.

What I most love about Lockport is its timelessness. Beyond the newer facades of Main Street—literally just behind the block of buildings on the northern side—is the Erie Barge Canal: this impressive stretch of the 524-mile New York State canal connecting the Great Lakes with the Hudson River and traversing the breadth of the state. For residents of the area who have gone to live elsewhere, it's the canal—so deep-set in what appears to be solid rock, you can barely see it unless you come close, to lean over the railing of the wide bridge at the foot of Transit Road—that resurfaces in dreams: the singular height of the falling water, the steep rock walls, the gritty, melancholy smell of stone, froth, agitated water; the spectacle of the locks opening, taking in water, and closing; the ever-shifting water levels bearing boats that seem miniaturized in the slow methodical ritual-like process. "Locks-port" might have been the original, more accurate name, since there are numerous locks, to accommodate the especially steep incline of the land. (Lake Erie to the west is on a much higher elevation than the Hudson River, and Lockport—"Uptown" and "Lowertown"—is built on an escarpment.) Standing on the bridge—"the widest single-span bridge in the world" as it was once identified—you feel a sensation of vertigo as you peer down at, or into, the canal fifty feet below; not so overwhelming as the sensation you feel staring at the legendary falls at Niagara twenty miles to the west but haunting, unnerving and uncanny. (Think of "uncanny" in the Freudian sense—*Unheimlich*—a sign/symptom of a deep-rooted turbulence associated with buried and unarticulated desires, wishes, fears.) In the midst of city-life, at the very noontide of day-life, there is the primary, primitive vein of elemental life in which human identity is vanished, as if it had never been. Falling water, turbulent water, dark frothy water churning as if it were alive—somehow, this stirs the soul, makes us uneasy on even cheery visits back home. You stare down into the canal for a long dazed minute and then turn back blinking—where?

You didn't let Joyce see, did you? Oh—Fred!

Not a thing for a little girl to see. I hope she didn't . . .

An early memory of being with Daddy—in Lockport—and there is a street blocked with traffic, and people—one of the narrow streets that run parallel to the canal, on the farther side of downtown—and Daddy has stopped his car to get out and see what is happening—and I have gotten out too, to follow him—except I can't follow him, there are too many people—I hear shouts—I don't see what is happening—unless (somehow) I do see—for I have a vague memory of "seeing"—a blurred memory of—is it a man's body, a corpse, being hauled out of the canal?

Joyce didn't see. Joyce was nowhere near.

Yes I'm sure!

(Yet years later, I will write of this. I will write of a little girl seeing, or almost-seeing, a man's body hauled from a canal. I will write of the canal set deep in the earth, in what appears to be solid rock; I will write of the turbulence of falling water, steep rock-sides, the frothy agitation of water, unease and distress and yet at the core, childlike wonderment. And I will write—repeatedly, obsessively—of the fact that adults cannot shield their children from such sights, as adults cannot shield their children from the very fact of growing up, and losing them.)

So strange—"uncanny."

That, between the ages of eleven and fifteen—through sixth, seventh, eighth and ninth grades—I was a "commuter student" first at John E. Pound School on High Street, Lockport; then at North Park Junior High in the northeast section of town near Outwater Park. (Though the term "commuter student" wasn't in anyone's vocabulary at that time.) For five grades, I'd gone to a one-room schoolhouse in Millersport—then for no reason that was ever explained, to me at least, I was transferred to Lockport, seven miles to the north—a considerable distance for a child, at the time.

In this era before school buses—at least in this rural corner of Niagara County—such "commuter students" were required to wait out on the highway for Greyhound buses. Decades later I can recall the sudden sight—at a distance of perhaps a quarter-mile—as the large bus seemed to emerge out of nowhere, at the intersection of Millersport Highway with Transit Road, headed in the direction of my family home which was on Transit Road. *The bus!*

Not a greyhound it seemed to me but a large ungainly beast—a buffalo, or a bison.

For my predominant fear, for years, was that I would miss the bus, and miss school, prospects to be dreaded. And there was the daunting fact of *the bus* itself—where would I sit each morning? With whom?—most of the other passengers were adults, and strangers.

Here began my "romance" with Lockport, which I experienced as a solitary individual mostly walking—walking, and walking—along the streets of downtown, and along residential streets; over the wide windswept bridge above the canal at Transit Street, and over the narrower bridge above the canal, at Market Street; on paths above the towpath, winding through vacant overgrown lots in the vicinity of Niagara Street; and on the shaky plank pedestrian bridge that ran parallel and unnervingly close beside the railroad bridge above the canal. Many days, after school I went to my grandmother Woodside's house on Harvey Avenue, and later on Grand Street, across town; after visiting with Grandma, I took a city bus downtown, or walked; to this day, I have a proclivity for walking—*walking, walking!*—I love to be in motion, and I am very curious about everything and everyone I see, as I'd learned to be, as a young child; and so I have felt invisible also, as a child feels herself invisible, beneath the radar of adult attention, or so it seemed to me at the time. For Lockport which I'd previously experienced only in the company of my mother, my father or my grandmother seemed very different to me, when I was alone. The small city—30,000 residents in the 1950s, now 22,000—became an adventure, or a series of adventures, culminating with the Greyhound bus to take me back home to Millersport.

Very few girls of eleven or twelve would be allowed today to wander alone as I did, nor to take a bus as I did; to be allowed, or obliged, to wait for long headache-wracked minutes—or hours—in the dreary Lockport bus station, located near Harrison's Radiator, Lockport's single large factory, a division of General Motors where my father worked as a tool and dye designer for forty years. (Why Daddy didn't drive me into Lockport in the morning, and take me home in the late afternoon, I have no idea. Was his work-schedule just too different from my school-schedule? There must have been some reason, but now there is no one left to ask.) What a desolate, ill-smelling place the Greyhound bus station was, especially in winter!—and winters are long, windy and bitter-cold in upstate New York; what derelict-looking individuals were to be found there, slouched in the filthy vinyl chairs waiting—or maybe not waiting—for buses. And I in their midst, a young girl with textbooks and notebook, hoping no one would speak to me, nor even look at me.

It was so, I was prone to headaches in those years. Not so severe as migraines, I think. Maybe because I strained my eyes reading, or trying to read, in that wanly lit, inhospitable waiting room, as on the jolting Greyhound bus itself.

How innocent and oblivious the 1950s seem to us now, at least so far as parental oversight of children is concerned. Where many of my Princeton friends are hyper-vigilant about their children, obsessively involved in their children's lives— driving them everywhere, calling their cell phones, providing nannies for sixteen-year-olds—my parents seemingly had no concern at all that I might be endangered, spending so much time alone. I don't mean that my parents didn't love me, or were negligent in any way, but only that, in the 1950s, in an era in which "sex crimes"—like "domestic violence"—had not yet been named and classified—there was not much awareness of such dangers; it wasn't uncommon that adolescent girls hitch-hiked on roads like Transit Road—which I'd never done.

The consequence of so much unsupervised freedom was that I seem to have become precociously independent. For not only did I take the Greyhound bus into Lockport but from the bus station I walked to school; while at John E. Pound Elementary, I even walked downtown at noon, to have lunch in a restaurant on Main Street, alone. (How strange this is—wasn't there a cafeteria in the school? Couldn't I have brought a lunch packed by my mother, as I'd brought lunches in a "lunch pail" to the one-room schoolhouse?) Though I rarely eat in any restaurant alone, as an adult, if I can avoid it, I loved these early restaurant excursions; there was a particular pleasure in looking at a menu, and ordering my own food. If any waitress thought it was peculiar that a girl so young was eating alone in a restaurant, it wasn't brought to my attention.

Later, in junior high, somehow it happened that I was allowed to see movies alone at the Palace Theater after school—

even double features. The Palace Theater was one of those ornate, elegantly decorated dream-palaces first built in the 1920s; there was also, across town, the less reputable Rialto where Saturday serials were shown to hordes of screaming children. Of the prominent landmarks of Lockport, the Palace Theater resides in my memory as a place of romance; yet romance fraught with some anxiety for often I had to run from the theater before the second feature had ended, leaving behind its baroque splendors—gilt-framed mirrors in the lobby, crimson and gold plush, chandeliers, "Oriental" carpets—to rush to the bus station a block or two away, to catch the 6:15 P.M. bus marked BUFFALO. It's doubly strange to think that, in late fall and winter, it would have been dark as night at this time, and bitter cold.

In the shadowy opulence of the Palace, as in an unpredictably unfolding dream, I fell under the spell of movies, as I'd fallen under the spell of books a few years earlier. Hollywood films—"Technicolor"—coming attractions—posters in the lobby: here was enchantment! These movies of the 1950s starring Elizabeth Taylor, Robert Taylor, Ava Gardner, Clark Gable, Robert Mitchum, Burt Lancaster, Montgomery Clift, Marlon Brando, Eva Marie Saint, Cary Grant, Marilyn Monroe—inspired me to a cinematic sort of storytelling, driven by character and plot; as a writer I would strive in my prose to the fluency, suspense and heightened drama of film, its quick cuts and leaps in time. (No doubt, every writer of my generation—of all generations since the 1920s—has fallen under the spell of film, some more evidently than others.)

It was so, from time to time, solitary men "bothered"

me—came to sit near me, or tried to talk to me—quickly then I would move to another seat, hoping they wouldn't follow me. It was safest to sit near the rear of the movie-house since ushers were stationed there. Once, sitting near the front of the movie-house, I felt an odd sensation—my foot being touched lightly—held, or pinched—as in a ghost-grip—to my astonishment I realized that a solitary man who'd come to sit in front of me had reached down somehow through the back of his seat to grip my foot in his fingers; I gave a little scream, and at once the man leapt to his feet and fled to an exit at the side, disappearing within seconds. An usher hurried down to ask me what was wrong and I could barely stammer an explanation— "A man—he was sitting in front of me—took hold of my *foot*."

"Your *foot*?" The usher, a boy of eighteen, or twenty, frowned in distaste at this prospect, as I did—my *foot*! In some old *shoe*!

As there was no comprehending anything so preposterous, so totally unnatural if not silly, the moment of crisis passed— the usher returned to his post at the rear, and I returned to watching the movie.

I don't think that I have ever incorporated this random incident into any work of fiction of mine—it hovers in my memory as bizarre, and singular, and very *Lockportian*.

It is not boasted in histories of Lockport and environs that, along with such renowned past residents as the late William Miller (Republican Barry Goldwater's vice-presidential running mate in the 1964 election, in which Democrat Lyndon Johnson was overwhelmingly elected), the late William

Morgan (inventor of volleyball) and more recently Michael Cuzzacrea (world record-holder for marathon running while flipping a pancake), the area's most "known" resident is Timothy McVeigh, our home-grown terrorist/mass-murderer. Like me, McVeigh grew up in the countryside beyond Lockport—in McVeigh's case the small village of Pendleton, where his family still resides; like me, for a while, McVeigh was bussed into Lockport public schools. Like me, he would have been identified as "from the country" and very likely, like me, he was made to feel, and may have exalted in feeling, marginal, invisible.

Unlike the downscale Rialto, the Palace Theater has been smartly renovated and refurbished, reborn as a theater that sometimes shows first-run films but more often is rented out to traveling productions, amateur local theater, and one-time events like this evening's. Before my presentation I am brought downstairs to the "green room"—a barren corridor of dressing rooms, a furnace room, closets—how unnerving this is, to find myself behind the scenes of the Palace Theater, the temple of dreams! And in this starkly lighted setting, so antithetical to romance, to be confronting my past—as in one of those dreams in which one's life flashes before one's eyes—Am I really here? *Here*—in the Palace Theater where long ago in the 1930s, before he'd started to work at Harrison's, my father Frederic Oates was a sign painter, making posters for coming attractions?

Onstage, I am greeted with tremendous applause. Perhaps I am perceived as one who has swum across a vast stretch of water, or climbed through an abyss.

Am I really here? Is this—possible?

Fifty years since I've left Lockport, more or less—and now for the first time I have been formally invited back to "speak"—I can't resist telling the audience that I hope this will become a custom, and that I will be invited back again in another fifty years.

He may have felt powerless, as a boy. He may have been watchful, a fantasist. He may have told himself *Wait! Your turn will come.*

In a piece I wrote for *The New Yorker* for May 1995, on the phenomenon of McVeigh, so cruel, crude and pitiless a terrorist that he never expressed remorse or regret for the many lives he'd taken, even when he learned that his victims were primarily young children and not employees of the detested "federal government," I observed that Lockport, well into the present, suggests a more innocent time imagined by Thornton Wilder or Edward Hopper, appropriated now by David Lynch: the slightly sinister, surreal yet disarmingly "normal"-seeming atmosphere of a quintessential American town trapped in a sort of spell or enchantment. That much remains unchanged over several decades—there is the Niagara Hotel on Transit Street, for instance, already seedy and disreputable in the 1950s when I had to pass by it on my way to and from school—is a consequence not of nostalgic urban planning but of economic recession. Harrison's Radiator Company has vanished, though its sprawling buildings remain, mostly vacant, renamed Harrison Center. As old churches scattered through the city have been renamed "centers"—"halls." The derelict bus station has vanished, replaced by a parking lot; Lockport High has long since vanished, moved to the southeast, newer side of town;

the stately old Niagara County Bank has been reborn as a "community college." But there the Lockport Public Library remains unchanged, at least from the street—the beautiful Greek temple-facade remains, and the jewel-like green lawn; to the rear, a multi-million-dollar addition has doubled, or trebled, its size. Here is unexpected change in Lockport—a good change.

And there remains the canal—dug by immigrant labor, Irishmen and Chinese who frequently died in the arduous effort, and were buried in the muddy banks of the canal—a waterway now placid, stately, a "tourist attraction" as it never was in its days of utility.

In America, history never dies—it's reborn as "tourism."

Postcript: *October 16, 2009.* As a guest of the Lockport Public Library inaugurating a lecture series in honor of a legendary Lockport resident, beloved teacher John Koplas, I have returned to my hometown city—in fact, to the Palace Theater! Instead of the twenty to forty people I'd envisioned in the library, there is an audience of over eight hundred crowded into the now "historic" theater, even in the balcony; on the marquee where once such names as *Elizabeth Taylor, Clark Gable, Cary Grant* were emblazoned now there is *Joyce Carol Oates Oct. 16* above *Hell Rell Oct. 17*—a local rock band.

Scattered laughter, murmurings. Is "Joyce Carol Oates" being funny, or—ironic?

Gently ironic, in any case. For truly I am tremendously moved and my eyes are welling with tears and I am particularly grateful that my brother Fred and my sister-in-law Nancy are here tonight in the audience—all that remain of my immediate family.

My presentation is informal, improvised, laced with "gentle ironies"—in fact, it's this very memoir of Lockport in an early handwritten draft. The audience seems appreciative as if they are all old friends—classmates of mine—as if I am one of them and not a visitor who will depart in the morning. More than once I'm tempted to shut my eyes and in a feat of verbal legerdemain recite the names of long-ago classmates— names as deeply imprinted in my brain as the street names of Lockport—a kind of valentine-poem, a sentimental homage to the past.

At the end of my talk, amid a wave of applause—warm, welcoming, buoyant—I am presented with a framed pen-and-ink drawing of the Lockport Public Library, by gracious Marie Bindeman who is the current director of the library.

How I wish that my mother, my father, and my grandmother Blanche Woodside were here with me tonight—that they were alive to share this extraordinary moment. *How proud we are of you, Joyce*—for pride is the life's-blood of family, recompense for hardship, endurance, loss.

Unexpected questions from the audience: "Do you think that there is a teleological purpose to the universe, and do you think that there is an afterlife?" Yet more unsettling: "Do you think that you would be the writer you are today if you'd had a middle-class or wealthy background?"

These questions, that seem to me not at all *Lockportian,*

stop me in my tracks. Especially the second. Beyond the blinding lights, eight hundred people are waiting for my reply. In the
exigency of the moment it seems that they really want to know.

Without Millersport and Lockport—would there be
"Joyce Carol Oates"?

THE WOMAN IN WHITE:
EMILY DICKINSON AND FRIENDS

1. At age fifty, bereft of what might have been a comforting fantasy of marrying her epistolary friend Higginson, Dickinson seems to have turned to Otis Lord; it's likely that, though the judge's portrait, reprinted in *White Heat*, suggests the very antithesis of Byronic romance, it was Lord in whose arms Emily Dickinson was reputedly once seen "reclining" in the Homestead parlor by her scandalized neighbor/sister-in-law Susan Dickinson. Unmistakably it's to Judge Lord that Dickinson wrote girlishly flirtatious love-letters: "Emily 'Jumbo'! Sweetest name, but I know a sweeter—Emily Jumbo Lord."

THE ART OF VENGEANCE: ROALD DAHL

1. Among Roald Dahl's most popular children's books are *James and the Giant Peach* (1961), *Charlie and the Chocolate Factory* (1964), *The BFG* ("Big Friendly Giant") (1982), and *Matilda* (1988); of particular interest to adult readers of Roald Dahl are *Boy: Tales of Childhood* (1984) and *The Wonderful Story of Henry Sugar* (1977), which contains the autobiographical essay "Lucky Break: How I Became a Writer." In his memoirist pieces for young readers, Dahl speaks with an engaging directness and honesty that suggests that his most comfortable mode of writing was in fact for young readers whose natural curiosity, lack of cynicism, and inexperience he could assume:

> I began to realize for the first time that there are two distinct
> sides to a writer of fiction. First, there is the side that he dis-
> plays to the public, that of an ordinary person like everyone
> else . . . Second, there is the secret side, which comes out in
> him only after he has closed the door of his workroom and is
> completely alone. It is then that he slips into another world
> altogether, a world where his imagination takes over and he
> finds himself actually living in the places he is writing about
> at that moment. I . . . fall into a kind of trance, and every-
> thing around me disappears. ["Lucky Break: How I Became
> a Writer," *Wonderful Story of Henry Sugar*]

Dahl's success as a writer of children's books far surpassed his success as a writer of prose fiction for adults and, according to Jeremy
Treglown, "part of [Dahl] always resented that he had become best
known as the author of what are known in American publishing as
'juveniles.' " Dahl would be particularly chagrined to discover that on
the Internet, "Roald Dahl" is celebrated almost exclusively as a children's writer; the official Roald Dahl website (www.roalddahl.com) is
so very antic, it's a challenge for an adult even to peruse it.

2. In *Boy: Tales of Childhood* and in "Lucky Break: How I Became a
Writer" Dahl writes in detail of having been the object of sadistic beat-
ings at the Repton School. In "Lucky Break" Dahl recounts having
been caned by the headmaster ("this giant of a man") for the most
trivial infractions of school rules: "That cruel cane ruled our lives."
In *Boy*, Dahl writes of having been caned by a school athlete/boazer
whose very strokes in the flesh of a boy's buttocks were perversely
admired. The sado-homoerotic undercurrent of Dahl's public school
boyhood gives to these memories an aura of romantic nostalgia:

> A ritual took place in the dormitory after each beating. The
> victim was required to stand in the middle of the room and
> lower his pyjama trousers so that the damage could be in-
> spected. Half a dozen experts would crowd around you and
> express their opinions in highly professional language.
> "*What* a super job."
> "He's got *every single* one in the same place!"
> . . . Once, I was still standing in the middle of the dormi-
> tory with my pyjama trousers around my knees when [the

boazer] came through the door ... "Pull those pyjamas up and get into bed immediately!" he ordered, but I noticed that as he turned away to go out of the door, he craned his head ever so slightly to one side to catch a glimpse of my bare bottom and his own handiwork. I was certain I detected a little glimmer of pride around the edge of his mouth before he closed the door behind him.

There is no male-female love scene in Roald Dahl's fiction for adults so exquisitely honed and so tender as this.

3. Roald Dahl's tales for children are affably narrated and are given a benign, not-very-distinctive comic-strip aura by the inoffensive illustrations by Quentin Blake, but demonic females figure prominently in such popular books as *Matilda* and *The Witches*, infusing the fantasy adventures with an air of sexual dread and revulsion. In *Matilda*, the young genius-heroine is persecuted by the demonic, deranged, and very ugly headmistress of her school, The Trunchbull:

[Miss Trunchbull] was above all a most formidable female. She had once been a famous athlete, and even now the muscles were still clearly in evidence. You could see them in the bull-neck, in the big shoulders, in the thick arms, in the sinewy wrists and in the powerful legs ... Her face, I'm afraid, was neither a thing of beauty nor a joy for ever. She had an obstinate chin, a cruel mouth and small arrogant eyes ... She looked, in short, more like a rather eccentric and bloodthirsty follower of the stag-hounds than the headmistress of a nice school for children.

When she marched—Miss Trunchbull never walked, she always marched like a storm-trooper with long strides and arms aswinging—when she marched along a corridor you could actually hear her snorting as she went, and if a group of children happened to be in her path, she ploughed through them like a tank, with small people bouncing off her to left and right.

(Canny Matilda defeats this monster through her superior mental powers, utterly.)

In *The Witches*, we are told:

The most important thing you should know about REAL
WITCHES is this. Listen very carefully. Never forget what
is coming next.

REAL WITCHES dress in ordinary clothes and look very
much like ordinary women. They live in ordinary houses and
they work in ORDINARY JOBS.

That is why they are so hard to catch.

A REAL WITCH hates children with a red-hot sizzling
hatred that is more sizzling and red-hot than any hatred you
could possibly imagine.

A REAL WITCH spends all her time plotting to get rid of
the children in her particular territory. Her passion is to do
away with them one by one . . .

A witch is always a woman.

"LARGE AND STARTLING FIGURES": THE FICTION OF FLANNERY O'CONNOR

1. In "Some Aspects of the Grotesque in Southern Fiction," O'Connor
remarks bemusedly:

> When I first began to write, my own particular *bête-noir* was
> that mythical entity, the School of Southern Degeneracy. Ev-
> ery time I heard about the School of Southern Degeneracy, I
> felt like Br'er Rabbit stuck on the Tarbaby.

2. In 2008, the Modern Language Association catalogued 1,340 entries
under "Flannery O'Connor," including 195 doctoral dissertations and
several book-length studies in addition to such meritorious earlier
books as *Conversations with Flannery O'Connor* edited by Rosemary M. Magee (1987), *The Art and Vision of Flannery O'Connor* by
Robert H. Brinkmeyer, Jr. (1989), *Flannery O'Connor: A Life* by Jean
W. Cash (2002), *Flannery O'Connor: A Biography* by Melissa Simpson (2005), and the closely argued and refreshingly unhagiographic
Flannery O'Connor's South by Robert Coles (1993). Gooch notes—
surprisingly, given the greater ambition, achievement, and international
acclaim of the work of William Faulkner—that the 1988 Library of
America edition of O'Connor's work "widely outsold" Faulkner's volume published three years earlier. (See O'Connor's misplaced dread of

the magisterial Faulkner in an essay of 1960: "The presence alone of Faulkner in our (Southern literary) midst makes a great difference in what the writer can and cannot permit himself to do. Nobody wants his mule and wagon stalled on the same track the Dixie Limited is roaring down." ["The Grotesque in Southern Fiction," *Mystery and Manners*.]

3. O'Connor's favorite among her stories, "The Artificial Nigger," has become virtually unteachable as a consequence of its blunt pseudo-racist title. Ironically, O'Connor had intended the "artificial nigger"— a crude black-face lawn ornament observed in a Southern town by the back-country Mr. Head and his grandson Nelson—to be a simulacrum of Jesus Christ and the story to evoke a tender sort of redemption unexpected in O'Connor's *oeuvre*:

> [Mr. Head and Nelson] stood gazing at the artificial Negro as if they were faced with some great mystery, some monument to another's victory that brought them together in their common defeat. They could both feel it dissolving their differences like an action of mercy.

4. *City Poet: The Life and Times of Frank O'Hara* (Alfred A. Knopf, 1993).

5. Poor Regina O'Connor! We have only fleeting glimpses in Gooch's biography of this pretentious "hide-bound Southern lady (who) always wore hat and gloves in public" and who seems to have been the model for a number of O'Connor's acid-etched portraits of garrulous, overbearing, and peevish Southern matrons, several of whom come to rudely abrupt, violent ends. In *A Jury of Her Peers: American Women Writers from Anne Bradstreet to Annie Proulx*, Elaine Showalter has provocatively suggested that Flannery O'Connor was "among the American writers of the fifties who confronted matrophobia, or the fear of becoming one's mother. Hating one's mother was the prefeminist enlightenment" of the era.

IN ROUGH COUNTRY I: CORMAC McCARTHY

1. Typical of the sharply divided opinion on McCarthy's work is A. O. Scott's entry on McCarthy in *The Salon.com Reader's Guide to Contemporary Authors* in which Scott says of *Blood Meridian* that it is

"by any criterion a masterpiece and one of the great American novels of the last quarter century" while the *Border Trilogy* is "sentimental, crowd-pleasing cowboy fiction" in which "some parts read like bad Hemingway, others read like bad Hemingway retranslated from the Spanish."

2. See "Cormac Country" by Richard B. Woodward, *Vanity Fair*, August 2005.

ENCHANTED! SALMAN RUSHDIE

1. The metafictional impulse to shatter narrative verisimilitude is boldly counter to the ambitions of "realism" and of the "historical novel"—to evoke distinctly credible worlds, carefully researched and replicated, in the hope of convincing the reader *This is not fiction but a window into the "real."* The device can be very funny, if disorienting, as in the sudden revelation in *The Satanic Verses* that there is a "Supreme Being," an author, inventing the trials of the hapless Gibreel Farishta:

> [He] was not abstract in the least. [Gibreel] saw, sitting on the bed, a man of about the same age as himself, of medium height, fairly heavily built, with salt-and-pepper beard cropped close to the line of the jaw . . . the apparition was balding, seemed to suffer from dandruff and wore glasses.

2. In an interview in the *Spectator*, April 9, 2008, Rushdie said:

> Not that [Akbar] ever thought quite like this, but I wanted to show that these ideas—the sovereign individual self, the plurality of the self—are not exclusively Western ideas . . . I suppose there is an unspoken subtext here, which is that there are such things as universals. There are ideas which grew up in the West, and in a slightly different way they grew up in the East—the idea of freedom, of open discourses, of tolerance, of sexual freedom even to the level of hedonism . . . So to say that we must now consider them to be culturally specific . . . is a denial of human nature. If there is an author's message in this book, it was actually the discovery that I made that the worlds of the book were more like each other, than unlike.

3. Rushdie's portrait of Niccolò Machiavelli as a sexually adventurous Florentine youth is substantiated by Maurizio Viroli's excellent biography *Niccolò's Smile* (1998), though of necessity Rushdie conflates and abbreviates the philosopher's political career and the range and depth of his writings.

A PHOTOGRAPHER'S LIVES: ANNIE LEIBOVITZ

1. Though the photographs of Susan Sontag *in extremis* will strike some observers, including this reviewer, as needlessly unsparing, taken at a time when the subject can scarcely have been aware of the photographer's presence, and could not have given permission to the photographer, it is clear from Annie Leibovitz's thoughtful commentary that she sees the inclusion of such photographs as enhancing, and not diminishing, her subject: "I edited this book with [Susan Sontag] in mind, as if she were standing behind me, saying what she would like to see in it." Elsewhere, quoted in the *Newsweek* cover story, Leibovitz acknowledges: "I think that Susan would be really proud of these pictures—but she's dead. Now if she were alive, she would not want them published. It's really a difference. It's really strange."

MARGARET ATWOOD'S TALES

1. See *Waltzing Again: New and Selected Conversations with Margaret Atwood*, edited by Earl G. Ingersoll (Ontario Review Press, 2006).
2. In *Negotiating with the Dead: A Writer on Writing* (Anchor Books, 2002), Atwood remarks:

> By the time I was born, my father was running a tiny forest-insect research station in northern Quebec. Every spring my parents would take off for the North; every autumn, when the snow set in, they would return to a city—usually to a different apartment each time. At the age of six months, I was carried into the woods in a packsack, and this landscape became my hometown.

3. As Atwood remarked in an interview with Geoff Hancock in 1986:

> I'm an optimist. I like to show that the Third Reich, the Fourth Reich, the Fifth Reich did not last forever.

In fact, Orwell is much more optimistic than people give him credit for ... He has a text at the end of *1984*. Most people think the book ends when Winston Smith comes to love Big Brother. But it doesn't. It ends with a note on Newspeak, which is written in the past tense, in standard English—which means that, at the time of writing the note, Newspeak is a thing of the past. [*Waltzing Again*]

4. *The Molecular Gaze: Art in the Genetic Age* (Cold Spring Harbor Laboratory Press, 2004).

ABOUT THE AUTHOR

Joyce Carol Oates is a recipient of the National Book Award and the PEN/Malamud Award for Excellence in Short Fiction. She is the Roger S. Berlind Distinguished Professor of the Humanities at Princeton University and has been a member of the American Academy of Arts and Letters since 1978. In 2003 she received the Commonwealth Award for Distinguished Service in Literature and the Kenyon Review Award for Literary Achievement, and in 2010 the Lifetime Achievement Award of the National Book Critics Circle.